Partnership for the Americas

Western Hemisphere Strategy and U.S. Southern Command

James G. Stavridis

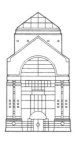

National Defense University Press
Washington, D.C.
2010

Opinions, conclusions, and recommendations expressed or implied within are solely those of the contributors and do not necessarily represent the views of the Defense Department or any other agency of the Federal Government. Cleared for public release; distribution unlimited.

This edition published by Books Express Publishing
Copyright © Books Express, 2010
ISBN 978-1-9780392-27-1
To purchase copies please contact info@books-express.com

To Simón Bolívar and the people he inspired and
liberated throughout the Americas

Contents

Figures

Photos

Foreword

Since its creation in 1963, United States Southern Command has been led by 30 senior officers representing all four of the armed forces. None has undertaken his leadership responsibilities with the cultural sensitivity and creativity demonstrated by Admiral Jim Stavridis during his tenure in command.

Breaking with tradition, Admiral Stavridis discarded the customary military model as he organized the Southern Command Headquarters. In its place he created an organization designed not to subdue adversaries, but instead to build durable and enduring partnerships with friends. His observation that it is the business of Southern Command to launch "ideas not missiles" into the command's area of responsibility gained strategic resonance throughout the Caribbean and Central and South America, and at the highest levels in Washington, DC.

Pursuing his vision for the Americas with limited resources, Admiral Stavridis made the most of every ship, airplane, Soldier, Sailor, Airman, Marine, and Coastguardsman committed to the region, employing each on constructive missions designed to create goodwill and mutual respect.

Perhaps Jim Stavridis' most enduring contribution to Southern Command is the newly constructed headquarters complex in Miami. The new building, which finally creates a permanent lodgment for the command in the city that the Admiral correctly describes as the "Gateway to the Americas," is a testimonial to his persistence, persuasiveness, and credibility within the Department of Defense and the U. S. Congress. More than a building, the new headquarters is tacit recognition of the importance of the command and acknowledgment that Miami is the single right location for the institution that, as much or more than any other, expresses our commitment to peace and stability in this hemisphere.

Admirals and Generals leave their marks on the organizations they command in different ways. Some solve the problems of the day; others set courses that will influence events and relationships for decades. Clearly, Admiral Stavridis is in the latter category. He has set wheels in motion that will transform our American culture to a culture of the Americas.

This thoughtful book should be required reading for those who recognize that the security of the United States, and indeed our destiny, are inextricably intertwined with those of our neighbors to the south.

General Charles E. Wilhelm
United States Marine Corps (Retired)

Preface

Consider the Americas of the 15th century: one vast stretch of relatively undeveloped land; lightly populated by indigenous peoples in varied and thriving societies, all blissfully unaware of the pending arrival of the conquistadores. From what is today Ellesmere Island in remote northern Canada to the tip of Tierra del Fuego in the far south, natural resources—water, timber, arable land, a wide variety of minerals—were plentiful and available.

Spring forward to the 21st century—half a millennium later. Five-hundred years of developing those resources have left us with a legacy of prosperity and progress beyond anything the conquistadores imagined. But was that progress evenly distributed? One would think so. Given the relatively even distribution of resources, it would be reasonable to expect there to be some rough similarity in how the stories turned out across the Americas, at least in terms of wealth, education, and development.

And yet, in the north—the United States and Canada—some 400 million people live at a standard of economic development that many in the south—from Mexico through Central America, the Caribbean, and much of South America—can only dream of. In some cases, even the dreams may seem out of reach to the nearly one-third of the population who live on less than 2 dollars a day. In a part of the world blessed with extraordinary natural wealth and highly advantageous geographic location, such poverty are tragedy of the highest order. This division of wealth and the inequities it represents are fundamental and challenging aspects of relations between the United States and its neighbors to the south.

In addressing Latin American diplomats and members of our Congress at a White House reception nearly fifty years ago, President John F. Kennedy said: "This new world of ours is not merely an accident of geography. Our continents are bound together by a common history . . . our nations are the product of a common struggle . . . and our peoples share a common heritage."

It is a common heritage that has at times been overshadowed by the unbalanced, and often resented, history of U.S. military and political intervention in the region in the 19th and 20th centuries. This particular legacy of heavy handedness and gunboat diplomacy still poses challenges to the building of bridges between north and south. But we've made great strides to develop a legacy of partnership and cooperation over the last few years.

As Commander of U.S. Southern Command, I was charged by the Secretary of Defense and the President with all U.S. military operations and activities in Central America, the Caribbean, and South America as part of a broader effort to build those bridges. This included leading operations in support of counternarcotic activities as well as leading the broad efforts of the Joint Interagency Task Force–South in Key West. I was also responsible for connecting U.S. and partner militaries to conduct training and exercises, respond to humanitarian crises, and conduct medical training and medical diplomacy missions like the voyages of the hospital ship USNS *Comfort*.

After spending decades studying and, most recently, living and working in this region, I wanted to spend some time writing about my observations and reflections on this beautiful, culturally rich, complex, and fascinating part of the world. Recognizing that quarrel is the daughter of distrust—and that distrust is born from misunderstanding—I write this book with one overarching goal in mind: to help close gaps of understanding between north and south and in doing so, to help galvanize the foundation of trust so vital to exchanging ideas, understanding each other, and cooperating with one another as we continue writing our common history.

This short book reflects a quarter of a million miles of travel to almost every nation in the region over the past 30 years, but especially during my time in command between 2006 and 2009. I have discussed its contents with some of the leading diplomats, intellectuals, political scientists, and security practitioners who have made focusing on Latin America and the Caribbean their life's work. Their insight and advice have been enlightening in the extreme. My interagency partners, especially at the State Department and the Agency for International Development—dedicated Americans whose heavy lifting in the areas of diplomacy and development daily pave the way to continued progress and prosperity—have been especially thoughtful and helpful.

I have also benefited immensely from my many superb colleagues at U.S. Southern Command. These are all passionate individuals who every day contributed their expertise, the ideas, and their views to help shape my own. My experience at U.S. Southern Command was defined and enhanced through my exposure and collaboration with an amazing cadre of individuals: Ambassadors Lew Amselem and Paul Trivelli; Generals Glenn Spears, Keith Huber, Norm Seip, Ken Keen, Dave Fadok, Dave Garza, Biv Bivens, John Croley, Charlie Cleveland, Hector Pagan, and Mike Moeller; Admirals Nan Derenzi, Harry Harris, Jim Stevenson, Tom Meeks, Joe Kernan, and Rob

Parker; and civilian Senior Executive Service professionals Caryn Hollis, Todd Schafer, Tom Schoenbeck, and all the members of my Distinguished Advisory Panel without whom strategic connections in the region would have been impossible to make. My executive assistant for 3 years, Carol Maldonado, truly stood out in her efforts to help me understand the world to the south, not the least of which included assisting my own learning of the beautiful Spanish language.

As part of my "travel support team," I was lucky to rely on my director of strategic communication, Sarah Nagelmann; our leading cultural expert and linguist, Lieutenant Colonel Barbara Fick; my Commander's Action Group, including Captain Wade Wilkenson, Lieutenant Colonels Mike Gough and John Perez, Commander Juan Orozco, Lieutenant Commander Rich LeBron, Major Al Perez, and Lieutenant Rob Prewett; and my Special Assistant for Congressional Affairs, Lizzie Gonzalez, who not only helped me navigate the Halls of Congress, but helped me chart a course to better understand Cuba and Cubans. Each and every one of them made our trips true voyages of discovery that contributed to the final form of this work. I also wish to extend a special thanks to Commander Elton "Thumper" Parker, who brought his skilled pen to the final editing of this volume over the past year.

Above all, I owe an eternal debt of gratitude to my Commander's Action Group leader, Colonel Jorge Silveira—whose intellect is matched only by his humility and selflessness—for his friendship and counsel as we sailed together through the Americas living the adventures that brought this book to life.

Of course, at the center of it all are my wife Laura, and my daughters Christina and Julia, who always put up with Dad's "boring" weekend work of thinking, reading, and writing. To them I owe it all.

As always in a work like this, all errors of fact or judgment are mine alone, and I take full responsibility for them—with the concomitant hope that in some small way this volume will help increase understanding and engagement for the United States with our neighbors to the south.

James G. Stavridis
Admiral, USN

Introduction

If I have a single theme for you throughout the coming pages, it is that, collectively, we in the United States need to spend more time with, and pay more attention to, the vitally important region to our south—I hope to convince you of that as we go along. I also hope to persuade you how truly erroneous and disrespectful it is to refer to Latin America and the Caribbean as "America's backyard." This could not be further from the truth. It is my strongest conviction that this region, the Americas, is *our shared home*. It is a home containing a vast and diverse family with a shared stake in a common future. We, the United States, must also strive to ensure that our fellow residents recognize and believe that we are truly in this together; we want them to see the United States as the partner of choice in a cooperative approach to our shared destiny of a safe, peaceful, flourishing, and egalitarian home.

Traveling throughout the Caribbean and Latin America for 3 years as Commander of U.S. Southern Command (USSOUTHCOM), I've had the wonderful opportunity and privilege to experience all that this region has to offer. During my travels, I've been honored to meet with Presidents, prime ministers, defense officials, dignitaries, U.S. Ambassadors, and many others who are fully committed to the security, stability, and prosperity of the people they represent. As a student of the rich culture and heritage that define this hemisphere, I've walked among the ancient ruins of Machu Picchu in Peru, felt the solemn grandeur of sacred cathedrals in Colombia, and marveled at the sheer force of human will as I watched ships big and small traverse the wondrous Panama Canal. I've made it a point along the way to enjoy the traditional cuisine and wine produced in places like Buenos Aires, Santiago, Brasilia, and everywhere else I've visited in the region. I've seen grandiose buildings dating back to the age of the conquistadors and admired monuments of national pride in Managua, Guatemala City, Tegucigalpa, and San Salvador. I've made it a priority to not only learn but to converse in the principal languages of the region, something I am very grateful to have had the opportunity to do.

Again, wherever I travel, with whomever I meet, I convey this important point: The Americas is a home we all share. The United States has so much in common already with our partners throughout the region; as our demography shifts and our Hispanic population blooms, we find increasingly that we share common interests, values, and goals, and are profoundly dependent upon each other in many ways. The geographic, cultural, economic, political, and historical linkages that tie all of the nations of the Americas together are numerous and compelling. While each of us celebrates our uniqueness and diversity across the hemisphere, these tremendous linkages and natural alignments bring us closer together with each passing year. As our hemisphere "virtually" shrinks, each of our nations—working together—becomes more important in facing the challenges posed by this new century.

I am passionate about the ties we share in this hemisphere. At U.S. Southern Command, we dedicate a good portion of our time studying these connections, and firmly believe that the region is inextricably linked to the economic, political, cultural, and security fabric of the United States. Understanding each other helps us all make the best use of our collective and distinctive implements of national power in order to better extend peace and prosperity throughout the entire region. Perhaps the most important connection we share is that of respect for democracy, freedom, justice, human dignity, human rights, and human values. We are fortunate that all but one nation in the region are led by a democratically-elected government.

Throughout the hemisphere, among both the leaders *and* the people of these vibrant and diverse democracies, there is also a common understanding and recognition that the regional challenges to security, stability, and prosperity are threats to us all. The scourges of illegal drugs, poverty, and violent criminal gangs are transnational and thus cannot be countered by any one nation alone. Their eradication requires cooperative solutions; it requires security forces, international agencies, and humanitarian assistance groups throughout the region to band together to establish a *true* Partnership for the Americas. Fortunately, many of the nations of this community have courageous leaders at the helm to navigate this epic journey, as well as some well-developed structures in place to discuss these threats and to fashion regional synergistic strategies to counter them.

As evinced by the already strong linkages shared within the hemisphere, we believe that overcoming the region's challenges to security and prosperity will unlock the real promise of the Americas: a secure, prosperous, and democratic hemisphere that works together to face threats to peace and stability.

The word *promise* has two appropriate meanings for how U.S. Southern Command approaches its role in the region to achieve our mutual view of the future for this hemisphere. On one hand, a promise is a commitment honestly undertaken and executed by two or more parties. In this case,

Southern Command is committed to lasting and beneficial partnerships with the countries in the region. Encouraging, cultivating, and nurturing regional partnerships have been cornerstones of our strategy for many years and part of a formal strategic objective for the last 4 years. Our promise entails fulfilling the commitment of being a good partner and pursuing better cooperative security arrangements in order to confront together the tough challenges that face us now and into the future.

Promise can also mean *potential*—the potential to do something foundational and fundamental; the potential to be something special and extraordinary. We believe that through lasting partnerships, we can help achieve the security conditions necessary to create the enduring basis for prosperity and healthy democratic institutions in this important region. This is the promise of a hemisphere of shared trade, technology, commerce, science, and culture; a home free of gangs, drugs, human trafficking, money laundering, and terrorism. It is the promise of all of us together finding cooperative solutions to demanding security challenges. No one nation is as strong as all of us working together.

The goal of U.S. Southern Command is simple: we will work with our partners to help unlock this "Promise of the Americas." Everyday we strive to be engaged in a positive way with as many of our regional security partners as possible, and in doing so, enhance the security of the United States while simultaneously enhancing their own as well. The command strives to fulfill the promise of this region by building partner capacity and enabling partner nations to protect their sovereignty and provide for the security and well-being of their citizens. Even as we focus on security cooperation, our partners at the U.S. Agency for International Development (USAID) focus on development and our partners at the State Department focus on diplomacy.

Let me share a few examples of these partnerships and their benefits:

■ During the summer of 2007, the hospital ship USNS *Comfort* visited 12 countries in the region on a humanitarian assistance training mission. Working closely with various Ministries of Health and international charitable organizations, the 800-person crew performed nearly 400,000 patient treatments over a 4-month period. The *Comfort* mission offers a model for cooperation and partnerships across the Americas, and she returned in 2009 and again in 2010 responding to the Haitian earthquake. In embarking various nongovernmental organizations on *Comfort*—such as Project Hope and Operation Smile—we have only just begun to tap into the enormous resources and synergies of partnering with the private sector and nonprofit ventures.

■ Following the devastating effects of a major earthquake in Pisco, Peru, numerous countries in the region responded immediately to alleviate the suffering of residents there.

■ Regional and international relief efforts were again mobilized and deployed to Belize and Nicaragua in the aftermath of Category 5 hurricanes. Nicaraguan President Daniel Ortega personally thanked U.S. Soldiers for responding in his country's time of need.

■ Working with partners throughout the region, nearly 730 tons of cocaine were interdicted in the Caribbean and Pacific in 2006–2009.

■ The Panama Canal is often referred to as "the economic heartbeat" of the Americas, because of its crucial role in the economic well-being of the hemisphere. In both 2007 and 2008, more than 20 nations sent naval forces to participate in Panamax, making it the largest joint maritime security exercise in the world. We had even more outstanding participation and representation in Panamax 2009.

I'm encouraged by these and the many other examples of cooperative efforts in the region. Through these efforts, we are building partnerships in time of peace that will endure in time of trial.

Another example of a durable and vital partnership that has proven essential to the success of the command and engagement in our shared home has been the one that USSOUTHCOM shares with its own physical home, the wonderful city of Miami, Florida. In September of 2009, we celebrated the 13th anniversary of our move to South Florida. Thinking about our indispensable bonds with the city, what stands out most in my mind is the connection to this community that has welcomed and embraced the men, women, and families of Southern Command. Each day as I drive through the gate and enter the command compound and see our new headquarters buildings under construction, I also see the prospect of continued partnership with this important and vibrant society for many years to come.

Having been born in West Palm Beach, I personally love being here in South Florida. Miami is truly the "Magic City" and is utterly unique. It is fast-changing and fast-paced. It is culturally diverse, energetic, and exciting. And it is constantly transforming and reinventing itself, undergoing a continual and obvious metamorphosis that we see every day in Miami's skyline, in the continuous flux of the population and cultural influences, and in the business opportunities that are ever-evolving and growing. This mutable character is one of Miami's greatest strengths and each day it reveals even more promise for the future.

When U.S. Southern Command relocated from Panama, Miami's strategic location and access to the region were the deciding factors that brought us here. As a major transportation hub for the Americas, the Miami location of the headquarters has increased staff access to partner nation counterparts. Our location has contributed to strengthened military-to-military relations across the region. This is not just because it is easier for *us* to get to the *region*, but also because it is easier for our *partners* to visit *us*.

Miami also offers the opportunity for cultural immersion in the region in a way no other city could. It really is the best classroom for the cultural understanding we need to be good partners in the Americas: there are expatriate communities from every country in the hemisphere; major Spanish-language radio, television, and newspapers in Miami are recognized for their premier coverage of the Americas; and, Miami is home to numerous academic centers focused on the hemisphere. This has afforded Southern Command the opportunity to engage in constructive dialogue with many regional experts, gaining a broader perspective and understanding of the region. Miami is also the first home (or a second or third home) for many Latin American and Caribbean or Hispanic American musicians and artists, all of whom add to the richness not only of this community but of the entire country.

Finally, Miami is the "Gateway to the Americas" for more than just business interests and the rich cultural influences of the region. Numerous nongovernmental and governmental organizations focused on Latin America and the Caribbean have a strong presence in Miami. U.S. Southern Command has capitalized on their presence by organizing to integrate and synchronize activities and resources within the region. This interagency group has become the seed for a major transformation of the command into a new vision of integration, with over 20 interagency partners represented.

In short, Miami is a dynamic, effervescent, and transformational city that represents new promises every day; it has been the optimal location for U.S. Southern Command to lead the way in evolutionary and innovative approaches to interaction with Latin America and the Caribbean. We've had a fruitful partnership thus far and it will inevitably continue to grow and expand in new directions, exploring new connections with our community every day. A magic city indeed—especially for U.S. Southern Command.

Allow me to leave you with this final introductory thought: We are living in an age of rapid change facilitated by advancing technologies and increasingly networked systems, societies, and economies. In order for security agencies to be successful in this complex environment, those organizations must be flexible, open, and forward-thinking. As globalization deepens and threats emerge and evolve, security organizations will need to continue fostering and building relationships with willing and capable partners to face transnational and multinational challenges. The security of the United States and that of our partners depends largely on our capacity to leverage joint, international, interagency, and public-private cooperation, all reinforced by focused messaging and strategic communication.

Despite all the references to change, evolution, transformation, and the like, our core mission at U.S. Southern Command has been left unchanged—we remain a military organization conducting military operations and promoting security cooperation in Central America, the Caribbean, and South America in order to achieve U.S. strategic objectives.

The ensuing pages will attempt to describe the characteristics, beauty, and vastness of the diverse region to our south. I will explore the tremendous linkages that we share with Latin America and the Caribbean—important geographic, cultural, economic, and geopolitical linkages. I will then also outline some difficult underlying conditions faced by the region—led by poverty and unequal wealth distribution—and how they contribute to specific challenges such as crime, violence, and illicit trafficking of drugs, people, and weapons. Finally, I will spend the majority of this work describing some innovative approaches and key initiatives USSOUTHCOM has underway to fulfill our mission more effectively and detail our efforts to modify our organization to meet current and future security demands. I will showcase some of the positive results and real success stories that we—both specifically at USSOUTH-COM and as the region as a whole—are seeing from the innovative approaches and initiatives in progress.

We are all in this together. The fortunes of those who call the Americas home will rise and fall together. We in the United States want to contribute as appropriate and necessary to the well-being of our home. There are a wide variety of mechanisms available, ranging from intelligence and information-sharing, to mutually beneficial exchanges of trainers, to transfers of equipment and technology. Our message is truly a message for the entire region: the United States is a caring friend and partner—we genuinely welcome the opportunity to discuss ways we can cooperate on regional security concerns.

At U.S. Southern Command we are ready to discuss issues and craft solutions to challenges and threats to our shared security, stability, and prosperity. Our pledge is to work with joint, combined, multiagency, multinational, nongovernmental, and private sector partners to achieve our collective goals in the region. In support of these, we employ a theater security cooperation strategy that calls for building host nation security capabilities. Over time, these capabilities will ensure our partner nations have the means to control their borders and protect their citizens, while also deepening the roots of good governance. We also envision our partners being able to work together in a collective environment so they can counter emerging and adapting threats. To this end, most of our military-to-military engagement is in the form of training and education programs, joint exercises, peacekeeping, and other partnership programs.

Latin America and the Caribbean are not "America's backyard"—that is an expression that is wrong in every dimension. The Americas is a home that we share together; and in this home, we must all work together to help each other face the security challenges of this turbulent but ultimately promising 21st century.

Jim Stavridis
Miami, Florida
Spring 2009

Chapter 1

We're All in This Together

The United States can make an enormous contribution in this new stage of global development by helping deepen hemispheric cooperation and political dialogue. If successful, this will lead to a better future for our peoples.

—H.E. Michelle Bachelet
President of Chile

During the last 3 years, many people have said to me, "Admiral, what you're doing at Southern Command is so important because that's America's backyard." If I accomplish nothing else in these pages, I will consider this piece a resounding success if I can convince you to remove that phrase from your lexicon—if I can get that out of your vocabulary. This is not our backyard, nor is it our front porch. Those are clearly the wrong images. My thesis for you is this: the Americas are a home that we share together.

Looking south from the United States through the lens at U.S. Southern Command (USSOUTHCOM), what I have discovered is a unitary hemisphere of enormous diversity, beauty, and potential. It is a vast and varied region of the world and it defies easy categorization. Essentially, I have witnessed, and found myself a member of, a house in which nearly half a billion people live together in relative tranquility when compared to other houses in other neighborhoods of the world; and, as family members are wont to do, they both share and compete for resources, languages, cultures, and familial ties. If we fail to spend more time thinking about these members and engaging them, we will find that as time goes on, our family members in this part of the world will have drifted away from us. We will become a house divided. And that would be, in my opinion, extremely deleterious to the security and the future of the United States of America.

U.S. Southern Command is responsible to the Secretary of Defense and the President of the United States for U.S. national security interests through roughly one-half of this hemisphere—31 countries, 10 territories or protectorates, and approximately 460 million people. All told, it is about one-sixth of the Earth's land surface and almost half of the population of the Americas. It is obvious, though too often underappreciated, that we in the United States have much in common with our partners throughout the region; we share common interests and are dependent upon each other in so many ways. The Americas is an interconnected system—a very diverse, yet interrelated, community. It is a community fundamental to the future of the United States.

There are numerous and compelling geographic, cultural, economic, and political linkages that tie all of the nations of the Americas together. These ties are manifested in the present, ranging from our shared economic activity to our comparative democratic ideals, as well as from mutual social and cultural appreciation to similar geography and climatic systems. There are also historical linkages based upon European colonial exploration and conquest, the insertion of Christianity and other foreign religions, and the way all of this impacted the indigenous peoples throughout the region that were here long before the Europeans arrived. For example, take the great cathedral in Santiago, Chile—it was a magnificent structure by the year 1600, when the highest edifice north of the Rio Grande was probably two floors and built of wood. There is a real pattern to the development in and of this region that evolved from the Catholic Church and it is worth knowing and understanding that. One cannot merely focus on the existing superstructure of the house without acknowledging and seeking to understand the historical linkages and foundation upon which the house is built.

Another comment I hear frequently during my travels is, "Well it must be great to be SOUTHCOM, Jim, because you know, all the countries down there are pretty much the same." Wait a minute. Consider for a moment the following contrasting examples. Brazil—for most, the name conjures up the iconic image of the statue of Christ the Redeemer, one of the new Seven Wonders of the World. It sits above the gorgeous city of Rio de Janeiro, in a country of almost 200 million people, where they speak Portuguese, not Spanish. Brazil is a very vibrant and unique culture, a massive state that is emerging in a global way. Contrast that to Belize, a tiny, African-descended country on the Caribbean, tucked away in Central America, where the language spoken is English. Can there be two more different countries?

Think about Chile, a First World country in every sense, where 16 million people have created a strong and vibrant economy. Chile has more free trade agreements than any other nation in the world and Spanish is its primary language. Contrast that with Haiti, the poorest country in the hemisphere and among the poorest in the world. The language spoken there is not French—rather, they speak Creole, which is an amalgam of African dialect, Caribbean slang, a great deal of French, and some English. It is a very diverse language in and of itself. Chile and Haiti, Brazil and Belize—utterly different. This is a region of enormous diversity and we need to appreciate that here in the United States.

A House United—Linkages

With the theme of a shared home in a vast and diverse neighborhood hopefully omnipresent in your mind, let me walk you through some of the streets of this neighborhood—the linkages between the United States and the rest of the nations in this region of the world. To appreciate our linkages, one only has to look at a map. Of course, we benefit from our physical connection by a plethora of land, sea, and air routes. Our proximity lends itself to a very natural tendency to depend upon each other. But we are also connected by so much more than physical means—we share environmental, cultural, security, and economic ties that inextricably link the fates of every nation, every resident of this house, in our hemisphere. In every sense, we share the same DNA in this region.

Continuing with this human metaphor, one might argue that the most important linkage between a nation and the nations around it and around the world is demographics. According to the August 2008 U.S. Census Bureau report, about 15 percent of us—just over 46 million—are of Hispanic descent. When undocumented Spanish-speaking workers are added to the count, it is fair to assume that the United States is now the second-largest Spanish speaking country in the world, only after Mexico. For added perspective, more Hispanics live in the United States today than there are Canadians in Canada or Spaniards in Spain. Meanwhile, the purchasing power of our burgeoning Hispanic population is pushing toward 1 trillion dollars, annually.

That's just today—what about the future? The Census Bureau report goes on to state that by the middle of this century, 30 percent of the citizens of the United States—approximately 133 million people—will be of Hispanic origin. That's by 2050, which is, or hopefully will be, within most of our lifetimes. And where will these people be living? A little over one hundred years ago, the 10 largest cities in the United States based on population were, not surprisingly, located predominantly in the northeast corridor—New York, Boston, Philadelphia, and so forth. Today, of the 10 largest cities, 3 still exist in the northeast, but the other 7 are along the

Figure 1–1. Shared Home of the Americas

southwest border section of the country: Dallas, Houston, San Antonio, Phoenix, San Diego, Los Angeles, and San Jose. Seven of our 10 largest cities border this world to the south.

In addition to the physical and the demographic linkages, the bedrock foundation of our shared home is a common social and political sense that respects democracy, freedom, justice, human dignity, human rights, and human values. We share the belief that these democratic principles must be at the core of what we accomplish in the region and that free governments should be accountable to their people and govern effectively. This common belief is most evident as expressed in the first article of the Inter-American Democratic Charter: "The people of the Americas have the right to democracy and their governments have an obligation to promote and defend it. Democracy is essential for the social, political, and economic development of the peoples of the Americas."[1]

The rest of this tremendous consensus document of the Americas further reinforces our shared values and the goal of strengthening representative democracy in the region. The Charter's promise has been largely fulfilled as democracy has made great strides in the last three decades in the hemisphere: today, civilian constitutional leadership chosen by competitive, participatory elections governs every sovereign nation but one in the region—Cuba. Indeed, the last 3 years have been watershed years for elections, as more general, presidential, legislative, and local elections were held than in any previous time in the entire history of the Americas. The political linkages between the United States and this part of the world are profoundly better today because of this evolution of the last 30 years. We look forward to the first time in history when our entire hemisphere is united in democracy.

The nations of the Americas are also increasingly connected and interdependent economically with our individual and collective fortunes intertwined. Trade between all of our countries is certainly growing and has become an important aspect of building the conditions for prosperity throughout the region. The Americas represents about a 2-trillion-dollar-a-year interwoven economy. Many in the United States normally think in terms of east and west when it comes to trade—in terms of Europe and Asia, respectively. In reality, however, more of the global trade of the United States goes north and south than goes east or west—40 percent of our trade stays right here within the Americas, half of which is with Latin America and the Caribbean alone. This huge volume of goods and services, this life-sustaining trade circulating throughout the hemisphere, acts like oxygen through our nation's bloodstream. As trade relationships mature and grow, we will see an increase in this economic symbiosis; the nations of the community will work together to forge stronger bonds and closer ties to increase their collective prosperity.

An important example of this connection is that just over 50 percent of the U.S. consumption of crude oil and petroleum products is imported from within our own neighborhood, the Western Hemisphere, with 34 percent coming from Latin America and the Caribbean, far outweighing the 22 percent imported from the Middle East. An important facilitator to this critical trade through the Americas—the major causeway—is the Panama Canal, which sees almost 15,000 ships transit each year, of which two-thirds are going to or from one of our coasts in the United States. The canal, in effect, is the economic heartbeat of the Americas, since 7 of the top 10 nations whose trade passes through the canal are in the Western Hemisphere. Panama recently passed an important referendum to expand the canal for a projected twofold increase in throughput capacity, which will certainly build the growing economic interdependence of this region. The canal also provides an important strategic transit for the nations of this neighborhood if rapid positioning of naval or logistic vessels were required during an emergency.

Historically, we have had very close military ties with our partners in the region. For example, Brazil fought with us during World War II—the Brazilian Expeditionary Force, numbering over 25,000 troops, fought with U.S. forces in Italy from 1944 to 1945. During the Korean War, a Colombian infantry battalion and warship served with the U.S.-led United Nations Command. Beginning in the 1950s, several Latin American countries contributed military units to United Nations (UN) peacekeeping operations in the Middle East. Recently, in Iraq, troops from El Salvador served as part of the multinational presence and have now completed a noteworthy 11 rotations with over 3,000 total troops. The Dominican Republic, Nicaragua, and Honduras also dispatched troops to support the efforts in Iraq, and U.S. troops have worked shoulder-to-shoulder with friends from this hemisphere in UN peacekeeping missions around the world for decades.

These are all examples of our partner nations, our cohabitants in our shared home, fighting side-by-side with us in times of conflict. However, we also engage with these nations continuously during peacetime through various bilateral and multilateral exercises, conferences, and other training engagements. One example is the daily interaction the U.S. military has with future senior military leaders throughout the region at military establishments such as the Western Hemisphere Institute for Security Cooperation, the Center for Hemispheric Defense Studies, and the Inter-American Air

Forces Academy. The camaraderie developed among military officers at these institutions and the schools' strong emphasis on democratic values and respect for human rights are critical to creating military organizations capable of effective combined operations.

These bonds, these connections, these linkages—physical, demographic, political, social, economic, and military—are profound. They form the foundation of our shared home. They will contribute to an increased sense of interconnection between the United States and the other inhabitants of this region. However, as with any locality, the roving patrols of the neighborhood watch have revealed a number of elements that challenge or threaten the security and stability of its residents.

A House Divided—Challenges

Given the criticality of our profound linkages in the Americas, it is imperative that we understand the challenges that exist within our shared home, affecting each of its residents, albeit sometimes in different ways and to different degrees. The current challenges and security concerns that we face in this hemisphere fortunately do not involve any imminent conventional military threat to the United States, nor do we anticipate one in the near- or mid-term future. For the foreseeable future, we also do not see any major military conflict developing among our neighbors, the nations in Latin America and the Caribbean. Communication has been strong in our region and has proven itself over the last couple of years during some of the region's political tensions. This is evidenced by the peaceful mediation and resolution by regional leaders of the crisis between Ecuador and Colombia that occurred in March of 2008. The creation of the new South American Defense Council is another indication of the tendency to create forums to encourage dialogue and to reduce tension.

Despite this "peaceful" state of our shared home, at least from a state-on-state violence perspective, numerous security challenges undoubtedly still exist. Narcoterrorism, drug trafficking, crime, gangs, and natural disasters are the primary security concerns and pose the principal challenges to regional stability, and to the United States from the region. Additionally, mass migrations, humanitarian crises, and the specter of ideological extremist terrorism are of concern and warrant due vigilance on our part. These challenges loom large for many of the residents of this region; they are transnational, they are multinational; and they are adaptive and insidious threats to those seeking peace and stability. By their very nature, these challenges cannot be countered by one nation alone—they require transnational and multinational solutions. Within our own country, they cannot be overcome by the military alone—they require a truly integrated interagency community that brings to bear the synergistic effects of a unified, full-spectrum governmental and even private sector approach in order to best address and confront these challenges.

But before we examine the specific threats to this community, it is essential to comprehend the omnipresent influences that shape and in some cases exacerbate the above mentioned conditions. Despite the economic gains of the past decade, poverty and income inequality remain grave concerns for many people in Latin American and the Caribbean. These concerns drive social unrest and provide fertile ground for many of the region's public security challenges—the same ground upon which our foundation and fundamental linkage pillars are embedded.

To understand this region, the first thing you need to understand is that the world to the south is still very much an expanse in which poverty is the dominant problem. Poverty. According to the 2007 United Nations Economic Commission for Latin America and the Caribbean (ECLAC) report, *Social Panorama of Latin America*, almost 40 percent of the region's inhabitants are living in poverty, defined as an income of less than 2 U.S. dollars a day. That is roughly 180 million people—the equivalent of the population of everyone in the United States east of the Mississippi—all living on less than the cost of a cup of coffee in the states. Furthermore, nearly 16 percent are living in extreme poverty, defined as less than 1 dollar per day.

Combined with poverty is a disproportionate wealth distribution that is second only to sub-Saharan Africa. According to the World Bank's 2008 World Development Indicators report, the richest 20 percent of the Latin American population earns 57 percent of the region's income, earning twenty times that of the poorest 20 percent. By comparison, the richest 20 percent in high-income regions of the world earns only 7.7 times that of the poorest group. Without a doubt, a true and salient feature of our shared home is that much of this community has not yet emerged into the global economy—it is still, in some ways, in some parts of the region, locked in the past.

Thus, poverty and a large unequal wealth distribution as a result of failing to engage fully in a global environment are two of the fundamental undercurrents of the hemisphere. A third factor in the region that is key to one's understanding of our shared home is the characteristics and the influences of the indigenous cultures. Let me spend a brief moment describing Potosí, Bolivia—a place that very few people, particularly in the United States, would know much about. In the 1600s, Potosí was among the top five cities in the world in population, exceeding 200,000 at its peak. That's the good news. The bad news is that the reason it had a population of over 200,000 is that this was the location of the largest silver mine in the world. Eight million indigenous Indian slaves died there mining silver for the Spanish. Why do I tell you about Potosí? Because it is important to understand the depth of the emotion in the indigenous cultures in this part of the world, in the people who were residents in this home long before outsiders came in and started "remodeling," doing so-called "home improvements" and "upgrades." It is critical that we truly grasp the historical impact that centuries of colonization and conquest, millions of lives lost, and countless tons of natural resources extracted, continues to have on our partners in this region.

Our shared home has poverty; it is steeped in income inequality and has not yet emerged into the global economy fully; there are indigenous pressures moving through it, but does it have to be like this? To illustrate the point about the potential of this region, I give you this historical anecdote. In the mid-1600s, after an Anglo-Dutch war, the Dutch, as part of the peace and treaty process, were given the choice of which two possessions to keep, namely: Suriname, the old Dutch Guyana on the north coast of South America, or New Amsterdam in North America, a place we know today as New York City. The Dutch chose Suriname.

How did that choice turn out? New York is a city of 8.2 million people, the center of the global economy along with Hong Kong and London. Paramaribo, the capital of Suriname, still looks much as it did several hundred years ago—beautiful, tranquil, rural, but still largely locked in the past. Now, why do I compare and contrast these images? The point is this: if you draw a line, arbitrarily across northern Mexico, and you go back to the year 1500, everything above and below that line is very similar—same climate, same natural resources, same level of indigenous populations, conquistadores knocking at the door in both places; the two sections are almost identical in every aspect in the year 1500.

Now fast forward 500 years: the north is one of the richest parts of the world while the south is still a region in so much poverty. We could spend this entire book, and perhaps several others like it, talking about why that is, but my point here is to emphasize the enormous potential of the region to the south. There is no reason whatsoever why the nations to the south of us cannot emerge in the global economy and be part of a wealthy, forward-looking and -leaning society. However, the cumulative effects of poverty and income inequality in this region provide a fertile field for the seeds of social and political insecurity and attendant instability to sprout, take root, and grow into the weeds of drugs, crime, gangs, illegal immigration, and trafficking, among others.

Pressing Security Concerns

Taking all this into account, and stemming from these underlying conditions, let us now focus first on the three most pressing security concerns in the region: illegal drugs, gangs, and crime. And based upon the proximity and the linkages to the United States, these become significant security concerns for our nation as well. I will begin with the ubiquitous and most all-pervading of those threats—narcotics.

The global illicit drug trade remains a significant—perhaps the significant—transnational security threat as its power and influence continue to undermine democratic governments, terrorize populations, impede economic development, and hinder regional stability. The profits from this drug trade, principally cocaine, are an enabling catalyst for the full spectrum of threats to our national security, and present formidable challenges to the security and stability for all who inhabit our shared home. Illegal narcotics trafficking is the fuel that powers the car of misery, traveling on the streets in our neighborhood. Our success—or failure—to address this insidious threat and remove this source of fuel and eventually get that car off our streets, will have a direct and lasting impact on the stability and well-being of both developed and developing residents. And this will be true not just in our neighborhood, but in other neighborhoods throughout the world.

Allow me to focus on one specific narcotic that is particularly pervasive and devastating to our hemisphere: cocaine. The Andean Ridge in South America is the world's leading source of coca cultivation and, despite international efforts and record interdictions and seizures, the region still produces enough cocaine to meet the demand here in the United States and a growing demand abroad. Evidence of this global market can be seen in the fact that Spain just recently passed the United States as the highest per capita consumer of cocaine in the world. Still, every year in the United States, somewhere between 6 and 10 thousand U.S. citizens die as a result of cocaine that can be traced back to this region. Not from methamphetamines, not from heroin, not from prescription drugs—6 to 10 thousand die just from cocaine. That equates to two to three times the tragic loss of lives from 9/11, every year. And that number accounts for overdoses, criminal activity attendant to the sale of cocaine, innocent bystanders, and police officers—6 to 10 thousand a year.

From a business model standpoint, the drug trade is an enormous industry that equates to roughly $65 billion a year in profits. When you add the resources we use to address health and crime consequences—as well as the loss of productivity suffered from disability, death, and withdrawal from the legitimate workforce—the total societal impact cost to the U.S. economy exceeds $240 billion and grows at a rate of 5 percent per year. Extending this outward to include our fellow inhabitants of this region, it becomes an approximately $300 billion global commerce of illegal drug production, distribution, and consumption that is also devastating whole societies in Latin America and the Caribbean. The growing number of societies impacted is directly attributable to the fact that narcotraffickers are intrinsically transnational and continuously adjust their operations to adapt to law enforcement efforts by developing new trafficking routes and consumer markets. They are also highly innovative and keep investing in relatively low-cost and unique conveyance and concealment technologies to counter our detection systems. A vivid example of this is the self-propelled semi-submersible (SPSS) vehicle—low-riding, low-profile vessels that narcotraffickers use to skim along the water line to avoid visual and radar detection. These comparatively new vessels now bring literally tons of illicit cargo to market.

Although we have seen several variants in size, payload capacity, and range, on average, an SPSS can carry approximately 7–10 tons of cocaine; it typically has a crew of 3–4, can reach speeds up to 12–15 knots, refuel at sea, and travel about 600–800 miles unrefueled. SPSS vessels are being built in the jungles in Colombia for about 1/300th of the return on investment of each individual payload. In the last 3 years, U.S. and partner nation interdiction teams caught 6 of these in 2006, caught or tracked 40 of them in 2007, and interdicted 11 vehicles at sea on their way to market in 2008. By all estimates, we anticipate roughly 60 similar vessels in 2009 will ply the waters of our shared home, with a collective cargo capacity of 330 metric tons of cocaine. This is a significant problem. And it's not just because of cocaine—if you can move 7–10 tons of cocaine via a single SPSS into the United States or into one of our neighbors, what else can you put in these? This is obviously a big concern and a complex problem, as is the observation that traffickers have expanded their presence in West Africa as a springboard to Europe, while also exploring new Middle Eastern and Asian markets. Finally, we have noted that traffickers have shifted from high seas routes to multi-staging tactics along the Central American littorals, thus attempting to evade international interdiction efforts.

This sign of expansion, both in tactics and in associative elements, is particularly troubling as it leads to an area of increasing concern, namely the nexus of illicit drug trafficking—including routes, profits, and corruptive influences—and terrorism, both "home grown" as well as imported Islamic terrorism. In the Western Hemisphere, the illicit drug trade historically has contributed, and continues to contribute, significant financial resources to known local terrorist groups like the Fuerzas Armadas Revolucionaras de Colombia (Revolutionary Armed Forces of Colombia, or FARC) and the Sendero Luminoso (Shining Path) in Peru. In August of 2008, U.S. Southern Command supported a Drug Enforcement Administration operation, in coordination with host countries, which targeted a Hizballah-connected drug trafficking organization in the Tri-Border Area of Argentina, Brazil, and Paraguay. Two months later, we supported another interagency community operation that resulted in the arrests of several dozen individuals in Colombia associated with a Hizballah-connected drug trafficking and money laundering ring.

Identifying, monitoring, and dismantling the financial, logistical, and communication linkages between illicit trafficking groups and terrorist sponsors are critical to not only ensuring early indications and warnings of potential terrorist attacks directed at the United States and our cohabitants in this region, but also in generating a global appreciation and acceptance of this tremendous threat to security. As a consequence, nations which were once isolated from the illicit drug trade are now experiencing its corrosive effects. Most nations in the hemisphere are now struggling to counteract the drug trade's destabilizing and corrupting influence. Innovative and inclusive approaches and partnerships are needed to successfully confront this dangerous threat. It will take a coordinated and multiagency and multinational strategic approach that brings to bear the strengths and resources of diverse, capable groups to stem the rising tide of this sinister and cancerous threat.

Drugs—unquestionably—are at the top of the list, not only because of their own adulterating effects, but also because they serve as a gateway for other ills to enter into and take up residence in our neighborhood. For example, a close corollary to the spread of illegal drug traffic is the alarming growth of criminal activity and violence in the region—some of which is a byproduct of the drug trade, but the rest of which is another weed by itself, allowed to grow in the fertile soil of the region's extensive poverty and inequality. Violence is now among the five principal causes of death in several countries in Latin America and the Caribbean. Over the past decade, approximately 1.2 million deaths can be linked to crime in Latin America and the Caribbean. In fact, United Nations data places the annual homicide rate for the region as one of the highest in the world, with 27.5 homicides per 100,000 people—five times that of the United States and three times that of the world average. The Caribbean registers as the highest murder rate of any of the world's subregions, with 30 per 100,000. In El Salvador, the rate is over 55—a rate approaching the level of a war zone. Recent surveys in Guatemala and El Salvador show that two-thirds of the respondents cited crime as the number one problem facing their countries, six times the number who chose poverty.

These statistics are underscored by the growing influence of gangs in several countries and of delinquent youth in general. In Central America, Haiti, and Jamaica, in addition to major cities in Brazil, gangs and criminal violence are a security priority, with some gang population estimates reaching into the hundreds of thousands. Primarily, these are urban gangs whose ranks are filled mainly by disenfranchised youth. Central American street gangs—maras or pandillas—are known for their brutal initiations and their extortion of "protection money," or "war taxes" as the locals refer to it. These gangs do not just pose a concern in Latin America—rather, the more sophisticated groups operate regionally, and even globally, routinely crossing borders and operating inside the United States ranging from near our nation's capital in Northern Virginia to the West Coast in Southern California.

The costs associated with violence in the region are difficult to assess, to be sure, but the Inter-American Development Bank has estimated the losses from crime reach 15 percent of gross domestic product for the region. This cost estimate is not just human costs, but on the order of $250 billion annually in economic impact. This has become a major threat and a destabilizing factor in many nations in the Western Hemisphere, as this economic drain inhibits the efforts to alleviate the underlying conditions of poverty and inequality.

In a noble attempt to ensure social integrity, several nations in the region have committed military forces to counter threats that normally would be the responsibility of the police. Although this is clearly not a preferred solution—especially from the human rights perspective—the growing trend is born out of the simple necessity to counter increasingly powerful and socially destructive gangs, drug cartels, and criminal organizations. In most cases, the military has been deployed as reinforcement for undermanned and outgunned law enforcement units.

But as public security and national defense roles and lines of authority blur, the governments of our shared home will have to be particularly vigilant. The reasons for this include: military units are not normally trained for conducting domestic security; military doctrine is not oriented toward the tasks of law enforcement; and, finally, military weapons are not particularly suited to the task. Here in the United States, for example, the primary responsibility for helping our hemispheric partners solve these challenges resides with the Department of Justice, Department of State, and the U.S Agency for International Development (USAID). We in the Department of Defense seek to be supportive and helpful where appropriate; and through our vital and robust military-to-military linkages throughout the region, we continue to pass along this message to our counterparts: the complexity of the challenges facing the governments of our shared home only reinforces the need for coordinated multiagency and multinational solution sets.

The Terrorism Threat

Even as crime, drugs, and gangs remain a continuing concern and function as a modern day Cerberus, preventing some of our neighbors from being able to emerge into a stable and secure global environment, U.S. Southern Command also focuses on the potential threat terrorism poses to our foundation and our soil, both literally in the United States as well as figuratively in our shared home. And of course, in today's world, when someone says "terrorism," we tend to be spring-loaded to think of the terrorism of Islamic extremists. Here the use is expanded to comprise all types of terrorism, including narcoterrorism. And make no mistake— terrorist networks are active throughout our hemisphere. These networks include domestic narcoterrorists, such as the aforementioned FARC, who reside mainly in Colombia, as well as the Shining Path Maoist-style narco-terrorists of Peru. Islamic terrorist networks are also active, primarily involved in fundraising, proselytizing, and logistical support for parent organizations based in the Middle East, such as Hizballah and Hamas.

Throughout the neighborhood, particularly since 9/11, the potential for terrorist activity is a growing concern. We consider Latin America and the Caribbean to be increasingly likely bases for future terrorist threats to the United States and its neighbors. Our collective intelligence communities have demonstrated that pre-operational and operational activities have indeed occurred, as exemplified by the attempt to blow up the fuel pipelines at John F. Kennedy International Airport in New York in 2007 and the leading suspects' roots in the Caribbean. In addition to "home grown" terrorism practitioners and adherents, the foreign terrorist influence can be felt as members, facilitators, and sympathizers of Islamic terrorist organizations are also present throughout the region. Hizballah appears to be the most prominent group active in the hemisphere; while much of their activity is currently linked to revenue generation, there are indications of an operational presence and the potential for attacks. The Hizballah network in the region is suspected of supporting the terrorist attacks in Buenos Aires in 1992 and again in 1994. We suspect that a similar operational support network exists today and could be leveraged in the future.

But the outlook in this challenge area certainly is not all bad for our shared home. We have seen definite successes in mitigating Islamic terrorist activity in the region. Brazil, Paraguay, and Argentina have made much progress in working together to address terrorism and illicit criminal activity through the Tri-Border Commission. A Regional Intelligence Center, located in Brazil and staffed by agents from all three countries, is nearly fully operational. In the last couple of years, there have been dynamic and successful actions taken against terrorist-linked supporters and facilitators. In January 2006, for example, Colombian authorities dismantled a complex document forgery ring with alleged ties to indigenous and Islamic terrorist organizations. More recently, Brazilian authorities arrested a suspect linked to the assassination of Lebanese Prime Minister Rafik Hairir. Partner nations throughout the region are working together to maximize counterterrorist successes and ultimately deter, dissuade, deny, and disrupt terrorist and terrorist-associated activities in the area.

Colombia's Success Story

Continuing along this positive thread as we complete our discussion of some of the larger challenges to security and stability in our shared home, there can be no more fitting summation of everything that has gone before than spending some time discussing Colombia, now one of our closest friends and partners in the region. Colombia is a strategic ally, an important partner, and a crucial anchor for security and stability in this shared home. This beautiful and diverse country is the second oldest democracy in the hemisphere, and is truly one of the great success stories.

In the late 1990s, Colombia's government was on the verge of failure. The headlines coming out of the country resembled the worst of those to come out of any war-torn country: daily reports of shootings, beheadings, kidnappings, torture, and bombings. The country was embroiled in an internal conflict that, by any objective measure, was literally tearing it apart. Drug cartels had a wide reign and violence was rampant.

Today's Colombia is a completely different story. Through its own military and interagency efforts, and a stream of modest resources and support from the United States as part of Plan Colombia which started during the Clinton administration, Colombia has battled back from the brink of chaos to a far better situation in terms of peace and stability. There is real hope and pride in the country and its accomplishments. The Uribe administration—now leading the follow-on to Plan Colombia, the "Strategy to Strengthen Democracy and Promote Social Development," again with support from the United States—has the country poised for true advancement. Since 2002, homicides have dropped by 40 percent, kidnappings by over 80 percent, and terrorist attacks by over 75 percent. Further, 2008 marked the lowest homicide rate in two decades.

At great effort, the government has established security police force presence in all of its 1,098 municipalities, significantly deterring crime and terrorist incidents. This increased presence has been paired with military development that has produced some significant operational successes against the FARC. None of these was more impactful, perhaps, than the July 2, 2008, daring raid that freed 3 U.S. hostages and 12 others from FARC internment. The Colombian military deserves complete credit for the operation, but it is fair to say that their bold and brilliant tactical action was the culmination of almost 10 years of effort shared by the U.S. Congress, the Colombian government, U.S. Southern Command, and other U.S. agencies responsible for capacity building of the military. The end result was one of the happiest and most satisfying moments of my military career—Marc Gonsalves, Keith Stansell, and Thomas Howes were finally free after almost five-and-a-half long years of captivity. Welcome home, gentlemen—you truly are American heroes!

We have mentioned the FARC several times now, but who and what are they, specifically? Briefly, they are a pseudo-Marxist/Leninist group that originated as a group of ideologues in the militant wing of the Colombian Communist Party in 1964. It began like many militant organizations in the region, rising up out of a popular dissatisfaction with corruption and incompetence in the central government. It eventually started moving away from its ideological base and grew to become heavily involved in the drug industry, primarily through protecting the cartels' crops. Since then, however, out of a need for increased revenue generation, FARC has created its own drug operation and expanded into kidnapping, as previously mentioned. In short, these are bad people seeking to overthrow a legitimate government in Colombia.

But they have not succeeded. The FARC has been beaten back—key leaders at the strategic/secretariat level have been eliminated and they have seen a greater than 50 percent drop in their numbers. Their communications have been disrupted, desertions continue to accelerate, and morale is at an all-time low. The Colombians have done a magnificent job over the last 7 years of taking their nation back from this insurgency. Today, the

Admiral Stavridis (left) and Brigadier General Charlie Cleveland (center) welcome home Keith Stansell, Marc Gonsalves, and Thomas Howes after 1,967 days of captivity by the narcoterrorist organization FARC (Revolutionary Armed Forces of Colombia). The Colombian military freed the Americans in 2008 in a bold operation that marked the culmination of years of capacity building of Colombian forces by the government, U.S. Southern Command, and other U.S. agencies.

democratically elected government led by President Alvaro Uribe has approval ratings in Colombia of over 85 percent. The FARC approval rating is less than 2 percent. In February 2008, approximately 6 million Colombians turned out to march in the streets of their country—it was a sea of white as virtually every person was wearing a white T-shirt adorned with the slogan *Yo soy Colombia* (I am Colombia). They carried banners with emotionally charged statements like: *No Mas FARC* (No More FARC), *No Mas Muertes* (No More Death), *No Mas Mentiras* (No More Lies), and *No Mas Secuestros* (No More Kidnappings). From its earliest origins, the FARC touted themselves and their movement as "popular insurgency"; it is now the most unpopular group in Colombia.

Highly unpopular, yes, but still not completely eradicated. They still have close to 9,000 fighters in the field, down from about 18,000. They are still kidnappers, torturers, murderers, and drug dealers. This is essentially their "business model." The United States has been involved in a supportive way with the aforementioned Plan Colombia—a relatively modest program that included $5 billion over 10 years and less than 800 U.S. troops on the ground, total. This small number shows how an expert cadre can help a country address an insurgency. This is a real model of how to fight a counterinsurgency, and there is much to learn from our Colombian friends about how they have handled this saga.

As Colombian security forces and other government agencies have continued to expand their presence throughout areas that were previously dominated by illegal armed groups like the FARC, there has been an increase of reporting that highlights the atrocities committed by members of these groups. Many of the charges have centered on forced recruiting of minors and the abuses they have suffered at the hands of their illegal armed "commanders." Additionally, internally displaced persons in Colombia have become a source of reporting the human rights abuses, as the legal and security processes required to return them to their homes have been established and enacted by the Colombian government.

Focusing the human rights lens on itself as well, the government of Colombia continually seeks to improve its own human rights record. Most recently, the government dismissed 27 Colombian Army commissioned and noncommissioned officers—to include three generals—for failure to comply with established human rights procedures. The dismissal of security forces members involved in human rights violations has been historic and asserts Colombia's firm intention to confront and correct human rights violations. The government continues to aggressively pursue illegal armed group leaders who have perpetrated human rights crimes against Colombian citizens, as well as investigating inside its own military. This continues to have resounding effects throughout the armed forces, even heavily influencing the retirement of a former army commander.

In addition to investigation and punishment of violations, the government has taken swift action on the prevention and policy side of the equation. The Comprehensive Human Rights and International Humanitarian Law (IHL) Policy of the Ministry of National Defense is the framework document that provides the guidelines, sets the aims, and establishes the programs which the Armed Forces and the National Police are required to obey. The government's aim is to institute a clear structure of rules and regulations that becomes an integral part of all activities of the national security forces and is closely monitored in its applications. All state forces are required to receive mandatory human rights training. Although still in relative nascence, these policies and programs have produced some dramatic reductions in violence since they have been instituted. For example, according to the Colombian Ministry of Defense and the American

Embassy in Bogota reports, homicides have decreased by 40 percent since 2002—the lowest point in 20 years; homicides of mayors, ex-mayors, and councilors have been reduced by 83 percent; kidnappings have declined by 76 percent; and the victims of massacres have been reduced by 81 percent.[2]

Rounding out Colombia's success story, the government's and military's efforts against the FARC have also significantly impacted the drug cartels, as Colombia has extradited over 700 drug traffickers to the United States. And although cocaine production is still a critical concern, interdiction and seizures of cocaine headed to the United States, other neighbors in the region, and destinations abroad have more than doubled over the last 10 years. This increase indicates improved state control, successful governmental strategies, and overall better interagency and international coordination and collaboration. All this has directly contributed to the fastest sustained economic growth in a decade: greater than 5 percent annually for the past 3 years. It has also encouraged a real sense of positive momentum for the entire country. These hard-fought successes, however, need continued support and steadfast effort from the Colombian government in order to fully win the peace—a permanent and lasting peace—for their country.

I highly encourage all serious students of the region to visit and experience firsthand the tremendous overall improvements and strides this vibrant and trusted neighbor to the south has made. Gain a sense from the people that "this is the moment" for Colombia. This is the time for Colombia and the other residents of our shared home to make the final push to win true peace for their country—a peace that will be of great benefit to all who reside in this neighborhood. For as Colombia wins its peace, narcoterrorists will lose the capacity to grow, process, and transport illicit drugs; other forms of terrorism will lose a vital source of support and funding; U.S. and other neighbors' lives and resources will be saved; and, ultimately, the overall security and stability of our shared home will increase.

A Marketplace of Ideas

Let me close by discussing some of the political challenges in the region. Really, these are challenges of ideas—differences of opinion on issues, values, perspectives, and philosophy. We are fortunate as a hemisphere to have as our neighbors, as cohabitants of our shared home, democracies virtually all of whom share similar principles with us. Unfortunately, the realities of poverty, income inequality, and security challenges all contribute to a growing but frustrated expectation from the people for dramatic and rapid change. As evidence of this, a recent survey conducted by AmericasBarometer in the region underscores the current fragility of democracy: as recently as 2006, greater than 25 percent of the population of Latin America and the Caribbean would justify a military coup in the case of high inflation, and more than 20 percent would justify one in the case of high unemployment rates. Granted, these percentages tend to be higher among countries recovering from recent conflict and instability; nevertheless, with the present regional and global economic slowdown, this trend might only continue, thereby leading to further autocratic problems to the detriment of democracy in the hemisphere.

Taking advantage of this arable soil and then adding in an abundance of fertilizer in the form of rhetoric, we have seen instances in some countries where political "change agents" have successfully sowed the seeds of radical change, using promises of achieving sweeping results through unorthodox and unproven economic and political policies. There are external actors trying to exert influence in our shared home, as well. Some wish to do us and our friends and allies harm, while others merely seek to develop uniquely beneficial relationships based on trade and access to new markets and additional natural resources.

In summary, I mention all this in the following context: it is often said that we, the United States, are in a "war of ideas" in the world today. I would agree with the notion that we are in a war of ideas with radical terrorists and networks like al Qaeda. In our own neighborhood, however, we are not in a war of ideas—rather, we are in a "competitive marketplace," a marketplace amidst all the linkages and challenges previously described where the primary commodity traded is ideas. As such, it is incumbent upon us in the United States to demonstrate that our ideas (e.g., personal liberty, electoral democracy, human rights, rule of law, fair and open markets, and political transparency) are the right ones that help a society move forward in a positive way. We need to continue to improve our "acceptance rating" and our "market share." Again, we live and work in a competitive environment, so a great deal of what we need to do as a nation in this region is in the vein of contending with a variety of alternative models, some of which are dramatically different.

To compete in this marketplace, we engage proactively in the region and counter anti-U.S. messaging with persistent engagement and demonstrations of goodwill, competence, and professionalism. The U.S. Government, through the interagency community, assists our partner nations by addressing the underlying conditions of poverty and inequality; concurrently, we at U.S Southern Command help build security relationships and create innovative security initiatives with cooperative partners to confront transnational and multinational security threats. In some cases, we have the complex task of maintaining working relationships with a nation's security force in the face of strained or even antagonistic political leadership and attempts to spread anti-U.S. views and influence. This situation exacerbates the already difficult mission of achieving regional cooperation to address ever-changing and insidious transnational and multinational challenges.

Taken together, all this represents a formidable list of challenges, priorities, and potential areas for cooperation. And we still have not addressed additional specific challenge areas or focuses of concern like U.S.-Cuba relations, mass migration, human rights, humanitarian assistance, and natural disasters; but we will in the proceeding chapters. Clearly, today's situation requires a broader understanding of all aspects of our national engagement in Latin America and the Caribbean. And this broader view brings a better focus upon all our efforts in the region.

Thus far, looking south through the lens at U.S. Southern Command, we have perhaps only been witnessing the tip of the iceberg; but as the coming pages will illustrate, this broader lens has allowed us to start seeing and examining the capabilities of the real mass of the iceberg, the heretofore submerged portion. I am referring, of course, to the enormous hard work of the various agencies and departments of the U.S. Government—the interagency community—as well as those of our partner nations, our neighbors in this shared home. Going still deeper, this mass also encompasses what we truly think is a real untapped and vast potential: namely, the private sector. The coming chapters will highlight the capacity and the abilities of these various elements, as well as offering insight into how they can be brought together, synergistically, in innovative ways with creative and cooperative partnerships. The task before us, then, is to explore how we at U.S. Southern Command confront the myriad complex security challenges in this region and bring security, stability, and ultimately prosperity to the Americas, a home that we share together.

Notes

[1] Article 1, "Inter-American Democratic Charter," available at: <http://www.oas.org/charter/docs/resolution1_en_p4.htm>.

[2] American Embassy Bogota, Scenesetter Cable (U) DTG 13163Z NOV08 and Colombian National Defense Ministry, "Achievements of the Democratic Security Plan," February 2009.

Chapter 2

Have a Plan

The dusty dogmas of the past are insufficient to confront our stormy present. As our world is new, we must think anew.

—Abraham Lincoln

In reading these words by President Lincoln, I am reminded of something President Ronald Reagan said in his 1982 address to the British Parliament. Surveying the strategic landscape and assessing the global threats and challenges at the time, he commented, "the ultimate determinant in this struggle now going on for the world will not be bombs and rockets, but a test of will and ideas." He was, of course, referring to the ideological struggle between capitalism and Soviet communism; but his words ring as true today as when he uttered them.

The physical nature of the threats and challenges we face, as well as the entire range of opportunities present before us, has changed—that much is very clear. No longer can our nation's security organizations and processes focus myopically on a single overarching and potentially existential threat. Today's world is much more complicated and nuanced, with the challenges emanating not from a single peer competitor but from multiple sources, including a growing number of different types of potentially influential state and nonstate actors. In this multipolar (some would even argue "nonpolar") world, beset by shifting centers of economic and political power, the challenges to national, regional, and even global security are marked by greater complexity, ambiguity, and speed. And much of what and how we see is based on the lens through which we look. In fact, it might be more correct if we didn't think of it as looking at the world through a lens, but rather peering into a kaleidoscope. Every gaze—indeed, every rotation—will produce something enormously difficult to anticipate and virtually impossible to predict. To presume we have any way of knowing how the various fragments will combine, and which of a seemingly limitless number of mosaics will result, is optimistic at best and naïve at worst.

Though the world has changed and power balances shift continually, at the broad strategic level, the ultimate determinant between victory and defeat is, as it has always been, a contest of wills and ideas—"brain-on-brain" warfare, if you will. Our senior leaders, specifically within the military, do not spend enough time thinking strategically about how to win that competition. As I briefly mentioned in the preceding chapter, in Latin America and the Caribbean, we are in a "marketplace of ideas" and we need to increase our market share; in this chapter, I will articulate one manner and one forum in which to truly concentrate on the substance and delivery of such ideas—strategy and strategic planning.

A late 1980s study of U.S. military culture once characterized the different branches of military service as being "driven by glacial engines for stability."[1] Changing the military back then, therefore, was like trying to speed up a glacier—huge mass and implacable momentum inevitably carving out its own course. Despite improvements, to some extent, this is still true today for our military, and it continues to apply to many other large, complex, tradition-centric, and vertically oriented and integrated organizations. Indeed, the history of management over the past two decades will reflect this was the beginning of true postmodern organizations that developed the ability to couple strategic speed with global reach and purpose.

In the military's case, it took significant congressional legislation, a new integration philosophy, two decades of trial and error, and several intervening crises and conflicts to slowly increase the speed and change the course of our particular glacier. Today's military is more agile and capable than ever before. Yet creating an organization —especially of the size and scope of the military—that is able to adapt to 21st-century realities requires developing a culture that is change-centric and that has an adaptive structure to match external conditions and forces.

That is the first task before us, then: to take the long view, to think rationally, to ask tough questions, to challenge assumptions, to assess and mitigate risks. We undertake all this in the hopes of attempting to avoid repeating the mistakes of yesterday, shaping the environment today and creating opportunities for tomorrow—in other words, to think strategically.

In surveying our own strategic landscape, we find that the specific challenges we face today are not the same ones faced by those upon whose shoulders we stand. The challenges of the 21st century are far more complex and multifaceted, the speed with which they operate and interact is infinitely greater, and their reach is undeniably regional and increasingly global. This mix of complexity, speed, and reach has forced us to reassess our current paradigms and to ask critical questions. How can we work *together* to help create a more peaceful, stable and prosperous world? How do we act more effectively to confront these challenges, deter potential conflicts, and prevent new crises? How do we transition from a reactive mindset of simply responding to threats and crises, to a more proactive one that focuses on shaping and ultimately creating lasting peace and security in our shared home?

In answering these and other questions, we find that we must *adapt*, we must increase our *speed*, and our *reach* must also be global and our presence persistent. In crafting strategy, whether it is our new maritime strategy, Southern Command's regionally focused Command Strategy 2018, or the National Military Strategy, our vision must be properly focused, our views must be pragmatic, and our missions must be anchored by our values and ideals. We must also strive to remain realistic and inclusive throughout the process.

Military strategy must be envisioned and developed with the idealism embodied in the Constitution, but must be crafted in a realistic tone to ensure military employment remains scalable, flexible, and adaptable to a rapidly changing world. It is a very precarious balance, but it is a balance that must be achieved and maintained.

Sound military strategy must also address the entire spectrum of 21st-century challenges: from constructive humanitarian assistance and civic action, to low-intensity conflict, all the way to major theater war. Executing such a strategy in support of national goals and interests will undermine the base for transnational terrorists and criminal groups, as well as other state and nonstate threats to global stability and peace.

But as we develop strategy and refine it to meet new challenges, we need to lend the proper level of strategic thought and carefully shape the advice we provide our senior civilian leaders. The effective military strategist must be cognizant of the expanding complexity of what defines national interests. We, as military leaders, are typically not responsible for the definition of those interests—rather we are the defenders and protectors of them. In this manner, we can help ensure our strategies indeed reflect the vital national interests of the American people and help the United States remain the partner of choice in this region. We must be increasingly aware that these interests are often transnational in character, as our linked economies and advances in technology continue to shrink the globe. Our desired endstates, as well as our intended (and unintended) audiences, always have to be foremost in our minds when crafting these strategies and formulating messages; in other words, we need to not only *think* strategically, but *communicate* strategically, as well.

We need to be constantly mindful of the bigger picture; that is not always easy. What is easy, however, is to become focused on what pains us the most right now. This is a natural human reaction to distress. And what is most painful right now is the conflict in the Middle East. But to the degree that we narrow our focus solely on that region, we lose sight of other state and nonstate threats around the world, specifically including the region we call home—the Americas. We also start to lose focus on the opportunities to engage world populations at the grassroots level and promote the desire for liberty from within.

This brings me to the importance of being practical and possessing a certain degree of pragmatism in first articulating the principles, and then pursuing the conditions, that underline peace. In looking at things from 50,000 feet, I see that any strategy for success in the Western Hemisphere must be envisioned in the context of a broader global view. It must also be focused on our own vital and enduring national interests, which have to be clearly defined in our strategic documents. We must also remember that due to an increasingly globalized and interconnected region and world, our interests are inextricably linked with those of our neighbors to the South.

As players in the large global system, the security and prosperity of the United States depend as much on the well-being of the rest of this region—and the rest of the world—as the rest of the region and world depends on the well-being of the United States. As Secretary of State Hillary Clinton commented in her remarks at the Asia Society in February 2009, "America cannot solve the problems of the world alone, and the world cannot solve them without America." Today's global system is more economically coupled than ever, but remember, too, there are several *other* linkages that connect us to the many inhabitants of our shared home in the Americas.

Building on these linkages and crafting open and shared strategies to confront mutual challenges and multinational threats will require persistent engagement to foster new relationships, strengthen enduring ones, and build trust. Additionally, we will need to labor tirelessly to ensure that freedom and equality take root and grow, even in unaccustomed soil, blossoming into the regional (and perhaps eventually global) harvest of peace and prosperity we all hope to enjoy within our shared home.

Achieving peace and prosperity is not simply an idealistic dream; rather, it is a reasonable and realistic goal and we must therefore always ask what must be done to achieve it and then maintain it.

"Reason and free inquiry," wrote Thomas Jefferson, "are the only effectual agents against error." These words still resonate today, at times deafeningly. In this competitive environment in which we live, this marketplace, this test of wills and ideas, we must rely on reason and free inquiry—not just on sentiment—to gain market share. We must be innovative and act with boldness *and* restraint. We must have a willingness to pursue multicultural enlightenment to contend with the adversarial and inherently flawed doctrines of ideologically driven extremists, insurgents, politically aligned oppressors, and demagogues. We must recognize that these groups are unable or unwilling to contend with change, and therefore we must focus on presenting their intended disciples and followers with better alternatives. Success in this pursuit is defined by the empowerment of these people to break the chains that keep them shackled to the past, and then joining together in a combined pursuit of freedom and stability in our shared home and around the globe.

The Jellyfish Analogy

Change starts with vision, and from that, a strategy to achieve that vision. No organization can endure without an effective one. But who possesses this vision and then articulates it into an effective strategy? The leader? An elite collection of "seers"? An external consulting group? One flaw in many organizations is the belief that strategy should come *only* from the very top—from an Olympian viewpoint looking down on an organization, essentially formed by a "star chamber" approach. This approach and belief will fail.

Although the leadership of an enterprise provides vision, guidance, and strategic decisions, it is the *entire* enterprise that helps build and carry out a strategy. Much like a jellyfish, where every cell is a sensor and part of the cerebral nervous system, leaders must sense the strategic environment through the sum of the enterprise's parts. To survive in the 21st-century environment, an organization needs each member to be a sensor: no one of us is as smart as all of us together. The entire organization has to exist as a living, breathing, adapting, fluid, and evolving organism.

How do we create an organization like this?

To create an enterprise that can sense both itself and the world around it with an imbedded culture connected to strategy, it is tremendously important to flatten the organization and its information flows. Technology, combined with unencumbered decisionmaking processes, can help us do that. With technology, we can potentially tap into the entire organization from almost anywhere in the world. Figuratively, we can hold the entire enterprise, if not the world, in the palms of our hands. With technology, we can potentially minimize stovepiped information flows, reduce redundancies, speed up communication, and move the strategic message both internally and externally.

But throughout, leadership needs to remove friction and open up access to the organization—access to email accounts, inboxes, and office doors—and to allow this information to come in mostly unimpeded. Leaders need to be capable of processing vast amounts of information and moving or acting on it swiftly.

All of this creates special challenges in the military and other large, bureaucratic organizations, where the ability to access leadership and information across the enterprise often collides with a rigid and vertically-integrated culture. In the military, for example, we are particularly fond of hierarchical structures with strict reporting processes, where entire publications are devoted to organizational charts and information flow models. These old models, however, simply do not stand up to today's fluid security and information environment. The leadership challenge in the military—and in many large, hierarchical companies—is to develop a culture that does not alienate the experience base, yet clearly and inexorably pulls information flow into the modern age.

Another key concept in flattening the organization and removing stovepipes is what Stephen M.R. Covey portrays as the "speed of trust."[2] Especially in a military organization, where there is usually a high turnover of people in a given unit—normally every 2 to 3 years (including the commander)—there is great need to create trust rapidly. Fortunately, in the military, our system is based on the ingrained concept of trust. But to operate and adapt rapidly to the changing global security environment and to compete in a 24/7 instant news cycle, our system of trust must adapt to allow flattened communication flows. As Covey writes, "Low trust slows everything—every decision, every communication and every relationship. On the other hand, trust produces speed."[3] It is this speed that is required in a large, complex organization living out in the world in today's globalized society.

Mythology and Strategy

Let me introduce you to three figures from Greek mythology whose stories illustrate some aspects of strategy.

Sisyphus

Simply put, strategy generation and strategic planning is a Sisyphean endeavor. It takes discipline; it takes a culture of planning across the enterprise; it requires constant attention; and, it never ends. Just when you think your strategy is complete, the world shifts, and you could be back at square one, just as in the myth Sisyphus was condemned to roll a boulder up a hill only to have it roll back down, and to repeat this task eternally. Publishing a strategy is the easiest part of strategy development. It is strategy execution, building enterprise-wide understanding, and the constant feedback for adjustment that require constant leadership attention and a process for continual strategy "re-development." In this context, one could say that Sisyphus is actually pushing two boulders—one boulder is "strategy the process" and the second is "strategy the document."

Focusing for a minute on the second stone, a strategy is a military organization's theory about how to produce security, first and foremost for itself and then for and within its own immediate environment. How the organization defines itself and its environment, and how and where it places or sees itself within that environment, are the primary steps in beginning the strategic planning process—pushing the first stone up the hill. In so doing, both process and document must clearly enumerate and prioritize threats and challenges, and potential remedies and counteractions to confront and minimize those threats and challenges. In addition, it must recognize the entire range of opportunities present in the *current* strategic environment to shape the *future* one, thus attempting to prevent the emergence of those challenges and threats. In all three categories—challenges, threats, and opportunities—the complete strategy should unmistakably justify the prioritization, particularly in reference to clearly stated vital and enduring national interests, as well as provide some description of how resources will be applied to achieve the desired results. Make no mistake, however—a strategy is not a rule book; rather, it is a set of concepts and arguments that need to be revisited regularly.[4]

Furthermore, the purpose of strategic planning is not solely to produce a single, comprehensive document or an assortment of secondary documents, or to try and prepare for an endless array of specific contingencies. Recalling the jellyfish analogy, the true milieu of strategy is information, primarily in the form of ideas and concepts via sensory interaction with the external environment; thus, the proper aim of strategic planning is really to inform and support the deliberations of leaders throughout the organization as they attempt to make long-range strategic decisions that affect the security of the organization and its environment. As Aaron Friedberg puts it, "The true nature of strategic planning should be heuristic; it is an aid to the collective thinking of the leadership of all levels of the organization, rather than a mechanism for the production of operational plans."[5] In competitive situations, this thinking would lead to creating or exploiting a decisive asymmetry and advantage. In noncompetitive situations, it would result in the steadfast commitment of resources to shape or build an envisioned future.

Tantalus

Tantalus provides an appropriate second metaphor for strategic planning, as we are too often tantalized by the search for the *perfect* strategy. In the myth, Tantalus is punished by the gods by being placed for eternity in a pool of water under a fruit tree; when he reached up to satisfy his hunger, the tree branch would rise beyond his reach; when he bent down, the water would recede, preventing him from getting a drink. We often feel that with just a little more effort, a little more time, we can write the perfect strategy. Somehow, it always seems to elude us, resting just outside our reach; yet we refuse to relent, thus fixating on it to the exclusion of other, more fruitful pursuits. We should never let the pursuit of the perfect strategy be the enemy of the very, very good one. When we develop a strategy, we need to recognize that it will not be perfect—that it will *never* be perfect; but after well thought-out, enterprise-wide effort, it *is* time to get the strategy out. We need to let our organization see it, our partners see it, and if appropriate, the world see it. And then, of course, we need to adapt—*constantly* adapt, on all levels. This analogy and concept will be explored in greater detail in describing the transition from academic discussion to real world application, and how honest and critical assessment is an invaluable tool. Further emphasizing the value of the process and downplaying the worth of the product, General Dwight D. Eisenhower once remarked, "In preparing for battle, I have always found that plans are useless, but planning is indispensable."

Prometheus

The end of the process, publishing and explaining a strategy, brings "light" to the rest of the organization, much as Prometheus brought fire to give light and innovation to mortals. His efforts came at great cost to him, however, which is the third and final leg of the planning metaphor: transparency—letting light through—has a cost. If you open your strategy up to others, inside or outside the organization, you expose yourself to risk, but a necessary one.

Without illuminating the organization, without informing partners, a strategy is useless. Learning from Tantalus and allowing that the perfect strategy is never attainable, transparency will enable criticism, both constructive as well as destructive. This can provide enlightenment internally, as well as arm external competitors to find faults with your organization. The difficulty lies in judging the opportunity costs of transparency. In many cases, the benefits of an open strategy, both during development as well as once complete, outweigh those of a closed one.

First, resources are invariably scarce; thus, if a strategy includes clearly delineated priorities, it provides a guide for the distribution of these scarce resources, in addition to shaping the discussion of development of future procurement efforts. Second, in the interdependent and cooperative region and community in which we live, multiple large and complex organizations—both governmental as well as nongovernmental—must work together and collaborate to achieve shared security goals. Detailed orchestration of this synergy could prove difficult. An open, perhaps even jointly authored, strategy helps these multiple partners better coordinate their activities. Third, as we have already stated, we exist in a competitive marketplace of ideas; thus we have a vast external audience, both intended and unintended. We must be able to communicate messages of deterrence and persuasion to potential adversaries, as well as reassurance and support to allies and friends—both groups must understand that diplomacy is always preferable to the use of actual force, but that we stand ready and able to utilize *all* tools at our disposal when needed. Open strategies communicate these ideas and interests—those produced in isolation and shrouded in secrecy do not. Finally, clearly stated strategies assist internal accountability. They permit criticism and correction when they are proposed; they organize public discourse when new projects are suggested; and they allow for evaluation of such policies after the fact.[6] Again, this may be painful, but it is ultimately beneficial in the end, as the organization will be better for bringing "light" to their strategy.

The moral of these stories is not that strategic planning is a punishment, although to some it may seem that way. The enduring images of these three ancient myths drive home the point that strategy development and execution are grueling, unending, and never will be perfect.

Hits and Misses

A key cornerstone of any viable organization is a culture of learning: the entire enterprise needs to be a learning organism. This involves setting goals for continued learning in areas that benefit the enterprise, as well as in areas that may only benefit the employee. Leaders throughout the organization need to allow time for learning; good leaders will make it a subtle requirement. In the military, continued learning, called professional military education, is actually a requirement for advancement. There is a minimum continuing education requirement for each rank of service, but for further or accelerated advancement, going above and beyond the required learning is encouraged and rewarded.

A critical element of a learning organization is innovation. When commenting on the value of innovation, particularly in a highly aggressive and volatile market where one is in direct competition with another organization, Steve Jobs, the founder and CEO of Apple, remarked, "Innovation has nothing to do with how many R&D dollars you have . . . It's not about money. It's about the people you have, how you're led, and how much you get it."[7] In a perfect world, we'd have all the resources we need to accomplish our mission. With national, regional, and even global commitments, however, the simple fact of life is that we do *not* have all we want; thus, we have to rely upon innovation in all we do. And when we do, we find that innovation often comes from unexpected sources, so it needs to be part of the culture of any modern organization—not just the culture of engineers or technical experts, but the culture of the entire enterprise.

Innovative ideas, to include technical breakthroughs, often bubble up from nontraditional locations. During the World Wide Developers Conference in June 2008, Apple introduced new software for its iPhone. Amidst a list of traditional and expected sources of new ideas for software—like Sega, eBay, and Intuit, among others—an *insurance worker* from England demonstrated an idea for a virtual instrument player, an idea that looks to have genuine promise.

In military organizations, innovation also comes from some unlikely sources. Since our organizations are populated by a cross-section of society, each Sailor, Soldier, Airman, Coast Guardsman, and Marine represents a potential innovator due to their unique backgrounds. Examples abound, such as the Army Sergeant in World War II, whose welding experience and innovative spirit helped quickly modify Allied tanks and solved the challenge that the coastal hedgerows of Normandy posed to the tanks of General Omar Bradley's 1st Army.[8]

Recognizing the great potential of innovative talent inherent in the military, each branch of service has an "ideas" or "innovation" program that actually provides a monetary stipend and personal recognition for inventions that save lives or resources. Moreover, these novel ideas and inventions are often outside the normal technical field of the individual Servicemember and frequently save numerous lives and millions of taxpayer dollars. But to incubate ideas from concept to reality requires the innovators have the ear of, or at least a clear path to, the decisionmakers. Good ideas need quick resourcing for evaluation—and the organization cannot have a zero-tolerance mentality for failure.

In this regard, innovation can be like baseball: if you are batting .250, you are having a rather good year. That is one in four successes—or, put another way, three in four failures. If you are batting one-for-three (.333), you are destined for Cooperstown and the Hall of Fame. Ty Cobb has the

Hall of Fame record for career batting average at .366 and it has been over 60 years since anyone had a season average of over .400. Innovators hit . . . and innovators miss. The key is to know when you miss and to not continue swinging away in hopes of hitting a ball that is already in the catcher's mitt.

The problem of innovation in the military is that the stakes are so high (some might argue too high). "Failure is not an option," is the cultural mind-set. And we are deeply predisposed to repetitive practice as the highest value good in preparing for operations, which is quite the opposite of innovation. Yet not all innovation in the military involves national security—in fact most of it does not. Still, the mindset prevails with many leaders.

Not long ago, an external consultant group rated a group of brand new Navy Admirals on numerous common attributes of senior leaders and compared them to the civilian sector. The new Admirals had fairly high marks across the board—decisiveness, vision, determination, intelligence—but surprisingly, they ranked at the bottom for *risk-taking*. This seems counterintuitive for a group of military leaders who presumably have spent their lives flying airplanes over enemy shores, launching missiles, driving ships at high speed, and engaging in countless other risky behaviors. Yet when you consider it carefully, it makes sense.

When it comes to physical risks and the dangers of combat, military leaders are good at mitigating and accepting risk. It is what we do. But when it comes to less tangible risk—essentially "career risk"—like betting on an untested idea for networking and information flow, or trying a new technique, we sometimes have difficulty committing. This is a direct reflection of the high risk of failure and the culture of conservatism and repetitive training.

A strategist, therefore, needs to understand and work hard at breaking that culture to improve large organizations in today's world.

How Goes It?

It is often said that even the perfect plan does not survive the first contact with the enemy. In the execution of our acknowledged "very good, yet still imperfect" strategy, we need a mechanism for making adjustments. We need to be able to assess our performance and our effectiveness. And if all your indicators tell you everything is going great, look out! As comedian Steven Wright once said, "When everything is coming your way, you're in the wrong lane."

Honest, unbiased assessment, like strategic planning, is hard work and often very difficult to do, if done at all. Perhaps in the traditional business sense, the bottom line of sales figures provides an objective assessment of effectiveness, but certainly there are many intangibles in sales that also need weighing. In the security business, however, the measure of effectiveness is not so black and white—especially when we consider that the *prevention* of crisis and conflict provides the majority of our military history when compared to combat operations.

Dedicated and rigorous assessment leads right back to strategic culture. The sensing strategic organism must have assessment as one of its core organizing concepts. Each cell of the organism should understand its role in measuring success through objective and subjective metrics, all of which are linked back to intermediate and strategic goals.

This personal assessment needs to start right from the highest levels in the organization. A common mistake many leaders make is to allow themselves to become too engrossed in the details, too fascinated by the tactical aspects of the enterprise. This is understandable since whether it is security matters or sales of a particular product, the ultimate terminal transaction—or tactical level of execution in military parlance—all tend to be more exciting and draw us in. The toughest job for the leader, then, is to trust in the strategy, trust in subordinate leaders, and trust the sensors to do their jobs to report the right information; in so doing, they should be able to stay out of the thicket of tactical execution.

Every day, the leaders need to ask the question "Am I part of the solution or am I part of the problem?" As leaders, we need to be part of the solution, and that involves rising above the tactical level to maintain sight of the big picture. Leaders need to set tempo, direction, and goals; the only way to do this, however, is by maintaining a ruthless standard of self-examination, making sure we are part of the solution. We need to focus on ensuring we can extract the nuggets of strategically important information amidst the deluge of background noise in the daily grind of the organization.

Assessment must also include an exacting analysis of external factors as well. As previously described, we are engaged at the strategic level in a competition of ideas and wills; as such, it is not sufficient for us to simply choose one particular course of action and then blindly stick to it until we have reached our desired endstate—there is another participant in this venture. And unless this adversary is completely outmatched, overcome, or otherwise inert, he will react and his actions and his own strategy will almost always necessitate alteration and perhaps even a completely new approach on our part. Without a constant focus on assessment and evaluation, taking into account both our own moves as well as the moves of our opponent—in addition to external factors that exist in the strategic landscape—we will not be able to judge our progress or adapt and evolve to overcome the emerging environment and its challenges. Aaron Friedberg makes this point when he observes:

> Although it is always conceivable that a combatant may stumble into victory simply by "staying the course," there is also the danger of blundering into defeat. Like a sailor in heavy winds and high seas who fails to consult his sextant and compass, a nation that does not regularly assess the performance of its strategy and that of its opponent is likely to wander far from its intended destination.[9]

Despite all that you do, and all the calculations, forecasts, and approximations of what the opponent might do and what he might not do, there will still be surprises; this is because there are still factors outside your or your competitor's sphere of influence. Like the old saying goes, "Man plans, fate laughs." Expect the unexpected to occur, both good outcomes and bad ones, and develop a culture and organization capable of dealing with it. Many times in military history, unexpected success created as many problems as unexpected failure. Your organization needs to be able to adapt to both—actually, the most secure strategic organization is the one that has evaluated and assessed the possibility of multiple future outcomes and positioned itself based on some factor of probability and consequence: namely, risk. Returning to Friedberg, because the interplay of all these actors and forces can never be predicted with any degree of certainty, "this kind of calculation is always imprecise and becomes even more so the farther into the future it attempts to project. Yet, for nations as well as individuals, some attempt to identify and evaluate different paths forward is the *sine qua non* of rational behavior."[10]

One such attempt to articulate these different paths and the variables that can be juxtaposed to create them is a methodology called *scenario-based planning*. This approach is a technique by which organizations develop and test strategies using a systematically created range of multiple alternative futures or scenarios. Scenario-based planning centers on developing strategies for managing future uncertainty, instead of focusing on specific conflicts or events as occurs with wargaming and contingency planning. Considered a best practice in the private and public sectors, scenario-based planning is a proven means of creating strategic and operational alignment across diverse and even conflicting organizations.

The power of the approach derives not from the merits of any one scenario, but rather from the strategic insight gained through using a set of scenarios that covers the fullest practical range of relevant and plausible future potential outcomes. Thus, the methodology allows for the creation of broader "platform" scenarios usable at the enterprise level that can be subsequently customized for use by component organizations.

Scenario-based planning is a technique for managing uncertainty, risk, and opportunity, and differs from traditional strategic planning processes by not "assuming the future." It not only yields remarkably strong strategic frameworks and practical bases for immediate operational action, but also—by virtue of being highly inclusive of diverse perspectives— serves to cultivate strategic thinking and alignment across large organizations and between diverse partner organizations. By systematically considering the future and by including multiple perspectives, scenario-based planning seeks to avoid institutional "failures of imagination."

Underlying your assessment strategy, there also needs to be a clear understanding of "that which really scares you." Certain triggers, trends, or metrics should be identified as critical to your organization's survival or mission accomplishment. When one of these triggers is reported back through the organization, there needs to be a plan to deal with it; and as all plans go, the organization needs to have a mechanism to adjust based upon the realities on the ground. Thus, the sensors throughout the organization need to understand the strategic vision—the commander's strategic intent, the big picture—allowing it to identify key trends and emerging issues of potential significance for ongoing or possible future strategic interactions. In the words of Richard Rumelt,

> Strategic insight is impossible if the problem is not defined. The quality of the strategy cannot be assessed unless the problem is defined. A good, succinct assessment of the situation—both *before* you start your strategic planning process, *and* once the first iteration is produced/published—helps generate good strategy; makes bad strategy more transparently bad; includes limits on resources and competence which promote focus.[11]

Once you have built a strategic culture rooted in planning and assessment, and you have a flattened organization based on horizontal as well as vertical information flow—perhaps you have even reorganized—then on a strategic level, you need to exercise some patience. In fact, patience is the key to leading change in any large, complex organization: patience to plan, patience to assess, patience for structural and process changes to take root.

Most of all, patience is needed not to make too many adjustments to your "very good" strategy.

There will be many tactical level victories and defeats. Neither of which, by themselves, heralds the success or failure of a given strategy. Strategic assessment takes time for the forces in play to settle out and to report a true measure of success. It is like the pilot struggling to keep a plane in straight and level flight. Sometimes aerodynamic forces result in a situation where every effort the pilot makes to maintain altitude tends to worsen the situation. This is called "pilot induced oscillations." In this case, the pilot is working too hard and is overcorrecting for the external forces. In most cases, the wisest thing for the pilot to do is to simply let go of the control stick and let the forces dampen out over time. Letting go is not a natural reaction, particularly for pilots, but we as leaders need to trust in the process and trust in our people—we are in the business of strategy, and that means having the long view.

To Reorganize or Not to Reorganize

Remembering Lincoln's counsel to "think anew," we need to take this a step further and actually *act* anew, as well. Inevitably, as we are all taught, form follows function. But form matters! Often, a reorganization is dubbed a simple "rearrangement of the deck chairs." Indeed, without rigorous attention to strategy and process, a reorganization might turn out to be just that. In today's environment, however, old hierarchical structures do not compete well. In today's military, our big military staffs are roughly organized in structures devised by the Prussians over a hundred years ago—a structure perfectly adept at moving men and materiel on the battlefield, but imperfectly suited to moving ideas and reacting to today's information environment.

U.S. Southern Command recently underwent an internal reorganization to flatten the enterprise, to match structure and process to strategy, and to build an organization better prepared to meet today's security realities. A common misperception among our personnel that we continually try to dispel is that the reorganization was an end in and of itself. Many think that after moving offices, changing phones and titles, and flattening reporting chains, the transformation was over. Reorganization is simply a tool, but creating a new culture with a 21st-century mindset is the real goal. And reaching this goal will necessitate continued change and continued strategic analysis and planning. To quote Winston Churchill, "To improve is to change. To be perfect is to change often."

An important challenge of attaining the right structure is connecting "islands of excellence" and breaking down cylinders of excellence, also known as stovepipes. Most organizations have an overall culture, but they also have numerous microcultures. From a competition standpoint, these microcultures promote new ideas, and competition among them impedes overall stagnation.

However, in a flat organization, these islands of excellence need to be connected so that the other parts of the organization benefit from the quality work being done, as well as to avoid undue duplication of effort. Too often, internal divisions are reluctant to share their work because of the very human (and professional) need to receive credit, praise, and reward. This tendency equates to reinforcing stovepipes and a vertical flow of information. The leadership challenge is to promote a culture of openness, create the proper structure and processes for information-sharing, and ensure credit and reward are appropriately placed.

A Lesson from the Opponent

Sitting outside our headquarters in Miami is a small nautical vessel that serves as a monument to innovation. It is a low profile boat about 30 feet long that can skim along just at the surface of the water. This innovative boat uses a diesel engine, has a crew of two, and is difficult to detect on radar and sonar, all with a payload capacity of a little over 1 ton of cocaine. The vessel was very cheap to make, and it went from design concept to operational status much faster than the norm in the defense establishment.

Sounds great, right? Real innovation!

The bad news, however, is that the vessel was not our idea or design. It represents the type of vessel being used by Colombian drug cartel transporters to bring cocaine to market in the United States and elsewhere, and they have made great strides in improving their design.

Perhaps it makes an unusual monument since many military bases have monuments of U.S. airplanes, ships, or ground vehicles. But since one of our organization's functions is to interdict illegal narcotics traffickers, we placed it there to drive home a very important point. Remembering that no good plan survives first contact with the enemy, we can further caveat this by acknowledging that the enemy gets a vote in the final outcome. And make no mistake: our enemies . . . our competitors . . . our opponents are innovators. They wake up every day trying to figure out how to defeat us. To view them in any other light is to do so at our own detriment. They have created flat organizations: networked, technology savvy, and quick to adapt—all great lessons for us. We cannot afford to stagnate. We also must change and adapt.

For our military, as for our industry, our current rigid, stovepiped, and slow moving institutions—our "glacial engines for stability"—simply will not do. We need a culture and a vision that is change-centric, one that can effectively meet the challenges of this unfolding 21st century and beyond.

A Southern Command Example

As mentioned earlier, over the last few years, U.S. Southern Command realized it needed to rethink itself to fit into the realities of the 21st century and 21st-century security. As Peter Drucker wrote in the *Harvard Business Review*, we realized we needed change, since "The assumptions on which the organization has been built and is being run no longer fit reality."[12] We needed a new theory of the business. We were doing many of the right things, but very much needed to renew our strategy, culture, vision, goals, processes, and structure. We needed to evolve.

As stated earlier, changing a military culture—one rooted in tradition and hierarchical structures—is not an easy task. National security is a "highest stakes" business. We could not afford to neglect our mission while we spent the time and effort to adapt and re-grow our organization. Like retooling a car's engine while driving 70 miles per hour, our core functions needed to remain intact, even while we made significant changes to the enterprise.

Our change initiative began with a lot of thinking and rethinking. We held a strategic offsite with senior leadership, midlevel muscle, and nontraditional partners. We analyzed the strategic security environment, allowed for innovative approaches, and published a strategic vision to begin the change process. Some of our change proposals were obviously appropriate to a military organization while many others have stretched the established norms but are critical to matching strategy to effective execution and action.

Once new thinking was established, we went about the business of changing culture to match the vision and strategy; honestly, we are still in this phase, and probably will remain so for quite some time. In the success column, we have improved information flow to senior leadership. Paperwork that used to take weeks to get processed due to old formal protocols now gets done in days or hours. Innovative and collaborative thinking is also starting to take off. And a sense of real momentum has begun taking root.

Our most recent step in evolving the enterprise was to reorganize the hierarchical organization into a mission-focused, flattened model, with horizontal integration and matrixed functions. Seeded throughout the new structure, and at every level of the organization, are key nodes of input for our strategic planning, execution, and assessment cycles. As a military establishment, some of our key stakeholders exist outside the organization, both in the nations in our region of focus and within the U.S. Government. Central to our new process, therefore, is a strategic messaging effort designed to inform these key stakeholders and to process feedback for inclusion in our designs.

Our largest challenge so far has been resisting the temptation to rest and declare victory. There have been many successes in our change efforts, many road bumps, and some resistance from both expected *and* unexpected sources. For our change initiative to work, the evolution of the enterprise will require continued attention to strategic planning and execution, as well as a constant sense of rolling the first boulder up the hill. As a military organization, we also exist within a clearly defined relationship between the Executive and Legislative branches of our government. Any change at our level has to be understood and, to a certain extent approved, at the national level, which raises the importance of strategic messaging and a clear, transparent strategy—the second boulder.

As previously described, strategic planning is often viewed as a complex and punishing process. But as we have also pointed out, it is a worthwhile and necessary endeavor that if performed correctly and thoroughly leads to a more successful organization and secure environment. In attempting to define the primary product of this trying and arduous process, Harry Yarger comments, "In simplistic terms, strategy at all levels is the calculation of objectives, concepts, and resources within acceptable bounds of risk to create more favorable outcomes than might otherwise exist by chance or at the hands of others."[13] The official Department of Defense definition of strategy is "a prudent idea or set of ideas for employing the instruments of national power in a synchronized and integrated fashion to achieve theater, national and/or multinational objectives."[14]

As the method to produce this "calculation of objectives, concepts and resources" and "prudent idea or set of ideas," Southern Command uses a four-phase Strategic Planning Process (SPP) model to align its organizational mission with the resources needed to accomplish the strategy. This process ensures unity of effort throughout the command so that every element is working toward the achievement of the objectives set forth in the command strategy and Theater Campaign Plan (TCP).

This process is the foundation for how Southern Command sets command priorities and makes decisions for the allocation of resources to achieve the command vision. The Strategic Planning Process is a cross-functional, interagency, enterprise-wide process that requires broad-base participation to ensure success. It provides the corporate structure to develop strategic guidance, determine required capabilities, focus command-wide programs and activities, identify and program for resources, and measure progress toward achieving the commander's vision and theater objectives.

The SPP (figure 2–1) applies a simple strategy-to-task/resource methodology with clear linkages to both national-level as well as the commander's guidance. These linkages assist in determining and prioritizing capability requirements, focusing command activities and programs, defending and prioritizing resources, as well as identifying gaps and disconnects that increase risk. The SPP also enables the command to measure progress on how well command-wide operations, activities, and actions are achieving the Theater Campaign Plan intermediate objectives, as well as measure performance of the Enterprise Campaign Plan (ECP).

Figure 2–1. Strategic Planning Process Model

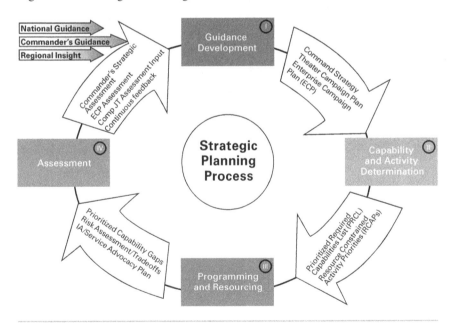

In the Southern Command area of focus, strategy development requires a whole-of-government approach to achieve the commander's vision. As a result, the command's SPP incorporates national, Presidential-level guidance and strategic themes from across the interagency, the commander's vision, as well as regional insight and analysis. Figure 2–2 below illustrates the methodology Southern Command utilizes for strategy development.

Figure 2–2. U.S. Southern Command Strategy Methodology

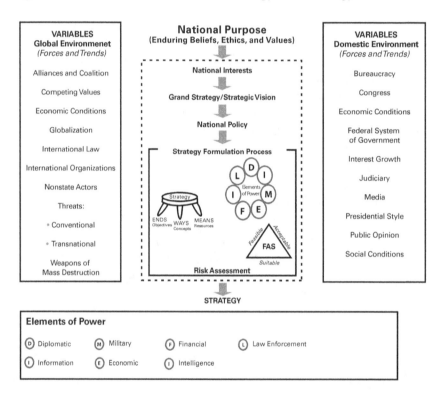

The product of this model—and the first output of the Guidance Development Phase of the SPP—is the Command Strategy, an enduring document that serves as the foundation for the command and has a 10-year timeline horizon. The current version is Command Strategy 2018 and provides the framework for achieving U.S. Southern Command's goals and objectives over the course of the next decade, setting forth and ensuring the efforts of the command are along the correct path. It defines the linkages, explores future challenges, and determines the ways and means for Southern Command to assist in fulfilling the commander's intent. The strategy will not remain static over this 10-year period; it is a living document and therefore we will make changes when needed to take advantage of emerging opportunities or address new challenges and threats.

Command Strategy 2018 includes two distinctive objective areas: Hemispheric (external) and Governmental Enterprise (internal). This division allows the command to determine external objectives for the area of focus along with internal objectives to accomplish required missions. The Theater Campaign Plan focuses externally, serving as the document that "operationalizes" the strategy's external objectives. The Enterprise Campaign Plan focuses on Southern Command internal processes and products to address the Strategy's goal to "Evolve the Enterprise."

Figure 2–3. Strategy Goal Linkages to the Theater Campaign Plan and the Enterprise Campaign Plan

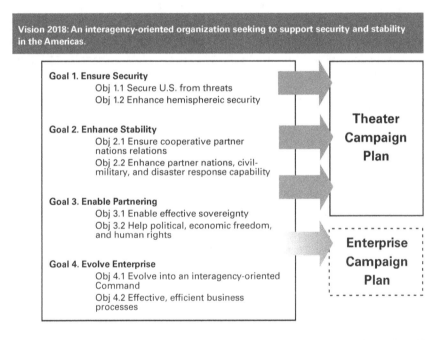

The Theater Campaign Plan is the second key output of the Guidance Development Phase. It derives its direction from national-level guidance and from Command Strategy 2018 and serves as the practical application of the command strategy. It provides the construct for focusing and prioritizing Southern Command's steady-state activities as they relate to current operations, security cooperation, and interagency and any preventive activities. It is created from page one with our interagency partners' input and is designed to enhance synchronization and prevent conflict. Southern

Command's Strategic Communication Framework, intended to fore-shadow strategic shifts, is an annex to the TCP. This framework should be used throughout the process to anticipate future events and assist with prioritization. It is also used as a standalone document to guide the various efforts in the command and is updated every 2 years or as required.

The TCP contains intermediate objectives which are linked to the Theater Strategic endstates, goals, and objectives from Command Strategy 2018. These objectives provide the command with a construct for focusing and prioritizing every operation, activity, and action, have a 2- to 5-year window of vision, and enable measurable and achievable progress toward goals. These objectives are evaluated annually through the Commander's Strategic Assessment (CSA) as phase IV of the SPP.

The TCP also defines the interrelationships of the various Theater Security Cooperation (TSC) governing documents. It drives and synchronizes security cooperation efforts in the region, as contained within Country Campaign Plans, Embassies' Mission Strategic Plans, and Country Security Cooperation Reports.

The Enterprise Campaign Plan is the third and final output of the Guidance Development Phase of the SPP. The ECP provides a 3-year roadmap for continuing the transformation of Southern Command toward the accomplishment of the Command Strategy goal to "Evolve the Enterprise." Transformation efforts to date have created tremendous potential for improving Southern Command's efficiencies, with macro reorganization as the first step. We now must develop the discipline of continual improvement and alignment in order to evolve into an interagency-oriented enterprise actively executing a strategic communications approach in cooperation with international and interagency partners and, where appropriate, the private sector.

In phase II of our SPP, the Capability and Activity Determination Phase, we determine the Prioritized Required Capabilities List (long-range) and Resource Constrained Activity Priorities (short-range).These capabilities and activities are based on a review of command guidance and emergent threats, and are linked to the TCP intermediate objectives to ensure the command has the best mix of programs and actions to support the objectives.

In phase III of our SPP, the Programming and Resourcing Phase, we address critical capability shortfalls associated with command activities and programs. During this step, we link the Southern Command Staff, Service Components, and sub-unified command programs, and use a joint inter-agency program review to identify, prioritize, and recommend disposition of critical capability gaps in the short (1–2 years) and long (5-year) fiscal year defense plan terms. As a first step, this capability gap analysis includes a validation of the funded baseline. This program review is an enterprise-wide entity that meets annually and evaluates each program on its efficiency and effectiveness in covering the command's requirements, ultimately providing the commander with a resourcing strategy for developing programs to meet the required capabilities.

The final phase of our SPP, the Assessment Phase, is a critical activity throughout the process. Periodic evaluations of strategies, tactics, and action programs are essential to assessing success of the entire process. A combination of multiple assessments done at various levels by a variety of sources provides enterprise decisionmakers answers to the following four questions:

- How well are we doing?

- Are we doing the right things?

- Are we doing things right?

- What's next?

These answers and the arduous process of asking all the right questions help to determine the overall level of performance and effectiveness and show progress toward stated objectives. A critical assessment identifies whether we are doing the right activities, and how well we are doing the right activities. Ultimately, assessments allow us to gain the insight necessary to reallocate resources, modify the objectives, or change the strategy in order to continue working toward the achievement of our vision.

Within this larger assessments phase, we have one specific effort, the Commander's Strategic Assessment (CSA). This is performed annually and answers "how well are we doing," identifying intermediate objectives where progress is lacking in order to focus the efforts of operational assessments. The CSA provides critical feedback to enterprise decisionmakers and informs and supports enterprise decisionmaking, program/activity prioritization, and resource allocation. Where an interagency partner has the lead for a program or activity, we work with that partner to obtain all the relevant data to incorporate in the CSA. Operational assessments allow identification of whether our activities and actions in the field are being conducted as planned. Finally, based on the knowledge of where we are, knowledge of outcomes of ongoing and completed activities, and an understanding of whether the results were due to execution issues or some other level in the process, decisionmakers can make informed recommendations on what to do next and where.

In summation, U.S. Southern Command's Strategic Planning Process is a four-phase process designed to align the organizational mission with processes and products that address our strategy-to-resource model and meet the strategic endstates contained in the higher level national strategic guidance, as well as the commander's vision. The SPP starts with guidance development as contained in the command strategy and two organizing campaign plans, one focused externally and one internally. During all four phases, the intent is to ensure unity of effort throughout the command so that every element, every sensor at every level, is working toward achievement of the same shared strategic objectives that define the strategic problem. We have an extremely robust assessments phase which actually permeates all three other phases and runs continuously. And omnipresent at every level and in every phase of our change-centric organization, ideas are the fuel that runs this engine, and the "speed of trust" is what keeps the engine revving high.

> I do not claim that strategy is or can be a "science" in the sense of the physical sciences. It can and should be intellectual discipline of the highest order, and the strategist should prepare himself to manage ideas with precision and clarity and imagination. . . . Thus, while strategy itself may not be a science, strategic judgment can be scientific to the extent that it is orderly, rational, objective, inclusive, discriminatory, and perceptive.
>
> —Admiral J.C. Wylie
> *Military Strategy: A General Theory of Power Control*

We—individually, and as a trusted and valued partner and neighbor in this shared home of the Americas—are in an era in which the strategic landscape has changed and is continuing to change. The nature of the challenges and threats to the Nation and partners, as well as the opportunities available to us to confront and mitigate them, are constantly emerging and shifting shapes and origins. What should remain constant and enduring, however, are our core vital national interests, as well as the shared vision of all free and democracy-loving peoples in the region. We must also factor into the ever-changing equation that resources are finite and increasingly scarce; thus, strategic priorities have to be established.

The intent, therefore, is a balanced approach to strategic risks: confront the most pressing and probable threats to the Nation today, while at the same time, posture the joint, combined, and multinational force to prevent, and if necessary, defeat the most consequential threats to tomorrow. The factors that influence strategic thinking—the prisms of the kaleidoscope we peer into—are multiple, and their possible combinations and permutations are infinitely variable. Even so, the barrel of the kaleidoscope contains the seeming "chaos" and we are able to manipulate the barrel to in some way influence and bring about new combinations and results. So, too, can the "scope" of strategic planning serve a similar function to establish boundaries and contain the risks of global events.

A key enabler in this balancing act is persistent engagement to build partner capacity, extend trust and confidence, and assure access to the commons and the natural resources therein. This is critical to fostering and sustaining cooperative relationships with friends around the world and contributes significantly to our shared security and prosperity. Ultimately, we will achieve enduring security for the peoples of the Americas in a stable and prosperous regional, international, and global system.

In the end, by anchoring the lofty ideals we value to the realities of the world we live in, we can and will overcome the test of wills and ideas that are defining the new era, but it will take time—years, decades even. Such is the way of strategy: it requires patience to let the forces at work play out and let the process work. We have a unique opportunity to use our reason and our free inquiry to influence the debate to help develop our future strategy. So I challenge you today to engage your organization's leadership and chain of command, bring them your ideas, and continue to help them stay dynamic and evolutionary, particularly in assessing and crafting our future strategies.

Notes

[1] Carl H. Builder, *The Masks of War: American Military Styles in Strategy and Analysis*, A RAND Corporation Research Study (Baltimore: The Johns Hopkins University Press, 1989), 202.

[2] Stephen M.R Covey with Rebecca R. Merrill, *The Speed of Trust: The One Thing That Changes Everything* (New York: The Free Press, 2006).

[3] Ibid.

[4] Barry Posen, "A Grand Strategy of Restraint," in *Finding Our Way: Debating American Grand Strategy*, eds. Michele A. Flournoy and Shawn Brimley (Washington, DC: Center for a New American Security, June 2008), 84.

[5] Aaron Friedberg, "Strengthening U.S. Strategic Planning," *The Washington Quarterly* (Winter 2007–8), 48.

[6] Posen, 84.

[7] Steve Jobs, *Fortune* (November 9, 1998), 24.

[8] Lida Mayo, "The Ordnance Department: On Beachhead and Battlefront", ed. Stetson Conn, *The United States Army in World War II* (Washington, DC: Center of Military History, United States Army, 1991), 253.

[9] Friedberg, 49.

[10] Ibid., 50.

[11] Richard Rumelt, "Some Thoughts on Business Strategy," CSBA Seminar, September 2007.

[12] Peter F. Drucker, "The Theory of the Business," *Harvard Business Review* (September-October 1994).

[13] Harry Yarger, *Strategic Theory for the 21st Century: The Little Book on Big Strategy* (Carlisle Barracks, PA: Strategic Studies Institute, U.S. Army War College, 2006), 1.

[14] Joint Chiefs of Staff, Joint Publication 1-02, *Department of Defense Dictionary of Military and Associated Terms* (Washington, DC: 2006), available at: <http:www.dtic.mil/doctrine/jel/doddict/data/s/05163.html>.

Chapter 3

Pulling the Oar Together

The unity of government which constitutes you one people is also now dear to you. It is justly so, for it is a main pillar in the edifice of your real independence, the support of your tranquility at home, your peace abroad; of your safety; of your prosperity; of that very liberty which you so highly prize. . . .

With slight shades of difference, you have the same religion, manners, habits, and political principles. You have in a common cause fought and triumphed together; the independence and liberty you possess are the work of joint counsels, and joint efforts of common dangers, sufferings and successes.

—George Washington, 1796
Farewell Address to the People of the United States

The nations of the Americas have always been linked through the accident of geography. President John F. Kennedy, in addressing Latin American diplomats and Members of Congress at a White House reception nearly 50 years ago, commented: "Our continents are bound together by a common history . . . our nations are the product of a common struggle . . . and our peoples share a common heritage." This, of course, is undeniably true; however, never have our linkages been as vital or as complex as they are today. With exponential advances in technology and strong natural connections, our societies are bound together inexorably, across the full spectrum of human contact. From migration and demographic changes, to a record level of commercial interaction and interdependence, to shared transnational security challenges, our countries' futures are tightly intertwined.

During my tenure at U.S. Southern Command, we concentrated on the strengths of this hemisphere of enormous diversity, beauty, and potential, while also seeking effective solutions to the complex and transnational security challenges shared throughout the Americas. At the same time, we understood that the realization of our hemisphere's long-term security, stability, and prosperity will only come through addressing—collectively—the underlying conditions of poverty, inequality, and corruption that affect vast portions of the region today.

Nevertheless, despite this growing interdependence, many claim the United States as a whole does not pay enough attention to Latin America and the Caribbean. Pointing specifically to the emergence of sharply anti-U.S. rhetoric emanating from several capitals in South America, some say the region is drifting away from us. Recent respected polls have indicated a decline in Latin America's positive opinion of the United States. Additionally, despite the shift in the political climate of the United States and notwithstanding the vast interaction we have with the region, many credible observers continue to counsel that the United States must pay more attention to this vitally important part of the world—and I could not agree more. To counter these perceptions and to facilitate an environment of cooperation, we need to better coordinate and communicate what we are already doing in the region, as well as to adapt, refocus, and innovatively increase our overall attention.

Focusing the spotlight inward as well, another important lesson we have learned is that our domestic partners—governmental and nongovernmental, public and private, state, local, and tribal levels of government—have

Ambulance donated by private enterprise is delivered to Argentina by U.S. Navy ships on 2007 "Partnerships of the Americas" deployment. U.S. Southern Command partnered with sister government agencies and private organizations in Project Handclasp—an example of SOUTHCOM leveraging the existing smart power capabilities of the United States.

never been as essential to our national security as they are now. None of us can take cooperation for granted, nor can we assume any longer that one department, one branch, or one level of government can go it alone in the face of myriad challenges or threats. We must renew our friendships, alliances, and partnerships while we work together to obtain a deeper and more comprehensive understanding of this new security environment. Additionally, we must update our rules and practices of cooperation to reflect the new challenges confronting us.

Internally and externally, we and our partner nations, agencies, organizations, and governments must work together routinely in peacetime, or we will be unable to work together in crises or contingencies. We will be unable to collectively deter threats to our common peace. We will be unable to create a cooperative security for our shared home.

To contend with the complex, multifaceted, and intricate strategic environment of the 21st century, U.S. Southern Command recently reorganized around a new strategic outlook that aims to better connect and partner inside the United States and throughout the region. Our new vision and organizational structure include employing a more holistic and integrated approach to national and international cooperation to better serve the security interests of the United States and those of our partners in this hemisphere. And as detailed previously, our new strategy involves understanding and harnessing the tremendous linkages we share with Latin America and the Caribbean.

The Three D's

There is little doubt that the United States has learned a great deal from the difficulties of its own recent past—the tragic events of 9/11, the death and destruction left in Katrina's wake, the challenges of Iraq and Afghanistan, and even our economic woes here at home. But we are a nation of courage, opportunity, and possibility, and this nation has mobilized to confront myriad threats and challenges, delivering valiant efforts to accomplish Herculean tasks. In the arena of interagency cooperation, however, our achievements thus far are eclipsed by the magnitude of the tasks before us. There is much more work still to be done.

Though we have made substantial headway, both doctrinally and organizationally, toward building a bridge to a new era of national security—a bridge that spans the preexisting gaps and connects the previously isolated islands of excellence—we have not been able to complete the journey. In fact, we've only just begun.

The recent rise in the level of national rhetoric reflecting this thinking, recognizing both the distance traveled thus far, as well as emphasizing the distance yet to go, is centered on taking a three-dimensional view of our nation's ability to serve as a force for good on the global stage. This new "3-D" paradigm of national power—development, diplomacy, and defense—will serve as the pillars, deeply rooted in the bedrock of our national values, upon which we will build the bridge to the future. Within the Executive Branch, there has been a renewed focus on enabling and empowering all the elements of our nation's capabilities, but particular attention has been paid to reconciling the mutually and necessarily codependent roles of development, diplomacy, and defense.

Starting with President Obama's Inaugural Address, followed by Vice President Biden's speech in Munich one week later, and reinforced by Secretary of State Clinton's remarks at the Asia Society on February 13, 2009, the resounding theme has been unanimous: "The United States is committed to a new era of diplomacy and development in which we will use smart power to work with historic allies and emerging nations to find regional and global solutions to common global problems."[1]

The Department of Defense (DOD) has been forward-leaning in this regard for some time. Defense Secretary Robert Gates and Chairman of the Joint Chiefs of Staff Admiral Mike Mullen have both repeatedly called for a "dramatic increase in spending on the civilian instruments of national security," insisting that "success will be less a matter of imposing one's will and more a function of shaping the behavior of friends, adversaries, and most importantly, the people in between."[2]

The halls of Congress also resonate with the sound of interagency cooperation and collaboration, as legislators strongly advocate revitalizing our civilian instruments of foreign policy. Chairman Ike Skelton and Representatives Howard Berman and Nita Lowey introduced legislation to create an interagency policy board. Representatives Jim Cooper and Mac Thornberry have written and thought extensively about this. Congress funded an important study led by Jim Locher, one of the architects of the Goldwater-Nichols Department of Defense Reorganization Act of 1986. The Lugar-Biden bill first passed in 2004 was the catalyst that created the Office of the Coordinator for Stability and Reconstruction at the State Department (S/CRS), which was ultimately enacted as part of the 2008 National Defense Authorization Act to much success.

Last year, 6 months of hearings on Provincial Reconstruction Teams (PRTs) led to a detailed House Armed Services Committee report which, among other things, changed the rules on how military officers can earn joint credit. This wise legislation allows military officers to now receive joint credit for interagency work with the State Department or the United States Agency for International Development (USAID), as well as serving on a PRT or Military Transition Team. Those experiences are vital to the military's collective knowledge base, and rewarding our officers for seeking to earn those skills and familiarity is of equal importance.

Additionally, legislation was enacted to grant the Defense Department global authority to train and equip allies using DOD rather than State Department funds. This authorization, which places such activities under the "dual key" of Defense and State, is invaluable when it comes to assisting our partners in learning how to provide not just for their own security, but also contribute to the security of the global commons and the points of commerce flow.

The totality of these efforts, combined with real world developments and the materializing 21st-century security environment, has produced some fundamental alterations to the existing structure, doctrine, and national security objectives of the U.S. Government as we pursue and protect our vital and enduring national interests.

To borrow from our National Security Advisor, retired Marine General Jim Jones:

> The whole concept of what constitutes the membership of the national security community—which, historically has been, let's face it, the Defense Department, the NSC itself and a little bit of the State Department, to the exclusion perhaps of the Energy Department, Commerce Department and Treasury, all the law enforcement agencies, the Drug Enforcement Administration, all of those things—especially in the moment we're currently in, has got to embrace a broader membership.[3]

Within the Department of Defense specifically, there is great momentum to integrate and coordinate military, interagency community, multinational, and private sector efforts on all matters of national security. In 2005, for example, DOD Directive 3000.05 declared stability operations were a core U.S. military mission, raising them to a level comparable to combat operations. Stability operations, by definition, demand civilian involvement—both government and private citizens—and this spurred the development of new Joint Operational Concepts and field manuals on stability operations in addition to counterinsurgency and irregular warfare.

Another seminal document signaling the shift from predominantly combat operations to a broader multinational and full-spectrum engagement is the Cooperative Strategy for 21st Century Seapower. This new maritime strategy was vetted throughout the Nation via a series of "conversations with the country" and it rightly emphasizes the need to foster and sustain international partnerships over time, building mutual trust and capability for steady-state security cooperation as a matter of course, and the desire to respond together in the case of crisis. We clearly recognize the inherent value and wholeheartedly embrace the need to build the capability and capacity of our neighbors to address the complex security challenges we share together, while simultaneously building upon the foundation of our common interests.

In its reorganization, U.S. Southern Command adopted an integrated, multiagency approach to security in its area of focus. While fully respecting the prerogatives of the State Department to execute diplomacy and USAID to execute development, our reorganization efforts included multinational, nongovernmental, and even private sector collaboration to enhance understanding of regional dynamics and amplify the benefits of cooperation activities. Although we cannot claim that our reorganization is *definitively* correct and final, we *can* truly attest to the fact that we are *definitively* more effective and responsive than we were just 3 short years ago. There has also been improved synchronization of operations and activities between Southern Command and other U.S. Government organizations operating in this part of the world. This is the direct result of innovation coupled with empowering courageous leadership at all levels to become a living organism that will continue to evolve and adapt as the environment and surroundings necessitate.

We have engaged interagency community partners and integrated personnel from these agencies into the Southern Command staff, not as liaison officers or external advisors, but as bona fide integral staff members—to include having a 3-star equivalent, former Ambassador as one of two Deputy Commanders, with all the requisite authority and responsibilities. We have also ensured all Southern Command exercises and conferences include participation from our interagency community partners. Finally, we have established the paradigm of pushing our innovative ideas and approach to the Joint Staff and the Office of the Secretary of Defense to support our interagency-oriented security command concept in future Unified Command Plans. It is important that we get this right.

One of the unique characteristics enabling such an energetic collaborative approach is that Southern Command has an entire directorate—the Partnering Directorate, lead by a Senior Executive Service civilian—dedicated to partnering with the interagency community and public-private sector. This allows for improved cooperation with interagency partners, and facilitates their involvement in strategic planning, resourcing, and operations. Additionally, a Stability Directorate was formed, responsible for executing activities that build partner nation capacity, and for integrating engagement projects with interagency, host nation, and regional activities.

Our new, flatter organizational structure and diverse interagency and international team members allow us to partner proactively with the U.S. Government interagency community and with the sovereign countries in the region. These efforts will ultimately improve our collective response to regional and transnational security challenges and help build relationships in the region based on trust, respect, and mutual understanding.

The entirety of the U.S. Southern Command concept and approach is articulated in our guiding strategic document called Command Strategy 2018. As mentioned in the previous chapter, this document is a living, breathing entity that serves as a foundation upon which to build the construct for joint and combined military/civilian operations. It contains our vision and strategy to respond to the ever-constant mandate to meet joint military requirements and to recognize the increasing importance of integrating all instruments of national capability to meet the challenges of the future throughout the hemisphere. As we continue to assist in building that bridge to the future, we see Southern Command as just one section of one span of that bridge, hopefully helping connect several islands of excellence here within our region. We are committed to helping build a focused, collaborative approach that will allow us to best support the State Department in carrying out diplomacy and USAID in executing development, even as we do our part in defense.

We also have a promise to fulfill with the American people. The military's primary goal is to fight and win our nation's wars; however, preventing war on conditions favorable to our vital national interests is of even more value than fighting. Diplomatic solutions are highly preferable and come at a much lower cost than military operations. That's where diplomacy by the State Department and development by USAID, together with the deterrent power of defense, find their most powerful sinews. As much as others may like to think—or default to the notion—that development is the purview of the military, it is not. Organizations such as USAID are there to fill that role, and the State Department does diplomacy. We do not want to convey the impression that we have any desires or intentions to usurp any other agency's priorities or mission sets.

USAID and other civilian agencies have very different perspectives and purposes derived from a different source of strategic guidance than does the military—and this difference should be recognized, understood, and embraced. Our National Security Strategy accounts for this and envisions a broad role for development assistance around the globe. Development is what USAID *does*, and they are good at it. But they need more people and resources, as does the State Department. As Hans Binnendijk and Pat Cronin point out,

> S/CRS made heroic efforts to organize and develop civilian capabilities for complex operations, but the new office was underfunded, understaffed, and unappreciated within the State Department. Whereas the Department of Defense had dedicated tens of thousands of military personnel to these operations, S/CRS had a staff of fewer than 100, most of them detailees.[4]

But the future *does* look brighter. As Secretary Gates recently put it, "The military and civilian elements of the United States' national security apparatus have responded unevenly and have grown increasingly out of balance. The problem is not will; it is capacity. Since 9/11, the State Department has made a comeback, Foreign Service officers are being hired again, and foreign affairs spending has about doubled."[5]

An expanded and enhanced USAID and State Department presence will enable the United States to implement its foreign policy in permissive environments. In nonpermissive or dangerous environments that are beyond the reach of diplomacy, the U.S. military sets the conditions for a secure environment—as it did in Iraq and is currently doing in Afghanistan—for development to take place. This capability stems from our logistic capacity, planning methods, experience, and the well defined chain of command. Through that chain of command, Theater Security Cooperation activities can pave the way for development, and development can pave the way for furthering U.S. strategic objectives using the tools of diplomacy. This is true whether it is U.S. Southern Command or any other combatant command.

Need for an Interagency Planning Process

Security, stability, and prosperity go hand-in-hand. When we cooperate in combating the threat of terrorism, when we prevent crises and turmoil, when we deter aggression, we help build the foundations for increased prosperity. But this formula works in reverse as well—when we work together to help build prosperity, we contribute to reducing the potential sources of threats to regional and global security and stability. This relationship highlights the complexity of the task we face in building a cooperative security and the inherent need for teamwork and partnering. However, it also emphasizes that our collective effort to deal with the volatility and potential sources of conflict can have a dual impact in shaping both a stable and prosperous world. All three variables in this equation must work together to face the challenges of the 21st century and strive to achieve our national strategic objectives. In addition, these objectives must be clearly defined, prioritized, and deconflicted by our civilian leaders, so we can take a whole-of-government approach—and a whole-of-nation approach—to national security.

Lacking coherent objectives and clearly defined and prioritized national goals will continue tipping the scales of military and civilian elements of U.S. national capability off balance. We must articulate our goals and establish an order of precedence among them; then we must formulate a national strategy that defines the ends, the ways, and the means that will ultimately lead to establishing the right balance between hard power and soft power—finding the correct setting on the rheostat of *smart power*—so as a nation, we can make the proper investments and focus on advancing national security. And it is important to emphasize that USAID must lead development, and the State Department must lead diplomacy. We must *not* militarize foreign policy. Our military does not want to be "the Peace Corps with guns." All of this must be planned and led by civilians, unless we are in a direct combat situation.

To arrive at the objectives, goals, and national level strategy described above—and drawing from the previous section on strategy formulation and strategic planning—it follows, then, that the U.S. Government requires a truly interagency strategic planning process for national security and foreign policy. The U.S. Government approach to interagency strategic planning represents a challenge for the Nation, given the characteristics of our current strategic landscape. This capability is a critical requirement for effectiveness in an emerging regional and global operating environment in which challenges and opportunities will proliferate, issues will become increasingly interdisciplinary, and the resources available to the U.S. Government may be significantly constrained. Therefore, this process must facilitate cross-agency issue prioritization, clarification of agency roles and responsibilities in crosscutting areas, greater visibility into budgetary resources by strategic area, and anticipation of emerging strategic issues. The solution should address traditional and nontraditional national security factors and therefore include the participation of all U.S. Government agencies that have a stake in these arenas.

As mentioned above, in such a setting, the U.S. Government must have the ability to prioritize among pressing issues; this necessitates a means for establishing prioritized strategic goals across the agencies and for having visibility into the interagency resources being spent to address these goals. Prioritized endstates will drive prioritized objectives; these, in turn, will drive prioritized capability development which drives resource allocation. The current atmosphere already features strategic issues that do not match up nearly with current agency structures—for example, the intersection of regional security, food availability, health, and the environment. Managing these issue intersections effectively requires both common orienting goals and regular assessments of performance *across* agencies to ensure all relevant capabilities are being brought to bear in a timely and coordinated fashion.

Our strategic environment also increasingly features nontraditional actors capable of highly unified, agile, and patient strategic action. To compete effectively for influence with such actors requires a means for closing the strategic and operational seams that such actors target. It also requires the ability to shape the environment. Given that many of the U.S. Government instruments of power best suited to shaping the operating environment reside in agencies not traditionally included in national security considerations, this highest-level interagency planning process must explicitly include them.

Globalization has distorted the boundaries and distinctions between national and international policy to the extent that more than 30 U.S. Government agencies now operate internationally. The new demands of homeland security and the rapidly evolving challenges of international affairs are converging increasingly into a linked set of regional and global challenges containing critical military, financial, homeland security, diplomatic, commercial, legal, environmental, and health components. Agencies previously considered mainly domestic now have vital global responsibilities with strategic linkages to traditional foreign policy agencies. Although U.S. Government agencies share highly interrelated goals, they often lack coordinated plans to achieve them, creating both strategic vulnerabilities and operational inefficiencies.

The value of a strategic planning process that is inclusive of interagency, public and private sector, and governmental and nongovernmental members and views from the outset derives from both enhanced effectiveness and efficiency in accomplishing the Nation's foreign policy and national security objectives. Effectiveness is strengthened both by increasing unity of effort and by managing performance across all elements of national power in accomplishing specific goals. Efficiency results from reduced duplication of effort, better visibility into and rationalization of investments in accordance with priorities, and anticipation of emerging strategic issues and gaps to enable earlier, more proactive action in lieu of more costly reactive responses.

As touched upon previously, even for a single agency or strategic command, conducting integrated strategic planning within today's strategic environment is a significant challenge, particularly for organizations composed of large, semi-autonomous agencies or bureaus. For many entities, the plethora of strategic plans, performance plans, and all other types of plans mandated by external factors and the resulting "urge to plan" creates a cacophony of white noise in the planning rooms throughout the organization. The result is that none of these plans is synchronized or aligned in any way, as different offices conduct strategic, performance, resource, and policy planning without a unifying framework. And this is still only talking about what goes on within a single institution. At the interagency level, particularly for agencies operating regionally and globally, these challenges are exacerbated, becoming even more difficult and imperative.

Stability operations, security cooperation, security assistance, humanitarian assistance, and disaster relief are all blurring the lines of authority. This blurring and overlapping jurisdiction between the development, diplomatic, and defense institutions are causing some understandable discomfort.

To ease that discomfort, we should recognize that stability and development are built upon the substratum of security. Without security, the other two are impossible to achieve. The United States and its international partners must focus on common interests, apply our collective wisdom, and leverage the shared *and* unique abilities of all partners to defeat those who seek to fracture the peace and disrupt the established global system of trade, commerce, and communication. The security challenges are not always traditional military threats, are often interrelated and transnational, and may involve both state and nonstate actors.

These threats, challenges, and conditions require using our 3-D glasses to see the blueprint for constructing an international partnering and interagency community approach on the foundational pillars of development, diplomacy, and defense.

Interagency partnering is an essential component of the Southern Command mission and enables the command to fulfill its full range of missions and effectively support our partners in Latin America and the Caribbean. These partnerships enable us to prioritize and synchronize efforts in a resource-constrained environment. Additionally, cabinet-level strategic plans and strategic plans from numerous independent establishments and government corporations provide valuable insights into the way these different organizations see a situation and how they approach a challenge or threat. This higher level guidance is but one factor that enables the synergistic development of a holistic strategy that synchronizes the efforts of our interagency community partners. This would not be possible if our Strategic Planning Process were not open and transparent from page one!

Bringing everyone together and openly sharing ideas and information is a vital step toward enlightenment and understanding the different points of view of our partners. But before we "understand," we must "see." Ultimately, we—the U.S. Government specifically, but also the Nation as a whole—need to view the world through others' eyes; it is not enough just to try and understand the other points of view, but truly understand where they are coming from and whence that point of view originates. We need to fully grasp the sources of grievance, and truly establish a permanent residence in the critical nodes in the international web of thought that drive political, cultural, and economic instability. We need to fully comprehend the sources of conflict and quarrel so that our thoughts, our words, and our deeds can serve as safety switches, not tripwires that set off unintended consequences.

Humanitarian Operations

Consider humanitarian operations, for example—such efforts foster goodwill and enhance the credibility of the United States. They solidify existing partnerships with key nations and open access to new relationships between and among nations, nongovernmental organizations, and international organizations. We need to always remember, however, that assistance provided by civilians can be viewed differently than assistance provided by personnel in uniform—even the vehicle from which this assistance is provided can influence perception and subsequently adulterate the mission. The former might be viewed as truly humanitarian, altruistic, and as part of a shared common interest. The latter could very easily be construed as serving some darker pursuit of national and military objectives.

One way to illustrate this "white hull vs. gray hull" mentality is shown in Nicaraguan President Daniel Ortega's remarks in August 2008: "Last year . . . the *Comfort* came to Corinto, and they were serving the people of Corinto, on the coast of Chinandega. They came to provide medical attention. They are ships of war! In other times, when these ships arrived in Nicaraguan waters, they would come to disembark troops. . . . Today we

In September 2008, local Haitians and Sailors from USS *Kearsarge* offload disaster relief supplies from Navy landing craft

U.S. Southern Command

have the *Kearsarge*, also in a plan of peace, with a plan of cooperation. Ships of war with a plan of peace." Understanding those nuances is crucial.

Civilian agencies and military organizations have different strengths to bring to development activities. USAID and its implementing partners have substantial experience in all types of development projects. They often combine this with extensive knowledge of the area where projects are performed, which is gleaned from a persistent presence (with a purpose) in country. This could aid greatly in ensuring the assistance—*and* the message that accompanies the assistance—is delivered to the proper audience in the proper manner.

Our Services, for example, have a long history of performing a wide array of humanitarian operations, including rescues at sea, transport of emergency personnel and relief supplies, community service, emergency relief, and medical services. These activities are an ingrained part of who we are and what we do. And though many observers often focus on the standard qualities of logistic capability and capacity, money, personnel, organization, and size as the most important comparative advantages held by the military, perhaps the most unique attribute the military has is its security mindset.

Whereas civilian development experts look at a situation and ask "what is the need," military actors ask the additional question of "what is the *threat*?"

This unique comparative advantage in providing security for itself and other U.S. agencies in hostile environments positions the military to be the only actor that *can* provide humanitarian or development assistance in situations of armed conflict.

Clearly, there will always be a need for humanitarian operations. Perhaps in our concept of maritime engagement operations, we should no longer constrain ourselves to the current force-packaging paradigm— carrier, expeditionary, and surface strike groups. If we are truly looking for a concrete way to implement the new maritime strategy and a new way to more completely take advantage of both traditional *and* nontraditional sources of national power, now is the time to give humanitarian missions a permanent, integral place in the spectrum of mission-tailored deployment options.

We could consider developing a new type of deploying group—call it a Humanitarian Service Group or HSG. As envisioned, an HSG could be organized from the keel up to conduct humanitarian relief and disaster recovery missions, but would benefit from the precise direction and focus of trained development and diplomatic professionals from USAID and the State Department being on board, in addition to a full complement from other departments such as Health and Human Services/Centers for Disease Control, Treasury, Energy, Commerce, Justice, Homeland Security, and the Environmental Protection Agency. Taking the hospital ships, USNS *Comfort* and USNS *Mercy*, as centerpieces, we already have the foundation for two HSGs—one for the Atlantic Fleet and the other for the Pacific Fleet. Each one would be home-ported in a place ideally suited for these ships to respond to crises or deploy to areas of most critical need. In addition, this would allow multiple participating agencies and their representatives to train and exercise together in advance of the deployments, much in the same way a carrier, expeditionary, or surface strike group goes through 6–12 months of "workups," honing their skills until they are in finely tuned synchronicity.

To accompany our hospital ships, we could assign escort ships from the Navy and Coast Guard, as well as assign permanent squadron command and staff and invite the various participating agency, nongovernmental, and public-private organization members to serve on that staff. The crews of these HSGs would focus their training on myriad humanitarian assistance, noncombatant evacuation, training and education, disaster recovery, health engagement, and community development missions. But regardless of how the HSG is ultimately organized, an inclusive mindset to work hand-in-hand and strive for complete integration with partners should be a core requirement.

We in the Department of Defense must expand our understanding of conflict and security beyond lethal means and reexamine all our operations, including peacetime engagement and training activities, as part of a single strategic framework. These are the new fundamental conditions of the 21st-century security environment:

- Attacks by organizations bent on ideological domination
- Nation-states fighting in unconventional settings with unfamiliar tool sets
- The "marketplace of ideas" at the root of conflicts, requiring sophisticated strategic communication to address
- A globalizing economy with perceived (and actual) winners and losers
- Exponential rise of environmental concerns directly linked to globalization
- Miniaturizing technologies producing powerful effects and dangers to security
- Diffusion of weapons of mass destruction—including biological and chemical

- Immediately accessible 24/7 news coverage from satellite radio and television

- Global communication at potentially everyone's fingertips—a "speed of thought" dialogue

- Exploding Internet dominated by bloggers and chat rooms, and threatened by hackers as well

- Cell phone cameras and pocket recorders, making everyone a "reporter"

- Sophisticated media engagement by transnational terrorists and organizations.

Pressing ecological issues, environmental disasters, rapid population growth, escalating demand for water, land, and energy—all these contribute to producing communities that lack the basic infrastructure to maintain even the most basic quality of life and health conditions that are essential to human welfare and civil development.

These new threats—not susceptible to combat operations but certainly exacerbated by bellicose behavior—tend to lurk in our intellectual seams and find our bureaucratic and cultural blind spots. Our self-imposed legal, political, moral, and conceptual boundaries defining what constitutes combat vs. criminal activity, domestic vs. international jurisdiction, and governmental versus private interest all provide operational space for potentially lethal opponents with no such boundaries to respect.

Countering such threats and challenges, and reacting to the informational realities of our age, require new organizational structures not predicated on traditional notions of war and peace. Our old model, wherein the State Department and USAID offer "carrots" in time of peace while the DOD threatens the "stick" should deterrence fail, provides solutions only when such black and white paradigms are readily distinguishable. Today we operate in shades of gray.

This all comprises a difficult set of conditions, to be sure. Accordingly, we must recognize that the 21st-century security environment is a thriving marketplace of ideas; we must also understand we are but one of *several* merchants in this marketplace where intended and unintended messages often carry equal weight, wherein every activity attributable to the United States communicates to some audience—either positively or negatively. Everything we do, therefore, must be guided with the thought of increasing our market share in a positive way. Thus, exactly what we wish to communicate and to whom we wish to communicate it—both the American population *and* the population of the country or region of focus—must be predetermined and guided throughout by a systematic, yet flexible and effective process; this process could perhaps be driven by a separate information agency which will ensure a more comprehensive, tightly integrated and synergistic interagency community effort delivers this national message.

The aforementioned set of challenging conditions comprises more than just a Defense Department issue, more than just a State Department issue, more than even just an Executive Branch issue—this is a whole-of-government crucible and it demands a whole-of-government approach.

The American people have a vested interest in this; Congress, as their elected representatives, should take its rightful place as an equal or leading power to set the agenda, identify problems, and enact solutions to ensure interagency cooperation, collaboration, and integration. Building greater transparency between the Executive and Legislative branches is essential for getting budget flexibility and the decentralized instruments we need to succeed. More collaborative planning and budgeting can help restore trust between the two branches and among the interagency community. We as a nation would fall short of that level of involvement to our own detriment.

Engaging all stakeholders in Congress is essential. To sustain support for the level of development activities essential for the Nation's interests, there must be a broad consensus among the American people regarding the importance of regional and global development for the Nation's security as well as its values. Building this consensus requires a concerted effort by a variety of advocates to educate both policymakers and the public. Some of this is already happening, as indicated by the increased level of focus on the 3-D approach. We must continue an assertive public engagement on the part of civilian development agencies.

Continuing on the theme of education, within the Executive Branch, we as members of the interagency community must become aware of each other's strengths and weaknesses, constraints, and restraints. We must find ways to mutually promote our common interests, and we must become intimately familiar with each other's goals and objectives, both in the field as well as in Washington. An example of this can be found at U.S. Southern Command as USAID and U.S. military officers are gaining a better understanding of each other and an appreciation for what they do through our exchange program. In the 16 countries in Latin America and the Caribbean where USAID operates, we find our valiant USAID personnel providing vital contributions and making a significant difference every day. We have also learned that objectives determined by headquarters may or may not match the needs and objectives of people and organizations in the country.

As remarkable as this learning process is, however, it is only the tip of the iceberg—we can and we must do more. The starting point is interaction and sharing, striving toward increasing the levels of awareness of how we each think and operate. But to truly institutionalize an integrated, coordinated, whole-of-government systemic approach, interagency national security training and education are needed across the U.S. Government. While we have made some modest improvements in this area for military personnel, the demands for increased civilian training, academic instruction, and interagency assignments and exchanges are compelling and immediate. This includes language and cultural training, but also a new system of personnel incentives similar to the military's changes following Goldwater-Nichols legislation more than two decades ago.

Interagency personnel need challenging assignments, regardless of their rank. In order to continue benefiting from interagency community expertise and perspectives, personnel need career-enhancing assignments. In the military, if personnel who work at an interagency activity or come to an interagency-oriented command are not promoted or sent to career-advancing follow-on assignments by their parent agencies, it is unlikely that strong interagency partnering will be sustainable or effective.

The demands of the 21st century will require even more interagency integration of planning, and the shortfalls in this area merit attention and resourcing. In many respects, we need to develop a new cadre of national security officers who can deploy and staff organizations across the whole-of-government. Particular attention must be paid to the development and diplomatic arenas; our desired endstate should be a new generation of national security officers and interagency community leaders who are just as comfortable practicing diplomacy, enabling development, or providing for our common defense and security.

> America must . . . balance and integrate all elements of our national power. We cannot continue to push the burden on to our military alone, nor leave dormant any aspect of the full arsenal of American capability. . . . This effort takes place within the walls of this university [NDU], where civilians sit alongside soldiers in the classroom. And it must continue out in the field, where American civilians can advance opportunity, enhance governance and the rule of law, and attack the causes of war around the world.
>
> —President Barack Obama[6]

The foundation of society rests upon the ability of a nation to provide security and stability for its people. Today, widespread poverty and inequality combined with corruption leaves many searching for the means for simple survival in much of Latin America and the Caribbean. A lack of opportunity and competition for scarce resources lead to an increase in crime and provide opportunities for gangs and terrorists to flourish. In many cases, these conditions lead to an environment that threatens the security of the entire region, and threatens democracies everywhere.

Addressing the challenges posed by gangs, drugs, and terrorist threats requires the application of all instruments of national power. Our nation must also deal with the underlying problems of unemployment, corruption, and a general lack of opportunity. The U.S. interagency community must encourage and assist in building partnerships across the region while working with intergovernmental organizations to ensure success. Given an environment of unceasing micro-conflict and constant ideological communication, "carrot and stick" must work not merely hand-in-hand, but hand-in glove—synchronized toward a single purpose and unity of effort, across national and tactical echelons, in ways previously unseen in our country's history.

We should not expect clear transitions between peace and war, and, thus, in certain regions, we need new standing organizations chartered to manage the entire spectrum of international relations conditions. Combatant commands must seek to maintain a vital regional perspective on security issues. Enabling truly joint and interagency activities requires additional modalities and authorities to provide effective synchronization of various U.S. Government agency resources. It also requires integration among the regional authorities of other interagency actor cells, particularly the State Department and USAID. We need to explore new standing organizations chartered to operate with today's dynamic and challenging international environment.

Joint Interagency Task Force–South (JIATF–South)

U.S. Southern Command is itself one example of such an organization at the combatant command level, but perhaps an even more impressive model can be found in the Joint Interagency Task Force–South (JIATF–South) located in Key West, Florida. The security and prosperity of the United States, Latin America, and the Caribbean are inseparably linked, and together we face some serious challenges. Fighting two of these in particular, narcoterrorism and illicit trafficking, is the very reason JIATF–South exists. This task force, which in February 2009 celebrated 20 years of excellence, is comprised of truly amazing individuals from all 4 branches of the military, 9 different agencies, and 11 different partner nations. This group, beyond doubt, is a team: a joint, interagency, international, combined, and allied *team*—a creative and innovative body that defines "synergy," the blending of experience, professionalism, and knowledge being greater than the sum of its individual parts. JIATF–South sets the standard of achieving unity of effort to accomplish great things in confronting the challenges that exist in our shared home.

JIATF–South's *raison d'être* is a task of enormous proportions, but the task force nevertheless continues to make incredible headway every year and produces eye-watering results. For example: JIATF–South's area of responsibility covers nearly 42 million square miles, almost 40 percent of the earth's surface; in the 20 years it has been conducting operations in this region, 2,300 metric tons of cocaine have been seized, 705,000 pounds of marijuana have been interdicted, 4,600 traffickers arrested, almost 1,100 vessels captured, and a grand total of approximately $190 billion taken out of the pockets of the drug cartels; in 2008, JIATF–South was responsible for greater than 50 percent of the total cocaine seizures in the world; and, while doing all this, JIATF–South set the benchmark for workplace quality in a recent nationwide study.[7] This kind of success demands total commitment from the entire organization—inspirational leadership, complete integration, collaboration, and partnership which pervade every possible sinew of the entity.

In an ideal world, the required resources for successful accomplishment of our missions would be limitless. With our national, regional, and even global commitments, however, the simple and honest truth is that we do *not* have all we want; more importantly, we do not have all we *need*. Thus we need to rely heavily on innovation and partnerships in all we do. JIATF–South is not just the frontline in our fight against those who threaten the region with drugs and other kinds of misery; they are the vanguard of creativity—a breeding ground for the kind of innovation and ideas that have transformed, and will continue to transform, not only this unit, not only U.S. Southern Command, but hopefully government at all levels.

The power of creativity—*the power of ideas*—comes not from secrecy and maintaining preestablished cylinders or stovepipes of excellence, but through open and honest communication and collaboration. For only through such a process can we hope to tap into the vast resource of experiences and enthusiasm to build the security and stability we owe the people of our nations, and tend to the needs of those who make this possible. This is what makes this team work so wonderfully; furthermore, it is helping to transform the face of government throughout the region. The team members' willingness to integrate, their desire to incorporate, and their creativity are the example—the catalyst—that will help lead all in government to work more cooperatively and efficiently.

Whenever I talk about this incredible organization, I describe it simply as a "national treasure" or the "crown jewel of Southern Command." And after being fortunate enough to witness it in action and see for myself all that this amazing organization represents—record-setting achievements year after year, and robust interagency and international partnerships that have been carefully cultivated by the leadership from the ground up and at all levels—I know what I am really observing at JIATF–South is the future of Southern Command specifically, and the model for future geographic combatant commands, perhaps even combined interagency *security* commands. The men and women of JIATF–South have been doing it for 20 years; their unparalleled achievements showcase them as a beacon to steer by for all thinkers and statesmen calling for better ways to integrate and implement the whole-of-government and whole-of-nation approach in confronting challenges to national and shared regional security. I have been extremely fortunate to have them as part of Southern Command as they have been an integral cornerstone as we continue to build our Partnership for the Americas.

In summation, cooperative security in this region must be anchored by the belief that only through constant engagement and aggressive development of our partnerships, at every possible opportunity, can our "forces" be agents that build regional stability and security. This fundamental principle must guide the thoughts, words, and deeds of all the elements of national power, as well as our friends and partner nations. This is an exciting prospect, as I believe this type of cooperative security is a shining example of a common tool that addresses human issues, while at the same time it preserves the pride of our own national heritage and the shared common heritage to which President Kennedy referred.

This inherent and elemental desire for security is the reason the nations of the Americas have each tailored unique military and police forces in their own right. From the protection of valuable natural resources and the preservation of human rights, to fears of potential existential clashes of political ideologies, our national needs have produced unique security forces and doctrines for their use. The previously described range of threats and challenges to our individual and collective security has also spawned a multitude of different meanings and definitions of security—but this should not be viewed as a problem. We probably will never reach a consensus, except on a very human level, on what security means to our nations, any more so than a meeting of all the Executive Branch agencies and departments could agree on a single definition of national security.

But that, in itself, is a positive thing—for those varied definitions of security have produced a magnificent array of capabilities, skills, and specialized strengths that contains an inner strength through its own diversity. This multiplicity is a veritable gold mine for all of us who will live and seek to thrive in the 21st-century. Where we have commonalities, we should leverage those and forge a stronger hybrid as a result. Where we have unnecessary redundancy and duplication of effort, we should look to maximize efficiency and effectiveness by channeling constrained resources into an area that may not be as well developed.

How do we mine this mother lode of extensive talent available to us? Access is, of course, limited by the reality of political constraints, both foreign *and* domestic. But political constraints are often overcome by the tremendously positive experiences we enjoy so often with and through constant interaction, cooperation, and transparent collaboration. It can begin in the classrooms at the Service war colleges and can extend to the many bilateral and multilateral exercises and humanitarian assistance and outreach programs throughout our shared home. To build a truly cooperative security for the 21st century, we must believe there are always new ways to operate together; there are always new forums for dialogue; there are always things we can learn from our partners; and, there are always new tools and solutions that bring both the largest and smallest players to the table.

We have recognized that the real thrust of 21st-century national security in this region is not vested in war, but in intelligent management of the conditions of peace in a volatile era. While remaining fully ready for combat operations, the defense function must work to support the practitioners of diplomacy and development—because their success will dominate so much of what unfolds for our nation in this volatile and unpredictable time. We in the Defense Department must undertake no task without first considering the valuable synergy of the State Department, USAID, and the entire cast of national security agencies, nongovernmental bodies, and the private sector, working together. We must also be equally inclusive of our international partners.

We have also learned that the entire organization must be mission-focused, informed and guided throughout by strategic communication, and integrated by function. I commented earlier that to survive and emerge even stronger from the 21st-century security environment crucible, we need a whole-of-government strategic plan and mindset; that is not enough—we need to truly mobilize all the elements of national power and capabilities, and truly bring to bear a whole-of-nation archetype.

Done correctly, this new way of doing business incorporates more fully the political, military, economic, humanitarian, ecological, and diplomatic dimensions of regional and global operations into a single, coherent strategic approach—an approach that keeps us on our journey toward completing that bridge to a new era of national security, a bridge built upon the "3-D" pillars of development, diplomacy, and defense, but constructed with, and supported by, the wrought-iron girders of all the elements of the interagency community, the nongovernmental organizations, and the private sector.

Notes

[1] Secretary of State Hillary Clinton, "Remarks at Asia Society," February 13, 2009.

[2] Secretary of Defense Robert Gates, "Landon Lecture," remarks delivered by Secretary Gates at Kansas State University, Manhattan, Kansas, November 26, 2007.

[3] Karen DeYoung, Interview with Assistant to the President for National Security Affairs James Jones, "Obama's NSC Will Get New Power," *The Washington Post*, February 8, 2009, available at: <http://washingtonpost.com/wp-dyn/content/article/2009/02/07/AR2009020702076.html?wprss=rss_world>.

[4] Hans Binnendijk and Patrick M. Cronin, eds., *Civilian Surge: Key to Complex Operations* (Washington, DC: National Defense University Press, 2009), 3.

[5] Robert M. Gates, "A Balanced Strategy, Reprogramming the Pentagon for a New Age," *Foreign Affairs* 88, no. 1 (January/February 2009), available at: <http://www.foreignaffairs.com/articles/63717/robert-m-gates/a-balanced-strategy>.

[6] President Barack Obama, *Address to National Defense University* in dedicating Abraham Lincoln Hall, March 12, 2009.

[7] 2009 Defense Equal Opportunity Management Institute (DEOMI) Organizational Climate Survey: JIATF-South surpassed the national average in every category (13 of 13). *U.S. Southern Command 2010 Posture Statement*, 18.

Chapter 4

Trafficking

Illicit drugs are a great enemy of the environment and also fuel terrorism. While Colombia fights to destroy harvests of illegal substances, other countries must address the role demand plays in the illegal drug trade. Indeed, whoever bought illicit drugs encouraged a child to become a part of the distribution system, helped to set off a car bomb in Colombia and encouraged the destruction of another tree in the rainforest. . . . We need help from the entire world, to be able to fight drug trafficking, which is finally the enemy of freedom.

—Alvaro Uribe
Colombian President
Address to 63ᵈ United Nations General Assembly
New York, September 24, 2008

Throughout my travels during my tenure at U.S. Southern Command, at meetings, conferences, and press events, people often asked me what I worried about as commander. Narcotics and other illegal trafficking impacts our national security immensely by presenting the following dilemma: how best do we remain a free and open society—a land of opportunity and a partner of choice for our neighbor countries— especially during a post-9/11 era in which criminals and terrorists seeking to do harm continuously exploit our borders on land, in the air, and at sea?

The enduring and vital national interests of the United States are best preserved by a hemisphere of sovereign democratic nations with capable, competent, and effective governments, free societies, and economies based on free and open-market principles. Such nations foster conditions favorable to increased development, improved standards of living, expanded opportunities, and stable and secure environments for their people. However, our interests are increasingly threatened by illicit trafficking which, among other things, can undermine democratic institutions and the rule of law throughout our shared home.

Yes, I worry about the trade in illegal narcotics; but I am also deeply concerned about the illicit trafficking of counterfeit items, dangerous goods, natural resources, money, cultural property, and even people by shrewd, well-resourced, and nefarious adversaries. Historically, within the U.S. Southern Command area of focus, the spotlight has been mainly on the transshipment of illegal drugs such as cocaine. However, illicit traffickers may also exploit their sophisticated transportation modes and networks to move weapons, people, money, and other contraband. Left unchecked, illicit trafficking poses a significant threat to the security, stability, and ultimately, the sovereignty and prosperity of nations throughout the Americas.

Two important events occurred in 2007 that received very little fanfare. In March, the U.S. Coast Guard, working with the Drug Enforcement Administration (DEA) and Panamanian authorities, seized the merchant freighter *Gatun*, carrying over 20 metric tons of cocaine—approximately 43,000 pounds, the equivalent of 10 Volkswagen Beetles—bound for Mexico. It was the largest maritime interdiction of drugs ever made in the Americas, and it denied drug lords over $300 million in revenue. Twenty metric tons would be enough cocaine for every single one of the more than 17 million U.S. high school students to take eight hits of 100 percent cocaine.[1]

Then, in September 2007, Colombian authorities captured Diego León Montoya Sánchez, one of the world's most dangerous drug traffickers and responsible for nearly two-thirds of the hundreds of tons of cocaine exported from Colombia each year. At the time, because of the nearly 1,500 murders attributed to this ruthless criminal, Montoya was near the top on the FBI's Top Ten Most Wanted list, behind Osama bin Laden and his deputy, Ayman Al-Zawahiri. Through fear and corruption, Montoya, like Pablo Escobar before him, played a huge, destabilizing role throughout Latin America and the Caribbean. His arrest marked a major milestone for Colombia—a nation that has labored for years to build a foundation for legitimate governance and rule of law.

Both events represented victories; but neither received significant notice. Twenty years ago, drugs were a leading concern in this nation and solving the drug issue was a point of routine debate and near the top of every political candidate's agenda. Newspapers featured daily "drug bust" stories on the front pages. Every television station carried stories about the latest efforts in what was termed the "War on Drugs," which in my view is the wrong expression. Congress passed the National Drug Control Act in 1992, creating the Office of National Drug Control Policy headed by what was then a Cabinet-level official reporting directly to the White House. Presidential candidates debated the best approach to take in solving the drug problem. As recently as the year 2000, the movie *Traffic* was a box office and critical success, nominated for five Academy Awards and winning four.

Today, however, little is heard about the war on drugs—and, incidentally, this was the wrong metaphor all along. Articles dedicated to the issue are relegated to the back pages of the papers, or several clicks away from their home page online. Yet, illegal narcotics and the associated illicit trafficking remain a national threat of significant proportion. What is missing is not only social consciousness, but political conviction.

Drugs kill tens of thousands of U.S. citizens annually. They undermine fragile democracies throughout the Americas, with enormous negative consequences in our nation. Drug trading and its associated astronomical profits fuel the vehicle of nascent narcoterrorism and misery throughout the region. The distortions and costs to the U.S. economy—and to those of the entire hemisphere—are enormous.

Here is a hypothesis: *Illegal drug use and illicit trafficking are huge national challenges that should return to the national spotlight and re-enter the national (and international) dialogue.* Every bit of effort devoted toward solving the crisis of drug abuse in this country on the demand side, and preventing the flow of illicit drugs on the supply side, is effort well-spent toward establishing control at our borders, stabilizing fragile democracies in our hemisphere, directly saving the lives of U.S. citizens, and enhancing our national security.

Furthermore, the impact is not restricted to just the United States; the costs of illicit trafficking in narcotics reach far beyond our borders. Nations who formerly saw themselves as largely immune to drug problems are experiencing the damaging effects of drugs first-hand, and are struggling to address them. For example, in less than two decades, Brazil has become the number-two consumer nation of cocaine in the world, second only to the United States in total consumption per year. Sadly, the region to the south of us no longer consists only of source countries, but now contains user countries, as well. In the source and transit zone countries, well-organized and increasingly violent drug traffickers are undermining democracy, the rule of law, and public institutions using extortion, bribery, and payment-in-kind as they advance their agendas for securing vast power and almost incomprehensible amounts of money. Internal and cross-border—via air, land, and/or sea—trafficking in drugs, weapons, human beings, money, and terrorists poses a threat to every nation's security and stability. Revenue from illicit trafficking has weakened state structures throughout the region, adulterated (and in some cases completely subverted) the rule of law, and ripped apart the fabric of social order. In extreme cases, illicit trafficking can overwhelm a state's ability to govern itself, thereby violating its sovereignty.

The confluence of money, power, and the ability to breach the integrity of national borders makes the illicit trafficking problem a significant security challenge for nations throughout the Americas. Border insecurity, rising health care costs, increased crime, public insecurity, corruption, weakening support for democratic institutions, and heavily burdened local, county, and state agencies are the byproducts of this illegitimate and criminal activity. It is estimated that illicit trafficking costs legitimate economies more than $245 billion annually. The illicit trafficking trade has devastating impacts on effective governance and economic growth, and it knows no boundaries. Simply put, illicit drug activity and its trafficking have a tremendously destabilizing effect on the people and partner nations throughout the Americas, our shared home.

The Challenges of Illegal Drugs in the United States

Here in the United States, drug abuse and related criminal activity have killed approximately 120,000 citizens since 2001. That is 40 times the number of deaths attributed to al Qaeda from the 1993 World Trade Center Bombing, the 2000 bombing of the USS *Cole*, and the 2001 September 11 attacks combined.[2] Nearly 20,000 people die from drug abuse-related causes in the United States each year, perhaps half of them from cocaine harvested from the jungles of Colombia.[3]

The drug challenge is enormous, and the underlying threat is real. Why? One simple truth: no business in the United States is more profitable or detrimental than the illicit drug trade. What is the largest cash crop in the USA? Wheat? Corn? Soybeans? Wrong. It is marijuana. In fact, the total illicit drug trade equates to a $65 billion per year industry in the USA. When you add the resources we use to address health and crime consequences—as well as the loss of productivity suffered from disability, death, and withdrawal from the legitimate workforce—the total societal impact and cost to our economy probably exceed $240 billion annually, growing at the rate of 5 percent per year.

Moreover, the negative effects of the drug trade reach far beyond sale and use of drugs in the United States. Throughout the Americas, illegal narcotics threaten delicate democracies. Today, 14 of the 20 leading source nations for drug shipments to the United States are located in the Americas. In source and transit zone countries throughout Latin America and the Caribbean, violent, well-organized drug-traffickers use threat of force, blackmail, bribery, and other alternative methods of influence to fan the flames of corruption and violence. Their actions constantly destabilize the still-settling foundation upon which the pillars of democratic principles are based, undermining governance in our neighboring nations.

In years past, governments sponsored and funded terrorism; however, international pressure following the September 2001 attacks has forced terrorists to rely on other activities such as arms trafficking, money laundering, extortion, kidnap-for-ransom, and drug-trafficking as their funding sources. The reasons for this strong link between terrorism and the drug trade are certainly not difficult to ascertain. Today, enormous profit margins and growing global demand for illegal drugs such as cocaine and heroin generate huge amounts of revenue to finance crimes against our society. This money assists rogue states and international terrorist organizations who are determined to build and use weapons of mass destruction. This all connects to national security by providing one set of reasons to traffic illicit cargo and violate our borders, while also being able to expand an extremely lucrative industry.

The stakes involved are huge. According to the 2007 United Nations World Drug Report, virtually all of the world's cocaine comes from coca leaf cultivated in Colombia, Peru, and Bolivia. Cocaine production estimates from these countries reached 984 metric tons in 2006. Worth nearly $21 billion wholesale, that amount of cocaine could retail on the streets in the United States for over $105 billion. The circulation of massive amounts of drug money on this scale would have a murderous effect on weak or small economies in the Americas, wreaking havoc particularly in those nations seeking to break free of the choking grip of corruption, greed, and violence. In the hands of terrorists, cocaine profits can easily fund thousands of attacks similar to the low-cost 9/11 plot.

On the human level, the illegal narcotics industry leaves tragedy and a trail of blood in its wake. Humanitarian crisis follows the drug supply throughout Latin America and the Caribbean region. Drug kingpins are notorious for their horrendous record of abuses, including frequent kidnappings, brutal tortures and murders, recruitment and use of child soldiers, and use of antipersonnel landmines. Widespread massacres, merciless killings, extortion, and forced seizure of land from civilians are also common.

Cocaine trafficking from source countries in Latin America through the Caribbean to destinations in Europe and the United States remains the leading cause of most of the violent crime throughout our region. The current murder rate in the region of 30 people per 100,000 inhabitants per year rivals even the most troubled areas of southern and western Africa. Largely due to successful interdiction at sea and in the air, land routes through Mexico have become the primary route for South American cocaine into the United States. As a result, Mexico now finds itself in the middle of an all-out war between competing drug lords. In northern Mexico, drug cartels seeking control of the lucrative drug trade murdered over 5,000 people in 2008 alone.

In addition to the cocaine industry, there has been an increase in the value and production of "precursor chemicals," compounds that may not be controlled substances in their own right, but are key ingredients in the manufacture of other highly addictive and destructive drugs. For example, Argentina has emerged as a leading provider of ephedrine, a stimulant used in over-the-counter medicines as well as a key ingredient for the production of methamphetamine—"meth," "crystal meth," or "speed." As ephedrine has become increasingly controlled and expensive, Mexican cartels who smuggle meth into the United States have turned to Argentina, where ephedrine is cheap and readily available. Mexican cartels have also begun using Argentina not only as a source for raw materials, but increasingly as a full-fledged producer country of designer drugs destined for Mexico, the United States, and Europe.

Humans are not the only species afflicted with the death and destruction of the illegal narcotics trade—there is also the ecological impact. Just over 2.2 million hectares of the Colombian Amazon forest have been slashed and burned to grow illegal coca in the last 20 years. To put this into perspective, 2.2 million hectares equates to just under 8,500 square miles, roughly equivalent to the size of the state of New Jersey—destroyed. Experts estimate that it will take between 100 and 600 years for each hectare to recover. Because cleared jungle land is not ideal for agriculture, coca growers use ten times more agrochemicals than growers of legal crops. Cocaine also needs to be produced near water sources, where waste such as ammonia, sulphuric acid, and gasoline is dumped. This is devastating to the fragile ecosystem that shelters the many endangered species of wildlife, including 13 percent of the world's amphibians and more than 6,000 unique plant species, found only in Colombia.

The illicit drug trade is the energy that feeds many public security ills in Latin America and the Caribbean—from criminal violence, to corruption, to political instability—but its toxic effects are not isolated to our south. West Africa is fast becoming a transshipment hub for metric-ton quantities of cocaine being transported to Europe by South American drug trade organizations. Andean Ridge traffickers are entrenched in West Africa and have cultivated long-standing relationships with African criminal networks to facilitate their activities in the region. Criminal groups take advantage of Africa's porous borders, poorly equipped and undertrained law enforcement agencies, and corrupt government officials to facilitate their trafficking operations. The Iberian Peninsula is Europe's main entry point for most drugs trafficked across the continent, according to a report published in July 2008 by the United Nations Office on Drugs and Crime, with Spain recently passing the United States as having the highest per capita cocaine consumption in the world. Cocaine is becoming increasingly entrenched in European society.

"War on Drugs": What's in a Name?

The term and concept first came into being almost four decades ago, when President Richard Nixon officially declared a "war on drugs" and identified drug abuse as Public Enemy #1 in 1971, 2 years after calling for the creation of a national drug policy. In a special message to Congress, he labeled drug abuse as a "serious national threat," citing a dramatic jump in drug-related juvenile arrests and street crime between 1960 and 1967. As part of his call for a unified national, state, and local antidrug strategy, President Nixon created the Drug Enforcement Administration in 1973 to coordinate the efforts of all other participating and responsible agencies.

At roughly the same time, at the heart of the drug darkness in Colombia, police seized 600 kilograms of cocaine—the largest recorded seizure to date—from a small plane in 1975. Drug traffickers responded with a brutality reminiscent of the Chicago gang wars of the late 1920s. In one weekend, 40 people were assassinated in what is now known as the "Medellin Massacre." The event signaled the new power of Colombia's cocaine industry, headquartered in Medellin. In 1981, the Medellin Cartel rose to power and the alliance included the Ochoa family, Pablo Escobar, Carlos Lehder, and Jose Gonzalo Rodriguez Gacha. These drug kingpins worked together to manufacture, transport, and market cocaine. As a result of these and other actions, the United States and Colombia ratified a bilateral extradition treaty.

In 1984, First Lady Nancy Reagan launched her "Just Say No" campaign, which included the *This Is Your Brain on Drugs* series of commercials as part of its aggressive ad campaign. Two years later, President Ronald Reagan signed the Anti–Drug Abuse Act of 1986, appropriating $1.7 billion. The act also created mandatory minimum penalties for drug offenses, which became increasingly criticized for promoting significant ethnic and social disparities in the prison population because of the differences in sentencing for crack versus powder cocaine. Possession of crack, which is cheaper to obtain than the powder form, results in harsher sentences; thus, the majority of crack users come from the lower income segment of society and were perceived to be punished with greater severity because they could not afford the "higher status" form of the narcotic.

Compounding this situation is the fact that drugs have thrived in our social fabric for many decades. As previously mentioned, the movie *Traffic* was a cinematic tour de force in 2000, winning four Oscars. *Traffic* was directed by Steven Soderbergh and explores the intricacies of the illegal drug trade from a number of different perspectives: a user, an enforcer, a politician, and a trafficker, whose lives affect each other though they never actually meet. The film is an adaptation of the British Channel 4 television series and even spawned a mini-series on the USA Network, also called *Traffic*. Hollywood produced additional blockbuster movies showcasing the use of narcotics and the vast amounts of money associated with the drug industry as *Blow* followed in 2001, *Cocaine Cowboys* in 2006, and *American Gangster* in 2007, all with Oscar winners or nominees as headliners and cast members. Drugs are very popular in this medium, and thus in our culture. Even if a movie is not specifically about trafficking, as these four are, drugs often figure prominently in the story line. In fact, from 2000 to 2007, no fewer than 150 feature films have featured the use of cocaine or other illicit drugs by a lead or supporting cast member.

General Barry McCaffrey, during his Senate confirmation hearing before becoming the Director of the Office of National Drug Control Policy under President Bill Clinton, stated, "The metaphor 'War on Drugs' is inadequate to describe this terrible menace facing the American people." He went on to comment, "Wars are relatively straightforward. You identify the enemy, select a general, assign him a mission and resources, and let him get the job done. In this struggle against drug abuse, there is no silver bullet, no quick way to reduce drug use or the damage it causes." During his tenure, General McCaffrey stressed the importance of understanding that there can be no total victory in this contest, and thus a military campaign is the wrong path to follow. Ultimately, particularly on the demand side of the equation, most of the people involved in drugs are not the enemy—they are the victims. His efforts led to a growing understanding of the requirements for and benefits of national drug treatment programs, healing the addicts to reduce the appetite for drugs that fuels the industry.

Experts estimate that people in the United States consume over 350 metric tons of cocaine each year.[4] As indicated above, the numbers of deaths and the profits being generated are staggering. Understandably, our neighbors in the Caribbean and Latin America often ask why we in the United States do not do more to curb the demand. In fact, the United States does attack the challenges on the demand side. Overall, in 2007, the

U.S. Federal Government spent over $13 billion combating drugs, and more was done by state and municipal governments. Over one-third of that money went toward programs to stop drug use before it starts and to intervene and heal habitual drug users.[5] Drying up the demand is, ultimately, the best way to finally stop the flow of illicit drugs and help us secure our borders.

In addition to attacking the demand side of the drug problem, significant effort is being expended on the production side of the equation in the source countries. Programs for eradication, alternative development, macroeconomic growth, judicial and police training, and human rights education all play a part in reducing illicit production of coca leaf.

Both demand and production efforts are vital and must continue; however, neither the demand side nor the supply side was in my area of professional concern at U.S. Southern Command. Instead, the primary role of the command in this mission area was and continues to be supporting *interdiction* by law enforcement via monitoring and detection, doing our best to prevent drugs from entering the United States. Interdiction efforts focus on stopping drugs and illicit trafficking through the transit zone between the producing countries and the market in the United States, Europe, and other areas. While actual arrests are made by law enforcement authorities like the Coast Guard and DEA, there is a significant support role for the U.S. military involving intelligence, communication, logistics, sensor operations, patrol, and force protection for law enforcement authorities engaged in interdiction activities. Again, Southern Command's roles in this mission are detection and monitoring in the transit zone and supporting our partners in law enforcement. It is a crucial mission—one that receives significant attention from all levels of the command.

A Vital Mission

As previously described, our area of focus at U.S. Southern Command is vast, including 41 nations, territories, and protectorates of Central America, South America, and the Caribbean, and covering over 16 million square miles—one-sixth of the Earth's surface. It is a region that is home to approximately 460 million people with a variety of cultures, languages, and histories. From the headquarters in Miami, over 1,500 people make plans and lead the military activities of roughly 7,000 military and civilians who fall under one-star to three-star component commanders from each of the Armed Services and the U.S. Special Operations Command. On any given day, thousands of Soldiers, Sailors, Airmen, Marines, Coastguardsmen, and DOD civilians are deployed in many countries throughout the region. In addition, hundreds more are routinely deployed in our Navy and Coast Guard ships throughout the maritime domain. Southern Command is committed to working closely with the entire interagency community to develop strategically important partnerships throughout the region for counterdrug programs.

Each year, the President develops the National Drug Control Strategy, which is the Nation's plan for combating the use and availability of illicit drugs. The National Drug Control Strategy has three key elements: (1) stopping use before it starts; (2) intervening and healing drug users; and (3) disrupting the market. The FY 2008 Drug Budget totaled nearly $13 billion, with about $940 million—7 percent of the overall budget—under the auspices of the Department of Defense for counterdrug operations.

The U.S. military's role in the drug control program was first mandated by legislation in the 1989 National Defense Authorization Act (NDAA), which directed the Department of Defense to assume the role as the lead agency for "detection and monitoring of aerial and maritime transit of illegal drugs to the United States." In addition to passive detection and monitoring of potential drug smuggling activities, we *support* lead Federal and other partner agencies (like DEA and Coast Guard) in the active element of interception of suspect craft to the full extent permitted by U.S. law and Defense Department policy. While providing this support, we must still observe the restraints of the Posse Comitatus Act, which specifically prohibits the military from acts of apprehension or arrest except in narrowly defined circumstances. This level of teamwork requires a close working relationship, one characterized by close coordination and trust, using a whole-of-government approach and leveraging the strengths and capabilities of our international partners. These efforts only constitute roughly 10 percent of the President's overall budget to address the drug problem, but I would argue they are a vital part of the overall endeavor.

The monitoring and interdiction process is incredibly complex because it requires a mix of sophisticated technologies and capabilities. It is sensitive because of the connections that must be established for varied organizations and nations to work together as a team without a comfortable margin of error. Interdiction also has to be dynamic because it deals with a highly capable foe with the capital to buy virtually whatever it needs to adapt to changing circumstances.

A primary operations center for all of this is what I referred to in a previous chapter as "the crown jewel of Southern Command," the Joint Interagency Task Force–South, or JIATF–South, located in Key West, Florida. Its focus is both air and maritime smuggling through a 6-million-square-mile area called

U.S. Navy Photo (Mass Communication Specialist 2ⁿ Class Ron Kuzlik)

Mexican ship ARM *Mina* sails in formation with other participants in the 50th iteration of UNITAS Gold, the longest-running multinational maritime exercise in the world. U.S. Navy ships trained off the coast of Florida with maritime forces from Brazil, Canada, Chile, Colombia, Ecuador, Germany, Mexico, Peru, and Uruguay to promote security in the Americas (2009).

U.S. Southern Command (Jose Ruiz)

In a realistic training scenario, a drone missile is shot from the deck of USNS *Hunter* in the live-fire portion of UNITAS Gold, a maritime exercise conducted with the naval forces of several nations (2009).

the "transit zone." With the help of 11 partner nations, JIATF–South has evolved into *the* model of interagency and multinational cooperation, achieving record-setting cocaine seizures every year from 2000 to 2006. From 2007 to 2008, JIATF–South was responsible, with international and interagency partners, for seizing more than 475 metric tons of cocaine in the transit zone. Put in a different context, that equates to over 190 hits of cocaine for the 17 million sons and daughters in high school here in the United States. In 2008, for the first time in a decade, we began to see a rise in the street price of cocaine and attendant scarcity in a variety of large U.S. urban markets. Working together with demand and production side solution sets, it seems that interdiction may indeed be having an effect on the market. At a minimum, we know that 475 *fewer* metric tons of cocaine are on our streets or in the hands of our children, families, and coworkers than would otherwise be the case over the past 2 years. Clearly, that's a staggering amount, but stopping even that much is not enough to solve the problem. We need to try to do more.

Innovation . . . Not Just a One-way Street

Each year, in spite of our efforts, illicit traffickers continue to prove they are ruthless, resourceful, and highly intelligent people who possess uncanny creative adaptability in the face of our countermeasures. The windfall profits they receive from their business model drive their innovation, making our job of trying to get and stay a step ahead of them very challenging. Utilizing both legitimate and illegitimate air, land, and sea methods of conveyance, traffickers have established an agile and viable infrastructure for transporting illicit cargo like narcotics to the United States and the global market. Just as legitimate governments and businesses have embraced the advances of globalization, so too have illicit traffickers harnessed the benefits of globalization to press forward their illicit activities. In the end, there seems to be no shortage of people willing to subject themselves to mortal danger or incarceration for the sake of the money drug trafficking can offer. There also seems to be no shortage of people willing to supply drugs. Finally, there seems to be no shortage of routes or efforts traffickers will take to get their drugs into the United States.

We see feats of innovation month after month. For example, there are people acting as drug "mules" on commercial airplanes, ingesting up to 90 sealed pellets of cocaine or heroin. A typical "mule" can carry about 1.5 kilograms, enough to bring in over $150,000 in retail sales. In addition, there has been an increase in the large-scale employment of semi-submersible watercraft, built to avoid detection from air and sea. A typical semi-submersible can carry between 1 and 10 metric tons of drugs or other illicit cargo. We will go into greater detail on this specific conveyance method later. Moreover, there are creative ways to hide drugs which are being transported. Just a few examples include:

- hidden within toys
- deeply buried in iron ore loads
- stitched into live puppies and exotic animals
- encapsulated in the buttons of clothing
- mixed with coffee
- sealed in fruit juices and purees
- hidden in cargo holds of frozen or rotten fish
- dissolved in diesel fuel
- transformed into odorless plastic sheets, undetectable through chemical testing
- hidden inside the shafts of golf clubs.

It is a boundless problem set. We must respond with innovation. This is classic 21st-century activity—brain-on-brain combat competition. We need to embrace innovation in the way we think, organize, plan, and operate. We need to welcome innovation in the way we adapt new technology to ever-changing challenges. In addition, we need to demand innovation in the way we communicate, including how we describe and frame our challenges—both with our partners and with the public in general.

Clearly, in a resource-constrained world, in an era in which the budget is tight and resource stewardship is constantly a matter of close scrutiny, we do not have the luxury to haphazardly throw away resources based on half-concocted notions; nevertheless, we must find ways to embrace change when it makes sense, as well as have the courage to experiment. As John Paul Jones once remarked, "He who will not risk, cannot win." Like our opponents, we must constantly try new things. Now, more than ever, creative solutions are paramount.

To be more effective—and, in turn, more efficient—we have to use innovative, nontraditional approaches to help forge a cooperative security in the region. This occurs largely by working with our regional partners abroad and our interagency community partners at home. We must strive to take advantage of every available opportunity to build cooperative partnerships within our area of focus. We have a duty to be agile, aggressive, and resourceful in our efforts to thwart this continuously morphing challenge and threat.

Flexible, scalable, and persistent maritime engagement capabilities are a welcomed and essential part of how the United States approaches its neighbors in the region and around the globe, and how it views itself as a contributor to—not the sole provider of—security and access to the maritime commons. Even with all the assets our nation might be able to muster, ensuring freedom of navigation and access in the waterways of our shared home requires more capacity than we individually have the ability to deliver. Designing a regional network of maritime nations voluntarily committed to building and maintaining cooperative security and responding to threats against mutual interests is the genesis of Southern Command's Partnership for the Americas. The natural outcome would be a combination of our own fleet working on an equal basis with partners and friends throughout this region, charting a course together toward a stable and prosperous future.

One manner in which we have begun to provide the basic building blocks of the partnership is through years of multilateral fleet and field exercises. For instance, UNITAS—a South American naval exercise with 16 partners, originating in 1959—has been instrumental in establishing enduring working relationships among U.S. and Latin American naval, coast guard, and marine forces. The friendship, professionalism, and understanding promoted among participants provide fertile ground to promote interoperability, develop a common framework for information exchange, and establish the command and control protocols we will need to achieve what might be called a Global Maritime Coalition.

In May 2009, we celebrated UNITAS Gold, the 50th Anniversary of this hemispheric maritime training exercise. This was the first event held in the waters off the northeast coast of Florida and the U.S. Fourth Fleet served as host, welcoming a record 12 nations, including more than 25 ships, 70 aircraft, and 7,000 sea-going professionals—an all-time record for participation. For nearly five decades, the participating nations have come together to exchange ideas, to understand each other, and to build mutual trust through a commitment to partnership and freedom. Sailors and marines—*mariners*—from Argentina, Brazil, Canada, Chile, Colombia, the Dominican Republic, Ecuador, Germany, Mexico, Peru, the United States, and Uruguay came together to, as the Commander of the Fourth Fleet, Rear Admiral Joe Kernan, put it, "renew the bonds of the sea in a spirit of cooperation and friendship."[6] The focus areas of the training and exercises were key topics for the regional and international maritime security participants, including:

disaster relief, peacekeeping, medical activities, humanitarian support, mutual professional training, and counternarcotics cooperation. By openly sharing information at sea through exercises such as UNITAS, and by cooperating at the individual level, we forge stronger relationships and build our collective capacity based on the foundations of transparency, trust, friendship, and cooperation.

Additionally, U.S. Southern Command was fortunate enough to be chosen as the test bed for a concept identified as a critical enabler for this coalition, the high-speed vessel (HSV) *Swift*. The *Swift* embarked on its first 4-month deployment in our region in the fall of 2007 for training and exchanges with our partner nations, and completed its 5-month deployment in the spring of 2009. These deployments, during which the *Swift* visited 10 different countries and made 29 port calls, provided valuable lessons-learned to help the U.S. Navy institutionalize the Global Fleet Station program; this program will result in flexible forward presence options to conduct theater security cooperation activities. These deployments were also part of Southern Command's Southern Partnership Program, an annual deployment of various specialty platforms whose primary goal is information sharing via training and exercises with navies, coast guards, and civilian services throughout the region. Although the *Swift* is not a combatant in the traditional sense, its capacity, shallow draft, and incredible speed give this ship unlimited potential.

Originally designed as a high-speed car ferry, the *Swift* is a 321-foot catamaran that can perform reconnaissance, countermine warfare, maritime interdiction, transport, and humanitarian assistance. It travels at well over 40 knots and has a maximum draft of only 11 feet when fully loaded with over 600 tons of cargo. The *Swift* is relatively inexpensive by modern standards—less than $60 million per copy for a fully militarized version— but it is optimized for exactly the kinds of missions we do in this region: training, disaster relief, emergency command and control, exercises, medical treatment, humanitarian assistance, and increasingly, counternarcotics. For example, with *Swift*'s speed and endurance, it can easily cover a lot of area in a short amount of time; even the fastest drug-running boats cannot outpace it for very long. Further, because of its unique flexibility and because it is so new, the complete mission set for the *Swift* is still evolving and expanding. Only through continued experimentation and deployment will we really be able to appreciate the incredible potential of this type of ship for use in maritime awareness and drug interdiction.

Another promising development in our arsenal against the flow of illicit narcotics and other cargo in this region is Project *Stiletto*. The *Stiletto* vessel can improve our counterdrug operations by offering

U.S. Southern Command (Jose Ruiz)

Experimental vessel *Stiletto*, manned by a crew of Army and Navy mariners and U.S. Coast Guard Law Enforcement Officers, trains for counter–illicit trafficking deployment to the Caribbean. An example of innovative design and construction, the *Stiletto* is lightweight, able to operate in shallow waters, easy to maintain, and fast (up to 50 knots in calm seas).

affordable cutting edge technology and mission flexibility with the additional advantage of being manned by a combined joint, inter-agency, and partner-nation crew. The current composition includes an Army mariner crew, a U.S. Coast Guard law enforcement detachment, a Navy technical representative, partner nation riders, and other inter-agency community representatives. Capable of 40- to 50-knot speed, the *Stiletto* can outrun most of the vessels typically used to support illicit trafficking in the Southern Command area of focus. Its shallow 2.5-foot draft allows the ship access to near-shore and riverine type areas often used by illicit traffickers as a sanctuary. Finally, the *Stiletto* uses a "plug and play" architecture and an electronic keel suited toward rapid installation and evaluation of new concepts and technologies used to stop illicit trafficking. Perhaps most impressive on the list of the *Stiletto*'s features is the price tag—it is built for approximately $6 million and can be fully outfitted for an additional $4 million.

But the *Swift* and *Stiletto* are just two vessels, part of a finite number of resources available to cover a vast amount of sea space. Even leveraging the numbers and capacity of our partners in the region, we cannot be everywhere at once. Each day, traffickers use more sophisticated communication, computer, and encryption technology to conceal their operations. Moving resources at every sniff of a threat is not feasible; we need fast, flexible, and properly vetted information that then becomes actionable intelligence and helps us pinpoint the locations where our forces and resources can do the most good—and with sufficient time to get them there. To coin a phrase, we seek"precision-guided intelligence."

Data we use to gain intelligence about drug trafficking can come from many different sources, including radar, infrared, and visual reconnaissance assets, as well as human intelligence and databases compiled by law enforcement and customs services. In essence, we need more relevant fusion technologies that allow all-source synthesis, distributed dissemination, collaborative planning, and multiple-node sensor resource management. Combine all-source data fusion with inexpensive, reliable sensors, and you have the basis for true "technological innovation" in counterdrug efforts. Here, we are looking to industry for smart solutions.

At U.S. Southern Command, we established a small innovation cell on the staff to research, explore, and test emerging technologies available commercially or through Federal research centers. In particular, the innovation cell works closely with the Defense Advanced Research Projects Agency (DARPA) because of its specific role in managing and directing selected basic and applied research and development projects for the Defense Department. Through this unique partnership, they pursue exploration and technology where risk and payoff are both very high, and where success may provide dramatic advances for the counterdrug mission. Examples include:

- unmanned aerial craft, especially those with the legs to have good transit and loiter capability
- remote laser infrared detection and ranging for foliage penetration
- high-speed, unmanned surface vessels for detection and identification to support maritime domain awareness
- commercial satellite sensors with the ability to detect "go-fast" boats
- next generation "over the horizon" (OTH) radars
- novel applications of existing technology.

This sample of initiatives represents a continuing effort to leverage innovative business solutions and technology to address the challenges posed by narcotics and illicit trafficking. This effort will require a long-term commitment of resources and collective will, but the security and sovereignty of both the United States and our partner nations demand it. But science is not enough—we need to advance and innovate philosophically, as well. We need to transform our way of thinking and operating from a "need to know" mindset to one of "need to share." In so doing, we will enable and start exercising our "push" mentality and muscles, in addition to our already well-developed "pull" ones. Meaningful partnerships are based on commitment according to fundamental notions of reciprocity, understanding, and cooperation. The security cooperation partnerships we seek to build require connectivity, interoperability, and a baseline for communicating mutual understanding. The key is to work toward significantly broader mechanisms of mutual trust with our partner nations. To do so, we need to be able to shed the veil of secrecy, on demand, and to share technology with our partners.

Today, no single arm of the U.S. Government has the ability or authority to coordinate the multiple entities required to execute an effective international antidrug campaign. But with imagination, one can envision an operational fusion of the best capabilities provided by joint, combined, interagency community, international, and public-private organizations in a way that coordinates efforts to tackle drugs and trafficking at every stage from source point to the streets. With such a capability at hand, real pressure could be brought to bear on the supply side. I have already described in great detail the ways in which JIATF–South sets the standard in this regard. However, we can and must continue to push the envelope further, finding new ways to draw from and bring together the immense talents and strengths of all the varied players in this mission area. Internally, at Southern Command, we conducted a headquarters staff reorganization in order to accomplish this vision, which involved restructuring the large staff to optimize our interagency community approach. The results include many new liaisons and personnel exchanges, as well as building directorates with interagency partner linkages.

Externally, an example of this approach is our partnering with the DEA to leverage the technology, infrastructure, and legal domains required for real-time leads to support drug trafficking interdiction and arrests. Our law enforcement agencies, including DEA, rely on sophisticated tools to stop major drug trafficking organizations. DEA has also developed advanced methods to compile investigative information, which ensures that all leads are properly followed and coordinated through their Special Operations Division (SOD). This mechanism allows all DEA field divisions and foreign offices to capitalize on investigative information from various sources on the spot, as cases are developed. Numerous major Federal law enforcement cases have already been developed with the assistance of the SOD, which is increasingly a central player in cocaine, methamphetamine, and heroin investigations. Through an innovative partnership with DEA—and with other interagency partners—we hope to reap similar benefit in the drug-interdiction realm.

The essence of interdicting drugs and other illicit cargo is communicating fused intelligence where and when it is needed. The time is right to expand our technology base for building partnerships—to build upon a long history of friendship and cooperation—especially in a region where our position is largely won by words and trust, not bullets or missiles. At Southern Command, we started this process by providing a common communication system called Combined Enterprise Regional Information Exchange System (CENTRIXS) to many of our partner nations. Each CENTRIXS node is part of a secure computer network that enhances operational situational awareness for everyone who is part of the link. It is connected with another innovative counternarcotic communication system known as Counter-narcotic Information Exchange System (CNIES).

Southern Command also trains, equips, and helps to sustain partner nation forces through a variety of Engagement and Integration (E&I) programs. One example is Panamax, a month-long, 20-nation, multiphase exercise. In 2008, participants included 31 ships and over 7,000 personnel, receiving training during the exercise to expand our partner nations' knowledge, capabilities, and confidence to conduct interdiction activities. Additionally, the State Department–led Merida Initiative assists Mexico and Central America by improving maritime and air capabilities to better counter illicit trafficking. Congress has been an integral member in these efforts, authorizing NDAA Section 1206 funds to provide our partner nations the tools to effectively conduct counterterrorism operations within their respective borders and counter the threat to the U.S. homeland created by illicit activities and the trafficking routes that are readily available for exploitation.

Air and maritime sovereignty programs are extremely important for the improvement of our collective ability to ensure that exploitable space is minimized while encouraging the flow of this traffic. An example of the application of such funds is the program Enduring Friendship, a multiyear maritime security assistance program that strengthens our Caribbean partners' maritime domain awareness and operational capabilities to anticipate and respond to threats. This program provides computers, interceptor boats, and the means to communicate with each other for mutual maritime security, thereby enhancing control over illicit trafficking lanes. It also enables information-sharing about possible threats affecting the region and our partners' ability to patrol their own sovereign waters.

Finally, Southern Command seeks not only to build partner capacity, but also the *relationships* with our partners in this region. Using the exercises and deployments previously mentioned as primary vehicles, we seek to develop these relationships in a way that encourages regional, multilateral cooperation among neighboring countries to address transnational challenges and confront serious transnational threats. This is a vital element of our strategic approach to counter illicit drugs and trafficking, and we are continually exploring innovative communication strategies to ensure this message reaches the residents and resonates in the halls of our shared home.

I have presented a few examples of innovation in the U.S. Southern Command area of focus: operational innovation like the *Swift* and *Stiletto*; technological innovation in terms of precision-guided intelligence, and federally-funded and commercial off-the-shelf solutions; organizational innovation to create change that better incorporates interagency, international, and private partnerships in the struggle against drugs and illicit trafficking; and finally, coalition innovation brought about through sharing information with our reliable partners in the region. With these types of inventive, forward-leaning, and adaptive approaches and ways of thinking, our efforts against drug suppliers and runners will no doubt improve; but innovation is never a one-way street—the enemy *does* get a vote and *does* have a say in the final outcome. With every positive step forward, it is only a matter of time before the very resourced, very intelligent drug traffickers respond with innovations of their own. Such a diminished effectiveness of each innovative leap over time is the exact reason why, at Southern Command, we must constantly strive for ways to do our job better.

A New Vehicle in Traffic

So often, we think of the Western Hemisphere as a place of relative peace, a part of the world without extreme threats approaching our shores directly—all true. However, as we have seen, trafficking and the narcotics trade in particular benefit immensely from determined, creative, and innovative criminals driven by profit through distributing poisons and their accompanying misery and death on the streets of our cities and neighborhoods. The criminals' hallmark is creativity and they exhibit physical and mental agility as they adjust methods of transportation, communication, and trade routes in response to (often in advance of) pressure from law enforcement. Maritime traffickers have a knack for discovering and exploiting vulnerabilities in counterdrug operations. Their use of the sea and rivers is not novel, but their methods are.

Despite efforts and cooperation that led to international and inter-agency partners stopping approximately 475 metric tons of cocaine at sea between 2007 and 2008, traffickers still managed to deliver an estimated *four times* that amount to global markets during that same timeframe. In 2007, for example, according to the Consolidated Counterdrug Database, more than 1,400 metric tons of cocaine departed South America for desti-nations worldwide, and at least 1,100 metric tons got through unscathed. This $240 billion-a-year business causes thousands of deaths in the United States, creates significant economic distortions, and threatens fragile democracies in the region to the south of us. Most of this business travels at least a major part of its long journey by sea. In fact, approximately 80 percent of the cocaine that departs South America travels by sea in the Eastern Pacific and Western Caribbean.[7]

Over the years, traffickers have created intricate methods involving multiple at-sea transfers between commercial fishing vessels, complex logistics chains along circuitous routes, hiding large shipments of drugs in commercial maritime cargo and fishing vessels, and extensive use of decoy vessels to confuse interdiction forces. When law enforcement placed a squeeze on those modes, via improved vessel registration and tracking systems, traffickers simply shifted to hundreds of "go-fast" boats to support movement of their valuable cargo—often successfully intermingling with local traffic during peak recreational boating times.

While it has been a highly effective tactic, cooperative strategies are in place to defeat go-fast trafficking, forcing traffickers to seek new forms of smuggling. As a result, unfortunately, this beautiful and diverse home we share together is now the world's vanguard in producing a new and dan-gerous threat technology: self-propelled semi-submersible (SPSS) vessels that can carry drugs—in addition to other illegal and deadly cargo such as terrorists or weapons of mass destruction—almost unobserved to our shores. These new vehicles' ability to deny detection, their capacity to carry tons of numerous types of illicit cargo thousands of miles, and their prox-imity to the United States combine to pose an ever-increasing grave threat to our national and regional security.

These stealthy, pod-like vessels first appeared in the mid–1990s. Early versions were little more than crude modifications of existing go-fast or Boston Whaler hulls. Later, as traffickers evolved, learning from what worked best, they began to build semi-submersibles designed from the keel up for optimal stealth. Current variants depart their expeditionary shipyards in the

Self-propelled, semi-submersible (SPSS) vessels show the growing sophistication and innovation of drug traffickers in adapting to U.S. and regional counterdrug capabilities. Designed to smuggle large quantities of cocaine over long distances, SPSS vessels have a low profile, are hard to see from a distance, leave little wake, and produce a small radar signature.

dense jungles and estuaries of the Andes region of Latin America as low profile, relatively small (60–80 feet), semi-submerged "submarines" that skim just below the surface. They are carefully ballasted and well camouflaged, and they ride so low in the water that they are nearly impossible to detect visually or by radar at any range greater than 2,000 yards. Loaded to a capacity of up to 15 metric tons of drugs (thus far), they plod steadily and generally unobserved at less than 10 knots toward designated drop-off points, depositing their payloads of misery and death for further transit to global consumer markets.

These vessels possess a range of approximately 1,500 miles and come equipped with GPS, allowing them to navigate independently without need for external communication. In short, the SPSS vessel offers drug producers and traffickers a sizeable advantage and innovative leap ahead from the previous conveyance methods of fishing vessels and go-fasts, while also adding a new dimension to the illicit narcotics struggle. The SPSS is harder to detect, has a longer range, carries larger and more profitable payloads, and launches and navigates in secrecy, depriving authorities of the actionable intelligence so necessary in aiding interdiction efforts.

As previously mentioned, JIATF–South supported record-setting cocaine seizures from 2000 through 2006. Then in 2007, maritime interdictions fell by 37 percent. Analysts explain the drop as a result of three significant narcotrafficking changes: (1) a shift away from more vulnerable, bulk shipments toward smaller, more distributed loads; (2) increased use of the littorals crossing multiple territorial boundaries—a technique that stretches the capabilities of coordination and interdiction response; and (3) a dramatic rise in the use of SPSS vessels to transport drugs.[8]

According to the Consolidated Counterdrug Database, SPSS vessels accounted for just over 1 percent of all maritime cocaine flow departing South America in 2006.[9] One year later, the SPSS share jumped to 16 percent. Between 2000 and 2007, drug traffickers launched only 23 total SPSS vessels. In the first 6 months of FY 2008, more than 45 SPSS vessels departed Colombia—with over 80 by the end of the year. So far, in total, less than 10 percent of known or suspected SPSS underway transits have been intercepted. Until authorities can disrupt significantly more of these deployments, the SPSS will remain a profitable and desirable link in the narcotics logistics chain and a serious threat.[10]

Experts estimate that SPSS vessels now account for over 30 percent of all cocaine traffic that occurs on the waterways of the Americas from South America to consumer markets; this percentage is likely to increase as the high return on a relatively low investment continues to grow. Recent captures demonstrate that many of the essential elements of successful detection, tracking, and eventual interdiction already exist to counter this latest wave of innovation. Indeed, every bit of success thus far can be attributed to the absolute cohesiveness and unity of effort of all players involved—joint, combined, interagency, and international. In addition, the U.S. Congress has been a crucial member in this endeavor as it signed into law the Drug Trafficking Vessel Interdiction Act of 2008, criminalizing the use of unregistered, unflagged submersible or semi-submersible vessels in international waters. Nevertheless, severe intelligence, detection, and interdiction gaps remain. Without doubt, the SPSS challenge demands a multifaceted systemic approach that includes increased international cooperation and interagency coordination, persistent presence and engagement in the transit and source zones, active and targeted information-gathering and -sharing, and effective legislation to ease the burden of prosecution. However, the transit side of the equation is of concern *not simply for the cocaine problem*. There is more to fear: the obvious nexus between drugs, crime, and terrorism.

Gangs and smugglers use their enormous profits to secure and preserve positions of power by whatever means necessary, resulting in mass homicides, corruption, and subversion of rule of law. We also know that drug traffickers use illegal drug money to assist rogue states and international terrorist organizations that are determined to build and use weapons of mass destruction, such as the FARC narcoterrorists in Colombia. In this sense, growing global demand for drugs such as cocaine and heroin directly links the world drug trade to international terrorism.

Semi-submersible, low-profile vessels transport drugs for profit, and they do so effectively. It does not take visiting the Oracle at Delphi to foresee what danger awaits us if drug traffickers choose to link trafficking routes and methods with another, perhaps even more profitable, payload. In simple terms, if drug cartels can ship up to 15 metric tons of cocaine in a semi-submersible, they can potentially ship or "rent space" to a terrorist organization for a weapon of mass destruction or a high-profile terrorist.

Illicit trafficking in weapons poses a similarly significant threat to national security. This trafficking includes illegal sales to insurgent groups and criminal organizations, illegal diversion of legitimate sales or transfers, and black market sales, all of which contravene national or international laws. The re-circulation of small arms and light weapons from one conflict to another, and illegal domestic manufacturing of these items, are also considered elements of illicit weapons trafficking. Another increasingly dangerous threat posed by illicit weapons trafficking involves the proliferation of weapons of mass destruction (WMD), their component materials and/or delivery systems, and the potential to transport them using existing trafficking routes.

Illicit trafficking in human beings is also a multidimensional threat. The impact of human trafficking goes beyond individual victims, as it undermines the health, safety, and security of all the nations it touches by fueling the growth of organized crime. By issuing Executive Order 13257 in February of 2002, the U.S. Government characterized trafficking in persons as a contemporary manifestation of slavery and passed the Trafficking Victims Protection Act. Several of the central aims of U.S. foreign policy—promoting democracy, respecting human rights, and just governance—depend on successfully addressing this challenge.

Finally, terrorism and illicit trafficking share many ties. Traffickers benefit from terrorists' military skills, weapons supply, and access to clandestine organizations. Terrorists gain a source of revenue and expertise in illicit transfer and laundering of money for their operations. Like traffickers and other organized crime groups, terrorists exploit countries and jurisdictions where state governance is weak. The September 11 attacks demonstrated the great danger that can emerge from territories where both terrorists and traffickers operate with impunity.

Given the emergence of this new threat technology and ability to transport multiple types of deadly cargo, we need to develop more effective counters. These will include long-dwell sensors capable of "seeing" such craft, better intelligence that provides cueing, maritime domain awareness that links systems together, more seamless interagency and international cooperation, and perhaps some new technologies that are on the fringes and outer limits of our visual acuity at this moment, but still must be explored.

Sometimes we cannot foresee the immediate payoff of investment in technological innovation and dedicated detection and interdiction assets. Criminals are never going to wait for law enforcement to catch up. They are always extending the boundaries of imagination; likewise, we must strive to push forward technology and invest in systems designed specifically to counter the semi-submersible. We need to be able to rapidly detect and interdict this new type of threat, both for its current effects via the drug trade, and—more troublingly—for its potential as a weapon in the hands of terrorists.

> A fundamental principle of American society is that the law must provide equal protection to all. Yet drug abuse and trafficking are having a disproportionate effect on our poor, our minorities, and our cities. . . . We must reduce the harm inflicted on those sectors of our society. There can be no safe havens for drug traffickers and no tolerance for those who would employ children. We cannot tolerate open air drug markets in our cities, markets fueled by suburban money and which exacerbate the drug crisis.
>
> —General Barry R. McCaffrey
> Director Designee
> Office of National Drug Control Policy[11]

A Look to the Future

As globalization deepens and threats to this intertwined regional and global system emerge and evolve, security organizations—from the United States as well as from our neighbors on *all* points of the compass—must continue fostering and building relationships that enhance our collective ability to face and thwart transnational challenges manifesting themselves ashore, at sea, in the air, and even in cyberspace.

Recognizing that no one nation can assure total security in a region as large and diverse as the Americas, in striving to develop and foster cooperative security, we place heavy emphasis on the word "cooperative." Working together and leveraging each other's strengths is a must. Our strategic approach in this regard rightly acknowledges that the vital interests of the United States—the safety of our citizens and that of our neighbors, our economic well-being, our territorial integrity and sovereignty, our regional security, and our assured access to the global commons and markets—are inextricably linked to the interests of other nations in the region and beyond.

The nexus between monetarily motivated and ideologically driven criminal and terrorist activity in the region is an area of increasing concern. The persistent presence of maritime partners throughout the region is vital to disrupting this potentially dreadful union. We must remain vigilant and work together throughout the Americas to stop transnational security threats of extreme consequence before they materialize.

To that end, U.S. Southern Command has worked to build strategically important cooperative security relationships and promote U.S. military-to-military partnerships throughout the region for source-country drug control programs and interdiction of traffickers. The primary aim of these efforts has been to limit the availability of illicit drugs like cocaine and marijuana—in order to drive up prices and discourage use—as well as seriously impede and disrupt their flow from source to market. This is vitally important work. Through innovative approaches such as the Global Fleet Station, Southern Partnership Station, Operation *Continuing Promise*, Partnership of the Americas, and the humanitarian deployments of USNS *Comfort*, USS *Boxer*, and USS *Kearsarge*, as well as multinational training and exercises like UNITAS and Panamax, we show our level of commitment and speak with a voice of goodwill, competence, and professionalism. We speak with a voice of *amistad y cooperación*—friendship and cooperation.

Clearly, the drug threat to the United States is of significant size and importance. It needs to be treated as such through a variety of solutions. Much of the work to be done is on the demand side, and there is a wide variety of policy ideas in place to address demand. On the supply side, there is much that can be done with producing nations to discourage growth and processing. Our focus in the military on detection and monitoring is likewise part of the solution set. We should devote more resources to this problem in every dimension: demand, supply, *and* interdiction.

U.S. Southern Command will build on the efforts and activities mentioned above by pursuing a strategy of trans-American cooperative security. The "lines of operation" of this strategy are: 1) supporting lead Federal agencies' counter–illicit narcotics and trafficking efforts; 2) synchronizing Southern Command efforts internally with its component commands and military groups, and externally with interagency and international partners, as well as members from the private sector; 3) strengthening partner nation capacity through training and materiel assistance; and 4) encouraging regional cooperative approaches to transnational security challenges. The tools we will use to execute this strategy will include innovative concepts and technological capabilities, mutually beneficial partnerships, prioritized resource expenditures that maximize return on investment, and effective strategic communications that match the right words with the right actions.

Key internal and external audiences need to be more fully engaged through overlapping, mutually supportive methods and synchronized activities to ensure intended audiences understand and support our counter–illicit trafficking approach and operations. Additionally, communication efforts need to highlight the continued impact of illicit trafficking on hemispheric security and stability in all available and appropriate venues. Frankness and transparency need to be cornerstones of our approach if we as a nation are to succeed in expanding the long history of friendship and cooperation we share with partner nations. In a region where both words and deeds matter greatly in terms of relationship-building and -strengthening, we must not fail in this regard.

U.S. Southern Command is working toward a safe and secure region that is free from the destabilizing and debilitating effects of illicit trafficking in all forms and all types of cargo. The illicit trafficking trade has escalated into a security challenge that requires the strongest commitment to regional cooperation. We live in a world where the tactics, techniques, and procedures of the producers and smugglers represent a real, and dangerous, toolkit for those who seek to do us harm.

By building upon our longstanding relationships in the region and by fully integrating the efforts across the services with those of our interagency, international, and public-private partners, we've mitigated human suffering, enhanced security cooperation, and made the region safer for those seeking to preserve the peace while simultaneously making it more challenging for those seeking to fracture it. But so much more needs to be done.

U.S. Southern Command's counter–illicit trafficking strategy represents a dialogue with a common goal of ensuring security, enhancing stability, and protecting sovereignty throughout our shared home, the Americas. The envisioned endstate is clear: illicit trafficking is sufficiently reduced to a point where it can be effectively controlled by domestic law enforcement agencies and no longer poses a security threat to the United States and the region. In so doing, we need to remember that our first, last, and constant emphasis should be on innovation: we innovate in what we do and how we spread the word; we need to avoid failures of the imagination and seek to leverage technology early and often, literally and figuratively; and we need to remember that human interests are at the heart of everything we do, and therefore continue to seek new and adaptive relationships based on common beliefs and trust.

With a land and air border that extends over 7,500 miles, a maritime exclusive economic zone encompassing 3.4 million square miles, greater than 500 million people admitted into the United States every year, more than 11 million trucks and 2 million rail cars crossing our borders, and 7,500 foreign-flag ships making 51,000 calls in U.S. ports every year, it is incredibly easy to be overwhelmed by the vast magnitude and scope of the drug challenge. That is, we can be overwhelmed only if we think sequentially and in isolation. But together, we can think, act, and work in parallel to solve the dilemma: by building partnerships that keep our borders open to legitimate trade and travel and reducing the threat of drugs throughout our society and our shared home in the Americas.

Notes

[1] It is estimated that users expend 180–400 milligrams per dose. See Peter Cohen, "Cocaine use in Amsterdam in non-deviant subcultures," in *Drugs as a social construct* (Amsterdam: Dissertation at Universiteit van Amsterdam, 1990), 82–100. According to the *Digest of Education Statistics*, 17.6 million students were enrolled in grades 9–12 in the United States in 2008.

[2] A total of 2,997 deaths resulted from: 9/11 attacks—2,974; 1993 World Trade Center Bombing—6; and the USS *Cole* bombing—17 Sailors.

[3] In 2003, a total of 2,448,288 deaths occurred in the United States. Of them, 28,723 persons died of drug-induced causes, and 19,543 were traced to causes related to drug abuse. Similar percentages occurred in 2004 and 2005. Source: *National Vital Statistics Reports* 54, no. 13 (April 19, 2006).

[4] Source: National Drug Intelligence Center, *National Drug Threat Assessment 2007*. Indicators of domestic cocaine demand show that the demand for cocaine in the United States is relatively stable. According to National Survey on Drug Use and Health (NSDUH) data, past year cocaine use (in any form) by individuals 12 and older has not increased or decreased significantly since 2002 (the last time the estimate of 350 metric tons was given). Also, according to the July 2006 interagency assessment of cocaine movement, between 517 and 732 metric tons of cocaine depart South America for the United States annually, feeding addiction, fueling crime, and damaging the economic and social health of the United States. See *National Drug Control Strategy* (The White House, February 2007).

[5] Office of National Drug Control Policy, *National Drug Control Strategy FY2008 Budget Summary*, February 2007. Total 2007 estimate: $13.128 billion.

[6] Rear Admiral Joe Kernan, Commander, U.S. Fourth Fleet, "Opening Remarks, UNITAS Gold," May 2009.

[7] For cocaine flow trends updated for 2007, see Consolidated Counterdrug Database (CCDB), February 15, 2008.

[8] Wade F. Wilkenson, "A New Underwater Threat," *Proceedings of the U.S. Naval Institute* (October 2008), 35.

[9] The Consolidated Counterdrug Database (CCDB) is a comprehensive data collection effort that captures the details surrounding every drug-related event submitted by U.S. and foreign counterdrug agencies. International and interagency partners gather quarterly to review all reported interdiction cases and vet the information for input into the database. They also revise, de-conflict, and validate data on overall counterdrug performance, trafficking trends, and regional cocaine flow. The information processed provides timely feedback for each participating agency to modify interdiction strategies and manage resources.

[10] Wilkenson, 35.

[11] General Barry R. McCaffrey, *Opening Statement*, Confirmation Hearing on the Nomination to be Director of the Office of National Drug Control Policy, Washington DC, February 27, 1996.

Chapter 5

People First, Human Rights Always

The United States must defend liberty and justice because these principles are right and true for all people everywhere. These nonnegotiable demands of human dignity are protected most securely in democracies. The United States government will work to advance human dignity in word and deed, speaking out for freedom and against violations of human rights and allocating resources to advance these ideals.

—National Security Strategy of the United States of America (2006)

Little more than a decade after a pattern of torture, killings, and "disappearances" focused worldwide attention on human rights violations committed by military regimes in Latin America and the Caribbean, there has been general improvement in institutional respect for human rights among the military and security forces of the region. With the return to democracy across the hemisphere has come a growing commitment to international humanitarian and human rights law, as well as a growing recognition that the safeguarding of human rights is not only a moral and legal imperative but an essential component of national security. Every citizen of the Americas has a moral obligation to uphold the principles of life, liberty, and human dignity; those of us privileged to wear a uniform have a legal obligation to do so as well.

U.S. Southern Command has played a role in nurturing this change in attitudes. Working with regional military and security forces in collaborative regional initiatives, we have endeavored to instill a culture of respect for human rights as a fundamental strategic objective. As testimony to our commitment to this process, the command has forged active partnerships with the international human rights community, bringing in the expertise and direct participation of experienced international and nongovernmental human rights organizations—including those who are often critical of the role played by the United States military in the region. What had once been an all-too-frequently adversarial relationship has evolved into positive linkages of cooperation guiding us toward two primary common goals: 1) ensuring that past abuses are not repeated; and 2), understanding that human rights are an integral component of military training and military culture throughout the region.

All of the democratic governments in the region have enunciated policies of respect for human rights and initiated programs to promote and strengthen support for human rights within their civil and military institutions. The very act of recognizing this ethical and international legal obligation is itself an important step toward healing the deep schisms caused by past abuses. Clearly, however, much remains to be done to fully transform the human rights vision of the region's democracies into reality. Inefficient, overburdened, and sometimes corrupt judicial systems continue allowing perpetrators of human rights abuses to escape punishment. Inhumane prison conditions, arbitrary arrest and detention, and instances of brutality—mainly by ill-trained and under-resourced police and internal security forces—remain problems throughout the region. Even so, the situation today stands in sharp contrast to the widespread and institutionalized abuses committed by the region's Cold War–era authoritarian governments.

From our headquarters in Miami, Southern Command professionals focus their efforts on realizing the command's vision of a community of nations enjoying lasting relationships based on trust, shared values, and common interests. These relationships are critical to delivering the cooperative solutions so necessary to address the varied and transnational security challenges facing the nations of the region today. Our motto "Partnership for the Americas" underscores the importance of working together as partners toward common goals.

Respect for human rights and the rule of law is unequivocally the cornerstone of these partnerships, and Southern Command plays a role in helping to foster that respect. In response to the widespread human rights abuses that rocked many of the nations of Latin America in the 1970s and 1980s, the leadership at Southern Command launched a human rights program that focused on ensuring correct behavior by U.S. military personnel and on encouraging the institutionalization of a culture of respect for human rights in partner nation military forces. In the two decades of its existence, this unique program has proven invaluable in strengthening support for human rights and helping to advance the Partnership for the Americas.

Human Rights: Concepts, Goals, and Role of the Military

As stated in the 1948 Universal Declaration of Human Rights, "All human beings are born free and equal in dignity and rights." As an evocation of fundamental principles, the term "human rights" is a powerful appeal to the loftiest aspirations of mankind; by the same token, it is purposely a general, perhaps even vague term. In practice, it is a notion that has often led to considerable confusion over what exactly constitutes a human right and what its basis is. Not surprisingly, different governments, institutions, and organizations have, at times, sought to define the term in unique ways that suit differing interests or agendas. Even among legal scholars, the concept of human rights is constantly evolving as it is debated and revised.

Yet over the last half century, a broad consensus *has* emerged among legal experts, human rights organizations, and governments on the scope and compass of the key principles of human rights to which all states must give deference. Many of these principles, as well as specific enumerated human rights, have been enshrined in international declarations, treaties, and laws. Among the basic human rights clearly recognized by international law today are: life, liberty, and personal security; freedom from slavery, torture, and arbitrary arrest; and, freedom of conscience, religion, expression, and movement.

Although deeply rooted in moral beliefs about the dignity of the individual found in almost every society, human rights in their modern legal conception are distinct in that they are specifically deemed to be rights that are *universal, inherent,* and *inalienable* possessions of all mankind—rights that no state may legitimately abridge. These rights are *universal* in that all human beings are entitled to them, regardless of race, religion, sex, nationality, or any other distinction. They are *inherent* in that they are a part of what it is to be human. Because they are inherent, they are also *inalienable,* thus meaning no one can take them away, and no one can give them up voluntarily.[1]

Human rights, accordingly, speak to how a state is obligated to treat its own people—regardless of the laws or customs of that state. Human rights are therefore distinct from civil rights, which are rights that citizens of a country enjoy because the constitution and laws of that country grant them. The government, and those who represent it, respect those claims because they have a duty to uphold the constitution and the law. The upholding of human rights, however, constitutes a higher duty that transcends even national constitutions and laws. Many human rights, such as the right to life and liberty, are also enshrined as civil rights. However, when a state includes human rights in its laws or constitution, it is not "granting" these rights but merely "recognizing" them. The distinction is important and goes to the very nature and essence of human rights. An authoritarian government may try to do away with civil rights by changing the constitution, or suspending it, or simply ignoring it. Other governments may fail to provide what is necessary for its citizens to enjoy their civil rights—things such as police protection and impartial justice. However, no government can abolish a human right, because, quite simply, it does not have the power to grant it in the first place. As stated in both the International Covenant on Civil and Political Rights and the International Covenant on Economic, Social, and Cultural Rights, human rights "derive from the inherent dignity of the human person." In addition to a person's safety and security, therefore, human rights include the social, political, and economic freedoms each person needs to realize his or her human potential.[2]

Because of this relationship between human rights and the state, in traditional human rights theory, only a state can violate a person's human rights. For example, an individual who takes the life of another person is a murderer, not a human rights violator; conversely, if a state orders or condones a murder by one of its agents (the police, the military, etc.), it has committed a human rights violation. In practice, however, this distinction is not rigidly applied, and human rights violations are commonly attributed to guerrilla and irregular forces, including terrorist organizations.[3]

Legal theory also acknowledges that human rights are not absolute; that is, the state may limit or suspend rights under certain conditions. For example, states do not allow children to vote—a recognized human right—until they are old enough to make a mature decision. Similarly, in a national emergency, states can limit people's freedom of movement to ensure public safety. However, as a general rule, such limitations must be as few and short-lived as possible, or they become abuses. Evidence of this premise can be found in Article 27 of the American Convention on Human Rights, which states that certain rights may be suspended in time of war, public danger, or other emergency, provided the suspension does not conflict with obligations under other international agreements, and is limited to the time and extent strictly required.[4] However, the article goes on to state that the foregoing provision does *not* authorize any suspension of the preceding articles of the

Convention, namely: Article 3 (Right to Juridical Personality), Article 4 (Right to Life), Article 5 (Right to Humane Treatment), Article 6 (Freedom from Slavery), Article 9 (Freedom from Ex Post Facto Laws), Article 12 (Freedom of Conscience and Religion), Article 17 (Rights of the Family), Article 18 (Right to a Name), Article 19 (Rights of the Child), Article 20 (Right to Nationality), and Article 23 (Right to Participate in Government). The article also recognizes the fundamental importance of the judicial guarantees essential for the protection of such rights.

Moreover, the relationship between the state and the individual that underlies human rights is reciprocal. All people have certain duties to a state that ensures their rights. They must obey its laws, for example, and pay required taxes to support it. They have to do their duty to the state because only the state can make sure they enjoy their rights. Article 29 of the Universal Declaration of Human Rights (UDHR) states this clearly: "Everyone has duties to the community in which alone the free and full development of his personality is possible."

Legal Underpinnings

The principle that certain fundamental rights of mankind are inherent and transcend the laws of any nation was definitively articulated in the United States of America's 1776 Declaration of Independence and in France's 1789 Declaration of the Rights of Man. Yet, it was not until the end of World War II that any international legal precedent or mechanism emerged to give effect to this ideal in practice. While traditional international law spoke to the relations between nations, it was virtually silent on what a nation did to its own people within its sovereign borders; each state decided the extent to which it would protect and respect the inherent human rights of its citizens, as well as which civil rights it would grant those under its power. There was no legal basis for any other state or international body to challenge these decisions.

In seeking to prosecute members of the Nazi government for the atrocities they committed against their own people, the victorious Allies were thus forced to bring a wholly novel charge of *crimes against humanity* at the Nuremberg Trials.[5] It was a precedent-setting step that helped establish the foundation for the modern system of international human rights law and treaties that have emerged in the 60 years since. As a result, the 1945 Charter of the United Nations became the first great international treaty to conceive of universal human rights as a practical matter rather than a vague ideal, calling on the UN to "promote universal respect for, and observance of, human rights and fundamental freedoms for all without distinction as to race, sex, language, or religion." In 1948, the United Nations set down these ideas in the Universal Declaration of Human Rights.[6] Other international agreements on human rights followed over the next half-century as the nations of the world committed themselves increasingly not only to respecting them, but also to making them part of the bedrock foundation upon which governments throughout the world were based.

Although lacking the force of law, the Universal Declaration of Human Rights is arguably the most important of the international measures on human rights because of its broad international support and because its 30 articles cover the minimum rights and immunities to which every human being is entitled. A number of subsequent binding treaties— in diplomatic terminology, such measures that carry the force of international law are also called *covenants, conventions,* or *agreements*—have given substantial credence to the principles of the Declaration. Of particular importance are the International Covenant on Civil and Political Rights and the International Covenant on Economic, Social, and Cultural Rights, both of which went into force in 1976.[7] Together with the Universal Declaration, these treaties are often referred to as the International Bill of Human Rights.

Besides international human rights law created by treaties, there is a growing body of what is termed *customary international law* that is based on precedents set by international tribunals and on widely accepted norms that states have declared and customarily followed.[8] Needless to say, determining precisely what precedents and practices have become legally binding and customary law is a matter of considerable debate and differing interpretation. Generally, however, no practice becomes part of customary international law unless it has become so customary that most, if not all, nations have consistently adhered to it. Currently, binding and customary international law unquestionably considers seven specific crimes violations of human rights. Those crimes are genocide; slavery and the slave trade; murder and "forced disappearance," in which a person is taken prisoner by the state and never seen again; torture or other cruel, inhuman, or degrading treatment or punishment; prolonged arbitrary detention; systematic racial discrimination; and a consistent pattern of gross violations of human rights.[9]

Categories of Human Rights

Legal scholars have divided all of the specific human rights that have been proposed, including those that are now generally accepted and those that are not, into three groups according to the era in which they first appeared. These three groups are conventionally called the three "generations" of human rights.[10]

The *first generation* consists of fundamental rights; these are generally assertions of what the state must not do. It includes civil and political rights such as the individual's right to life and liberty; freedom from slavery, genocide, and torture; and freedom of conscience and religion. Most of these freedoms were already generally accepted, at least in democratic countries, by World War II, and national governments have the authority to enforce them and punish violators.

The *second generation* of human rights covers social and economic rights. These are things a state must *do* for its people, such as seeing to it that they have at least the minimum diet and medical care needed to keep them healthy and access to education as well as adequate shelter. Most Western countries—the United States included—acknowledge second generation rights but do not consider them legally enforceable, regarding them rather as "aspirational" goals that states should progressively strive to attain.[11] Most other countries place economic rights on equal legal footing with civil and political rights—even if few have the means to in fact guarantee them.

The *third generation* of human rights is a mix of broader rights relating to the environment, culture, and development. In addition to the right to a clean environment, they include things such as the right to peace and the right to humanitarian aid. Few rights of that sort have yet appeared in international agreements or achieved very wide acceptance. However, some third generation rights are progressing toward possible espousal by the international community, such as the United Nations resolution on the Declaration on the Rights of Indigenous Peoples, adopted in September 2007, which is designed to protect the cultures and other group interests of indigenous peoples around the world.

Although the term "generations" suggests that human rights can be ranked hierarchically, most human rights advocates assert no right can be sacrificed to ensure another because all are equally important, and each one depends on the others. This remains an underlying tension between human rights theory and practice, because in practice human rights do follow a natural hierarchy: the right to an education, for example, means nothing without the right to life, whereas one can enjoy the right to life without access to education.

Human Rights versus International Humanitarian Law

The international law that governs the behavior of combatants in an armed conflict is called international humanitarian law. It is an ancient part of the law of armed conflict, popularly known as the Law of War, which evolved into its present form beginning in the late 19th century.[12] It is contained throughout a number of international legal instruments, including the Hague Convention of 1907, which governs weapons and combat operations, and the four Geneva Conventions of 1949 and their First and Second Protocols, which deal with how to treat the people those operations affect, including prisoners and noncombatants. International humanitarian law covers all types of conflict, internal as well as external.

International humanitarian law derives from many of the same principles as legally binding human rights and covers much of the same ground. Both are based on the concept of human dignity, and both set minimum standards for preserving and protecting that dignity. Precisely because it is intended to be humane, international humanitarian law requires specific treatment of people that mirrors in many respects the requirements imposed upon the state under human rights law. However, it differs from human rights law in one key respect: *it applies only to combatants involved in armed conflict.* It applies equally to all combatants, whether they fight for a state or as part of a guerrilla or irregular force. In contrast, human rights apply to states and all those who represent a state, not just to those who fight for it. Moreover, international humanitarian law applies only during armed conflict, whereas human rights apply at all times across the entire spectrum of human interaction ranging from peace to war.

Role of the Military

Speaking to senior Latin American military officers in 1994, then-USSOUTHCOM Commander, General Barry McCaffrey, stated, "For military leaders, human rights entail practical responsibilities rather than theoretical exercises."[13] The foremost of these practical responsibilities, General McCaffrey pointed out, is to support democratic government and the rule of law. This statement and view were in stark contrast to the false belief that resulted from the Cold War era in which democracy had to at times give way to authoritarian rule—most often military rule—in order to ward off the greater tyranny of communism that threatened the Free World. Instead of helping the cause of freedom, repression by authoritarian regimes spawned legitimate grievances that could be (and were) exploited by those willing to form radical subversive movements. Throughout history, however, humanist, liberal, and democratic governments have proven better at rallying the broad public support essential for stemming the tide of the threat of internal subversion and insurgency than has any form of despotism or authoritarianism.

Military and security forces throughout Latin America and the Caribbean now recognize that a state is strongest and most secure when its people can count on all government representatives to respect and defend their human rights. This is particularly true for members of the state who are trained to use violent means in extreme situations. Above all, military and security services must obey their country's elected civilian leadership—subordination to civilian government is essential for military effectiveness. When all military and security personnel are unquestionably accountable to the people—when they derive their authority and power through the consent of the governed—the risks of widespread abuses that would otherwise undermine the people's confidence in those charged to defend and protect them, are broadly mitigated. Strong, confident, and competent civilian control of the military helps to ensure those who bear the awesome responsibility of using force and might in the name of a state always wield them on behalf of, rather than against, those they are charged to protect.

In his 1994 speech, General McCaffrey also articulated many of the ways fostering respect for human rights can promote military objectives. For example, respect for human rights keeps a unit focused on its mission, as violations can distract the commander's attention from the goals the unit has been assigned. Additionally, it strengthens discipline since a willingness to violate orders with respect to human rights may often show up later in refusal to obey other kinds of orders. A publicized policy of such adherence can undermine enemy resistance because fear of death or torture if captured motivates an enemy to fight to the death; conversely, an enemy who is sure of receiving good treatment is more likely to surrender or defect. Finally, a fundamental belief in the primacy of human rights increases local public support for military operations—if the government forces are able to establish or maintain a good relationship with local residents, and if they, in turn, sympathize with government forces, the populace is more likely to volunteer intelligence on enemy movements. Ultimately, it helps turn military victory into a lasting peace as the cycle of recrimination and the ceaseless quest for vengeance that occur if a defeated enemy and its supporters have suffered abuses and outrages during the course of the fight, can be avoided altogether.[14]

It is important to note that some human rights activists have expressed concern that any discussion of the practical "return on investments" that comes from respecting human rights may tend to debase the moral underpinnings which are their true foundation. If respect for human rights is justified purely on the grounds of expediency, the argument goes, it becomes all too easy to rationalize ignoring those rights when it is equally expedient to do so.[15] However, in a region where military commanders have historically viewed human rights to be at odds with military effectiveness, pointing out the practical military advantages of a policy of respect for human rights and international humanitarian law has been an important step in changing attitudes.

To help further develop this still-nascent paradigm shift, we draw heavily from our own history and foundational beliefs. Promoting observance of human rights and international humanitarian law has long been a fundamental objective of U.S. foreign and national security policy. In fact, human rights and individual freedoms were the very seeds from which our nation was born and have always been supported and promoted by a strong bipartisan consensus in Congress and the executive branch. All military forces have a responsibility to respect human rights, but as representatives of the U.S. Government, the U.S. Armed Forces have an additional responsibility to promote respect for human rights by other nations. As heirs to a long tradition of subordination to civilian authority, the U.S. military can also serve as a model for forces in other countries seeking to overcome a legacy of abuse. Also, by making military-to-military engagement contingent upon the continued progress of improving the support of human rights, our military can positively influence long-standing and emerging partners.

Military-to-military cooperation is a core strategic function of U.S. Southern Command. By demonstrating commitment, military-to-military cooperation reassures our allies and partner nations of U.S. resolve to help protect our shared home, deter potential enemies, and contribute to internal and regional stability. It also improves the ability of other countries' forces to operate with those of the United States. Finally, it encourages positive reforms in many sectors.

U.S. Southern Command pursues many security cooperation activities in support of human rights reform in Latin America and the Caribbean. For example, we provide instruction in Spanish, host seminars and conferences as forums for dialogue, and provide ongoing security assistance and training in numerous exercises, operations, and outreach programs. These activities serve as excellent opportunities to encourage colleagues in other countries and to help them consolidate early initiatives into systematic programs. Southern Command's ultimate goal is to help make these achievements permanent by enabling regional militaries to institutionalize new attitudes and practices, creating an organizational culture in which observance of human rights can never be in doubt.

Southern Command's adoption of an explicit human rights policy in 1990, and its subsequent establishment of a dedicated Human Rights Division within the command in 1995, grew directly out of the turbulent history of the region—in particular, patterns of human rights abuses by the region's military and security forces that drew international attention and condemnation.[16] Events during the 1970s and 1980s in four countries—Guatemala, Chile, Argentina, and El Salvador—arguably had the greatest impact in raising international concerns about human rights abuses in Latin America and in catalyzing the new Southern Command policies and programs to help counter these abuses. These historic events thus form a critical backdrop to understanding Southern Command's current commitment to making human rights a core component of its military strategy for the entire region.

U.S. Response to Human Rights Violations

Promoting respect for fundamental human rights has been a principle of U.S. domestic and foreign policy since the Nation's founding. However, for most of the 20th century, the United States tolerated friendly dictators who could maintain stability and protect U.S. political, economic, and military interests, even if they resorted to repressive measures. This approach was rationalized by comparing it to the larger potential horrors, destructive results, and existential threat of the spread of communism. This was a tightrope to walk, and we eventually discovered such an approach devalued our fundamental ideals. In the words of Senator William Fulbright, "When we depart from these values, we do so at our peril. . . . If we are faithful to our own values, while following an intelligent, courageous, and consistent line of policy, we are likely to find a high measure of the support we seek abroad. But if we fail our own values and ideals, ultimately we shall have failed ourselves."[17] Inevitably, the breakdown in respect for human rights in Latin America and the Caribbean that accompanied the Cold War forced the United States to adopt a new approach.

Southern Command and Human Rights as the Strategic Core

On March 19, 1990, U.S. Southern Command's Commander-in-Chief, General Maxwell Thurman, issued a policy directive that explicitly defined the human rights responsibilities of all Defense Department personnel who served within Southern Command's area of focus. In unequivocal terms, the new directive stated, "one of our most important and universal foreign policy objectives is to promote the increased observance of internationally recognized human rights by all countries."[18] This memorandum established the requirement for all U.S. military personnel to immediately record and report through the chain of command any instance of suspected human rights violations. To ensure U.S. military personnel were aware of exactly what constituted a human rights violation, General Thurman also instituted mandatory human rights training for all personnel deploying within Southern Command's area of focus.

Established in mid-1990, the mandatory training included instruction in four key areas: the laws of war and international humanitarian law; U.S. Government human rights policies, objectives, and directives at the national and international level; the responsibilities of military personnel to support these policies; and procedures for reporting suspected human rights violations. This predeployment training was supplemented by a wallet-sized, quick-reference Human Rights Standing Orders Card that personnel were required to carry at all times. The card, with minor revisions, remains in use today. It reminds personnel of "the five R's of human rights" (Recognize, Refrain, React, Record, and Report) and lists Southern Command's standing orders concerning respect for human rights.

The command was acutely aware that failure to help improve respect for human rights in the region would ultimately jeopardize the success of its missions and undermine public and congressional support for essential military-to-military cooperation programs. Consequently, shortly after initiating the internal training program, Southern Command also made human rights instruction an element of all training it provided to partner nations' military and security forces.

Over the course of the next decade, subsequent commanders built upon the strong foundation forged by General Thurman. For example, General George Joulwan, who succeeded General Thurman in late 1990, significantly expanded the human rights initiative in two visible manners. First, he supplemented the training materials developed by the Staff Judge Advocate's office with a 10-minute video presentation in which he unambiguously laid out the responsibility of all command personnel to recognize and report human rights violations. In the video, General Joulwan articulated Southern Command's vision of human rights, emphasizing that the "issue is not one of conflict between the mission and human rights . . . [but rather] the mission includes human rights."[19] The content of the training video earned praise from the nongovernmental human rights community, although many in the community initially remained skeptical of the degree to which the command would be able to rapidly implement the policy as it was presented in the video.[20]

General Joulwan also oversaw a dramatic development in military-to-military contacts aimed at promoting human rights. Under the policy developed by General Thurman, Southern Command was to incorporate human rights instruction in all of the training it provided to partner nation forces. Typically, this type of training was conducted by mobile training teams, which traveled to the host country and returned after providing the required training. However, the goal of human rights training is to instill a long-lasting culture of respect for human rights, and Southern Command believed the typical mobile training mission was too fleeting to accomplish this.[21]

Through the Staff Judge Advocate's office, General Joulwan thus instituted a new concept of "training the trainer" within the host countries. The idea was to thoroughly train a cadre of partner nation instructors who could then present the material in their own courses. Southern Command believed this new approach would not only provide the more sustained instruction needed to foster a culture of respect for human rights, but would also minimize the cultural and language barriers that tend to hinder instruction of foreign military personnel by U.S. forces. General Joulwan later described the essence of the "train the trainer" initiative and the new emphasis placed on human rights training as an effort to help "turn the corner" in a region emerging from a devastating decade of conflict and human rights abuse. He also believed it was imperative that human rights be fully integrated into how all of the command's missions were analyzed and assessed.

The Human Rights Division

Continuing along this innovative path, General Barry McCaffrey, who succeeded General Joulwan in February 1994, looked for new ways to further ingrain a culture of respect for human rights within the command and its mission. He focused on creating an organizational framework that would help integrate human rights directly into U.S. Southern Command's daily operations. The approach was guided by the principle that human rights could not remain merely a philosophy or an abstract legal principle; rather, it had to be fully operationalized in order to achieve the type of progress the command was hoping to, both within its own ranks and within its area of focus.

The first step in such a process was to transfer responsibility for the human rights program from the Staff Judge Advocate's purview to a dedicated human rights office. The primary reason behind this decision was to emphasize the need to do much more than merely report on legal developments related to human rights and international humanitarian law. Instead, the mission would be to help inculcate human rights into the basic mindset of each member within the command, ensure consideration of human rights was taken into account in all aspects of the command's operations, and facilitate similar changes in regional military and security forces.

The new office was established within the Strategy, Policy, and Plans Directorate, a sector very adept in dealing with civilian and government organizations and the outside bodies who would ultimately be involved in the process of promoting human rights: the interagency community, nongovernmental organizations, and foreign military and security organizations. This was deemed the optimum location and position to directly impact the larger, long-range command and theater strategic documents, thereby providing the best possible manner to start changing *attitudes* about human rights and not merely change *behavior*. This was the fundamental goal Southern Command was striving to achieve.

General McCaffrey also formed a senior-level human rights Steering Group to provide him advice on human rights issues and oversee policy implementation. According to General McCaffrey, the reason for creating the Steering Group was to ensure that fostering respect for human rights became the concern of all the command's various components.[22] The Steering Group was chaired by the head of the Strategy, Policy, and Plans Directorate and included senior officers from all of the command's directorates, such as intelligence, operations, and command and control. The Steering Group was a visible symbol of General McCaffrey's commitment to fostering respect for human rights throughout Southern Command and impressed upon its members that he expected nothing short of a new mindset: respect for human rights and international humanitarian law was now an integral part of the command's mission. The Steering Group was instrumental in providing support and recognition to the fledgling Human Rights Division.

The Human Rights Division Today

Today, Southern Command's Human Rights Division is an institutional statement of the command's commitment to promoting, protecting, and preserving human rights throughout its region of focus. It remains unique across DOD, as Southern Command is the only combatant command with a separate office charged to monitor and coordinate human rights issues. The Human Rights Division has five primary responsibilities:

- Advise and report on human rights issues
- Establish and support human rights training programs

- Ensure that human rights are integrated into Southern Command exercises and operations

- Advance respect for human rights by supporting regional initiatives

- Serve as a liaison with other entities working human rights issues, such as the interagency community, international organizations, and nongovernmental human rights organizations.

In advising and reporting on human rights issues, the division monitors and analyzes developments in international human rights law. It ensures that personnel assigned to the Southern Command receive all the information they need to comply with DOD policies and directives and the command's own human rights policy. It prepares country-specific information for the commander's meetings with foreign dignitaries and supports congressional testimony by senior Southern Command personnel. The division also monitors allegations of human rights violations once they are reported, although it does not independently investigate such charges. Ultimately, it keeps the command's leadership abreast of important provisions in domestic laws related to human rights that affect many security cooperation activities. For example, the Leahy Amendment requires the termination of security assistance to any foreign military unit that either the U.S. Department of State or Department of Defense confirms to have engaged in gross human rights violations. There is a caveat that allows security assistance to continue if the Secretary of State finds the country in question "is taking effective measures to bring the responsible members of the security forces unit to justice."[23] To ensure compliance, each foreign unit receiving U.S. military assistance must submit to a vetting process overseen by the U.S. Embassy in that country.

In addition to the Leahy Amendment, U.S. laws impose other prohibitions on U.S. security assistance in certain areas where Congress has voiced concern over human rights issues. For example, the Secretary of State must periodically certify Colombia's progress in fostering respect for human rights before funding for bilateral security assistance can be fully released. Similarly, Congress currently imposes restrictions on security assistance to Guatemala because of concerns over the slow pace of human rights reforms. The Leahy Amendment and these other restrictions on security cooperation have further sharpened Southern Command's already intense focus on human rights in its area of focus and given even greater impetus to its robust and proactive human rights program.

In implementing its training responsibility, the Human Rights Division ensures all personnel assigned to the command or performing temporary duty in the region receive initial human rights training and that permanently assigned personnel receive annual human rights awareness training. To facilitate access to the training materials, the division uses a computer-based training module, available over the Internet via its Web site. In addition, the division supports other countries' efforts to develop their own human rights and international humanitarian law training. It does this in close cooperation with the Western Hemisphere Institute for Security Cooperation (WHINSEC) at Fort Benning, Georgia, and other military schools that have developed rigorous human rights training programs. To integrate human rights awareness into all of Southern Command's operations and plans, personnel are exposed whenever possible to realistic situations during military exercises that test their knowledge and understanding of human rights laws and expectations. The Human Rights Division helps prepare and evaluate the human rights scenarios incorporated into exercises.

The last two responsibilities of the Human Rights Division, supporting regional initiatives and providing liaison with the human rights community, help build networks and partnerships throughout the region and open up opportunities to foster understanding of the issues and respect for human rights. It is in these areas of initiatives and liaison that Southern Command has helped lay a solid foundation for even greater cooperation and progress in the future.

Engaging Regional Leaders

One of the most important contributions the Human Rights Division has made to U.S. Southern Command's human rights program has been to organize and host a series of regional conferences on human rights issues. The conferences, in turn, set the stage for the groundbreaking Human Rights Initiative. The first conference, which took place in Miami in February 1996, capitalized on the momentum created by the 1995 Defense Ministerial of the Americas in Williamsburg, Virginia. Attended by representatives of all 34 democratic governments in the Americas, the Defense Ministerial of the Americas produced the "Williamsburg Principles"—six principles affirming the commitment of the region's armed forces to respect human rights and to subordinate themselves to civilian and constitutional authority.[24] The Human Rights Division followed up the ministerial by organizing a conference to address the obligations of military and security force personnel under international human rights and humanitarian law, and to discuss approaches to human rights education and training. The conference was organized in cooperation with the Inter-American Institute of Human Rights (IIHR), marking the first time any U.S. military command had ever forged such a partnership with a private human rights organization.[25]

The conference, entitled "The Role of the Armed Forces in the Protection of Human Rights," brought together 186 participants and observers including human rights experts from throughout the hemisphere, 6 ministerial-level representatives, and 8 senior defense officials. General McCaffrey led the U.S. delegation and delivered the keynote address. The gathering provided a unique opportunity for senior defense officials and military officers to begin a dialogue with representatives of human rights organizations. In doing so, it helped break down deeply ingrained mutual suspicions. Initially, these profound divisions and feelings of mistrust were so strong that they led to self-imposed segregated seating. As the conference progressed, however, the participants gradually integrated and a growing amount of one-on-one dialogue began to overcome the perceived obstacles between what had seemed to be thoroughly incompatible organizations. In the end, the conference revealed a growing consensus on the importance of human rights and democratic governance and the crucial role of the region's security forces in protecting them.

To continue the dialogue, in February 1997, Southern Command— under the command of General Wesley Clark—collaborated with the Inter-American Institute on a second conference, titled "Armed Forces, Democracy, and Human Rights on the Threshold of the 21st Century." By the time it concluded, a consensus had emerged among the more than 190 participants from throughout the Americas that additional steps of a more concrete nature were now needed to keep the human rights agenda moving forward. Accordingly, General Clark invited the participants to join in a series of seminars intended to establish common criteria for measuring the progress made by military and security forces in respecting human rights.

The Human Rights Initiative (HRI)

The two human rights conferences, and the invitation to sponsor a long-term initiative of a series of regional seminars, marked a turning point in Southern Command's human rights program. Generals Thurman and Joulwan had focused on laying the foundation of a strong human rights program, implementing critical improvements to training and doctrine, and pursuing bilateral initiatives with regional militaries. Under General McCaffrey, the human rights program matured institutionally via organizational changes that brought respect for human rights and international humanitarian law more fully into the operational realm. Through the seminars proposed by General Clark, the program moved into an even more ambitious phase of promoting a multilateral approach to improving respect for human rights and international humanitarian law. As General Clark later recalled, the achievements made by the command's human rights program through 1997 had already changed human rights, in his words, "from an obstacle to a centerpiece" of the command's relationship with regional military and security forces.

In June 1997, Southern Command and the Inter-American Institute cohosted the first of the seminars. The meeting was held in Panama City, Panama, and included a small group of approximately 20 representatives of regional military and security forces, Southern Command, and the nongovernmental human rights community. Its theme was "Measuring Progress in Respect for Human Rights." The format, which remained the same for subsequent seminars, was designed to encourage dynamic interaction, allowing the participants to reach consensus on difficult issues by engaging in small group dialogue.

The seminar succeeded in its primary objective, which was to produce a draft "Consensus Document" identifying human rights standards and objectives for military doctrine, education, and training; effective internal control systems; and, cooperation by military forces with external control systems. The process of finalizing and ultimately implementing the Consensus Document became known as the Human Rights Initiative (HRI). The meeting also succeeded as a confidence-building exercise that helped diminish the initially high level of mutual suspicion between the human rights community and the regional military and security forces, which helped lay a solid foundation of trust for subsequent meetings.

From 1998 to 2002, Southern Command sponsored five additional hemispheric seminars to develop plans of action, objectives, and performance measures. By the conclusion of the final seminar in March 2002, military and/ or security-force officers from all 34 democracies in the Western Hemisphere had participated in drafting and finalizing the consensus document. Prominent nongovernmental organizations (NGOs), international organizations, and academic institutions sent representatives to serve as advisors. The final wording can truly be said to represent agreements reached between the hemisphere's military forces and the human rights community, writ large.

Overall, the Human Rights Initiative proved to be an excellent tool for engaging both military forces of the hemisphere and the human rights community in a collaborative effort to ensure that improved performance on human rights continues into the future. Southern Command's role has been instrumental in facilitating its progress. The Consensus Document embodies the principles of Southern Command, as well as those long espoused by human rights activists and NGOs. These include: fostering a culture of respect for human rights in the region's military and security forces; introducing rigorous human rights awareness training; establishing effective means of internal control, such as conducting investigations; sanctioning human rights offenders; prohibiting collaboration with illegal groups that commit human rights violations; and finally, encouraging full cooperation with civilian authorities. The Consensus Document also demonstrates an unprecedented degree of cooperation and dialogue on human rights, both among the region's military and security forces, as well as between the security forces and representatives of the human rights community. Merely achieving consensus among such a diverse group of participants on the points laid out in the Consensus Document, and on concrete measures to evaluate progress toward their implementation, was by itself a remarkable accomplishment.

The Consensus Document is the watershed final product of the first phase of the Human Rights Initiative, representing a broad consensus among the region's military and security forces and the human rights community that respect for human rights must be an integral part of their mission and their institutions. It establishes two ambitious goals for those services: fostering an institutional culture of respect for democratic values, human rights, and international humanitarian law; and measuring progress toward developing that institutional culture. To achieve the first objective, the participants agreed upon four broad consensus points in regard to military and security forces:

- Their doctrine should incorporate human rights and international humanitarian law principles and awareness.
- Their education and training should include human rights principles and principles of international humanitarian law.
- They should have effective systems of internal control.
- They should cooperate fully with civilian authorities.[26]

However, the Consensus Document is simply a means to an end—helping to solidify a culture of respect for human rights throughout the region—rather than an end in itself; much work still needs to be done. With the completion of the final draft Consensus Document, the Human Rights Initiative entered a new phase, implementation. Participants in the final seminar expressed the strong desire that the Consensus Document not become "just another document that sits on the shelf," but that it be implemented and deliver a "real world" impact. In a statement entitled "The Conclusions of Guatemala," participants specifically requested that Southern Command continue to support the HRI, focusing on three initial priorities during the implementation phase: 1) securing high-level support from the participating nations' ministries of defense and security; 2) maintaining the involvement and support of credible and influential nongovernmental and international human rights organizations; and 3) creating an executive commission to oversee implementation and a technical secretariat to support the process.

Implementation

In July and November 2002, the first two meetings specifically addressing implementation plans were held in Bolivia. By September 2003, the technical secretariat was established. It is administered by the *Centro de Estudios, Análisis y Capacitación en Derechos Humanos* (CECADH), known in English as the *Center for Human Rights Training*. Work began in earnest as CECADH and the Southern Command human rights team designed a strategy for approaching the countries of the region to promote participation in HRI Phase II. The first step of the process is a visit to each nation to inform the nation's military and government leaders about the history, goals, and objectives of HRI, and to invite them to make a formal commitment to implement HRI within their military and security forces. Following a visit, the partner nation's minister of defense typically informs Southern Command, through its military security cooperation office in the U.S. Embassy, when it is ready to move ahead with a formal commitment to implement HRI. That formal commitment is made through the signing of a memorandum of cooperation with the HRI secretariat. This emphasizes the important distinction that participation in HRI is not a commitment to the U.S. Government, but rather a commitment to uphold principles and standards agreed upon within the community of nations of the Western Hemisphere.

The second phase of the Initiative, now under way, is to implement the points contained in the Consensus Document within the military and security forces of the participating nations. The Human Rights Division, working in a unique partnership with the Center for Human Rights Training, will support the military forces of each nation in the region whose Ministry of Defense chooses to formally commit to implement the Consensus Document. As of the date of this writing, Bolivia, Colombia, Costa Rica, the Dominican Republic, El Salvador, Guatemala, Honduras, Panama, and Uruguay have all signed the document and are moving ahead with the Initiative.

Additionally, the *Conferencia de Fuerzas Armadas Centroamericanas* (Conference for Central American Armed Forces, or CFAC) is a participating constituent and includes militaries from member nations who have not yet signed the Consensus Document. Southern Command expects several other countries to join the group in the near future. The Human Rights Division will continue to sponsor periodic hemispheric meetings in which militaries participating in the Initiative can come together to report progress, share ideas, and discuss specific human rights topics.

Following the signing of the memorandum, Southern Command stands ready to sponsor a leaders' seminar and an implementation conference. The leaders' seminar familiarizes the small number of military officers and civilians charged to lead the implementation process with the Consensus Document and the methodology to develop unique national versions. The implementation conference is a larger event in which officers from all the military services, representatives of other government agencies, and representatives of civil society, including academia and human rights organizations, adapt the regional Consensus Document model to national realities. Conference participants produce a comprehensive plan showing timelines, institutions, offices responsible for execution, and measures of effectiveness for each specific action plan.

The core objectives of the document cannot be changed except by consensus in a future hemispheric conference. Participants in the national HRI events therefore work only with the specific action plans that affect actual implementation within their institutions. In this way, the Consensus Document both supports regional agreements on human rights and encourages innovation and appropriate activities that respond to the real needs of the military forces in each nation.

As of this writing, the HRI team has conducted 20 visits to 15 countries, concentrating primarily on Central America and the Andean Region. Eight nations have signed memoranda of cooperation and one has begun implementation independently. In November 2005, the Conference of Central American Armed Forces became the first regional organization to join HRI. For the years ahead, the focus will be on approaching the remaining Southern Cone nations, followed by the island nations of the Caribbean.

During the implementation phase, the HRI secretariat and Southern Command stand ready to provide technical assistance to the implementing militaries when requested. Some of the most noteworthy action plans have included printing and distribution of human rights manuals for soldiers, printing and distribution of new national security doctrine with a human rights component, human rights training courses for officers and soldiers in units throughout a national territory, and a 16-nation regional conference on human rights as the basis for combating terrorism.

In total, U.S. Southern Command has conducted over 60 HRI-related events involving thousands of participants. For those military and security forces who have implemented the HRI for a minimum of 2 years, Southern Command sponsors strategic progress assessment seminars (SPAS), thus completing the "plan-execute-assess" feedback loop. The SPAS provide a forum for partner nation action officers to assess progress made on the comprehensive implementation plan, to identify successes and obstacles, and to formulate follow-on action plans. In this way continuity of the process is ensured and real world achievements can be measured.

Collaborative Efforts and Continual Learning

A major objective of Southern Command's human rights program has been and continues to be the identification and cultivation of areas in which the command can work together with the human rights community on ways to achieve the mutual goal of ending human rights violations in the region. The task is particularly challenging because, in many cases, human rights activists and organizations harbor deep suspicions about the commitment of the U.S. Government, and especially the U.S. military, in promoting human rights. The divisive struggle in the 1990s over the U.S. Army School of the Americas is an example of how difficult it can be to reach common ground, as well as how counterproductive an adversarial relationship between the U.S. military and the human rights community can be. Southern Command therefore seeks to maximize opportunities to work with the human rights community and to leverage their expertise and experience to meet common goals.

The Human Rights Initiative has been the most visible collaborative endeavor between Southern Command and the community of human rights experts, and it represents a possible model for future efforts. Southern Command's involvement, and especially the personal commitment of visionary leaders like Generals Thurman, Joulwan, McCaffrey, and Clark, gave the effort legitimacy in the eyes of many regional military and security forces and encouraged their participation. In turn, the representatives of human rights groups brought a new perspective and valuable expertise, as well as organizational assistance, to supplement the limited staff and resources of the Human Rights Division. Partnerships with the nongovernmental organizations to manage the large conferences and seminars were the key to success. But perhaps most importantly, both Southern Command and the nongovernmental groups involved were able to formulate a common vision in which they would facilitate consensus among regional military and security forces while also giving them "ownership" of the process.

The focus of Southern Command's human rights program has always been both internal and external. Its responsibilities in the internal realm center on institutionalizing human rights within Southern Command and integrating human rights training and practices in all of the command's activities. It accomplishes this by ensuring its staff and Department of Defense personnel deploying into its area of focus receive human rights awareness education; working to incorporate human rights principles into command-sponsored exercises, training, conferences, exchanges, and operations; and advising the command's leaders on human rights issues. Its external focus involves building collaborative relationships with the human rights community and promoting a culture of respect for human rights within the military and security forces of the partner nations in its area of focus.

Military and security forces throughout the hemisphere have accepted their obligation to observe human rights and international humanitarian law, and they have begun to adopt and institutionalize a culture of respect for human rights with initiatives such as creating human rights offices, revising doctrine, and improving training programs. Although there is still room for improvement, the fundamental shift in institutional attitudes among the region's military and security forces regarding human rights has laid a solid foundation for continued progress.

The success of the first phase of the HRI has resulted in a concrete mechanism—the Consensus Document—that has the potential to move the region forward. The plans of action contained in the Consensus Document point the way ahead, and the accompanying performance measures of effectiveness provide a yardstick for objectively measuring progress. Moving the Human Rights Initiative ahead in its implementation phase will require broadening "ownership" of the Initiative across the interagency community, to draw upon a greater pool of both resources and expertise to assist with implementation. An additional aim will be to muster additional support in helping to gain approval for the Initiative among the senior ranks of the region's ministries of defense and security. Navigating the Consensus Document's implementation plan through the higher level ministerial offices throughout the region without reopening its consensus points to an entirely new round of negotiations will be a significant challenge.

Since its inception, Southern Command has regarded forming and strengthening partnerships with organizations that promote human rights as an integral part of our mission and as a force multiplier to our own efforts. Representatives of human rights organizations and academia contributed their valuable perspectives on the regional and historical human rights context as well as extensive technical expertise. The pivotal role played by the Inter-American Institute of Human Rights, among others, contributed in a decisive manner to the success of the early stages of the Human Rights Initiative. The Center for Human Rights Training provides invaluable technical expertise as the Secretariat in the second phase of the Initiative to the military and security forces of the region who commit to implement the Consensus Document within their institutions.

The Human Rights Division has benefited from strong leaders within U.S. Southern Command who have maintained the promotion of human rights as a central component of the command's mission, despite an environment of scarce resources and periodic budget cuts. Southern Command's human rights program is a product of the commitment and vision of a succession of leaders from the early 1990s to the present day—it is not a legislatively mandated program—and we remain the only regional combatant command that has such a formal human rights policy and a specialized office to administer it.

Finally, to continue making progress, U.S. Southern Command will also have to maintain its underlying commitment to fostering human rights through training, dialogue, and cooperation as an integral part of its overall regional strategy. This fundamental precept, adopted when the human rights program was launched, remains essential to the program's future success. The unique process of the HRI has yielded a wealth of experiences and lessons. The first lesson is the power of dialogue and collaboration between people of diverse backgrounds working toward a common goal based on shared values. Here, the Americas have a strong advantage. All of its member nations, save one, are democracies. This fact does not guarantee, in and of itself, that human rights are upheld to the same standard by all the different variations and practices of "democracy"; in fact, many of the most egregious violations of the basic tenets of human rights were carried out in the *name* of human rights. However, this *does* provide a powerful common framework within which to work. Even the mutual suspicion and distrust between military officers and civilians from human rights organizations, palpable during the first hours of every event, eventually wears away. By the end of every event, camaraderie and a sense of shared purpose prevail—such is the sense of mission, dedication to task, and enthusiasm for the projects developed in the HRI conferences held to date.

Additionally, the basis for forming a true Partnership for the Americas comes from an attitude based on genuine mutual respect. Human rights are an extremely sensitive subject in many, if not most, nations of the world. No nation has a perfect record, and the level of sensitivity toward any hint of criticism relates directly to how recently those abuses occurred and how severe they were. The HRI has continued to move forward—even in the polarized political atmosphere of the past few years—because the work is based on respect for all participants, whether they come from human rights organizations, the military forces, or other institutions of the partner nations. The message is twofold: 1) all participants are stakeholders working toward common goals based on shared values; and 2), all who participate and contribute have valuable insights to share. It is a message HRI team members take care to communicate consistently, in thought, word, and deed. Throughout, partner nation participants take the lead; Southern Command and secretariat personnel support and assist as requested.

The third and final lesson is that we must focus on the way ahead while understanding the past provides the context in which the HRI takes place. Events must not focus on seeking justice for previous human rights violations—that is the work of other organizations. Instead, HRI's objective should be to facilitate the creation and institutionalization of processes that will prevent future abuses.

Nontraditional Challenges to Human Rights

Advances toward worldwide recognition of universal human rights principles moved ahead rapidly in the second half of the 20th century, beginning with the Universal Declaration of Human Rights in 1948 and the conclusion of the Geneva Conventions in 1949. This continued through the ratification of numerous regional and international human rights treaties, the inclusion of respect for human rights in national constitutions and legislation in many countries, and the establishment of national and international human rights institutions. The role of nongovernmental organizations has also grown as these groups exert more influence over national legislation, the texts of international treaties, public opinion, and government policies.

Having made great progress in democratization, however, the countries of the region now face a daunting crisis of weakening economies, growing crime, and endemic corruption. Violations of human rights and international humanitarian law still persist. Thankfully, such abuses are much less frequent. More importantly, they no longer reflect official government policy, as they did in the 1970s and 1980s when dictatorships systemically tortured and murdered political opponents. On the contrary, countries throughout the region have adopted human rights legislation and begun to reform civilian and military judicial systems explicitly to protect the rights of their citizens. The efforts of the U.S. Government, with support from U.S. Southern Command, to help the region's military and security forces institutionalize a culture of respect for human rights and overcome a legacy of abuse, made an important contribution.

Military and security forces throughout the region also have taken concrete steps to institutionalize a culture of respect for human rights among their members. Many have, for example, established human rights offices at ministries of defense and high-level military commands, and they have integrated education in human rights and international humanitarian law into basic training, professional military development courses, and the curriculums of military academies. These institutional improvements by regional military and security forces have enabled the United States over the last few years to focus needed attention on helping to improve other areas critical to human rights, such as reforming overburdened and corrupt judicial systems.[27] Although many human rights challenges clearly remain, no other region in the world, taken as a whole, has made as much progress in respect for human rights over the past decade. As Dr. Martin Luther King, Jr., once wrote, "We must be able to accept finite disappointment, but we must never lose infinite hope."

While helping to overcome the legacies of past abuses throughout the region, we must also remain vigilant against new threats to human rights. Today, the region specifically—and the international community as a whole—confronts a host of nontraditional challenges to the further development and entrenchment of respect for human rights. These challenges and threats come in the form of international terrorism, narcotrafficking, and dangerously high levels of violent crime, together with more long-standing issues, such as endemic poverty, lack of economic development, income inequality, ethnic tensions, discrimination, and growing popular frustration with democracy's failure to provide solutions to these problems. We must also guard against any resurgence of old threats, such as instability and internal conflict, that could threaten the region's fragile democracies and pose persistent challenges to the safeguarding of human rights in the region.

In our shared home, many Latin American and Caribbean democracies face an uphill battle, not only due to the previously mentioned long-standing social and economic problems, but also because of the growing lack of confidence in the respective governments' ability to overcome these challenges. There is increasing popular dissatisfaction with some democratic governments, resulting in social tension, popular unrest, political instability, and a growing tendency to govern from the streets. Irregular changes of government have occurred in some countries in our region in recent years, and there are disturbing trends toward undermining or simply overriding the democratic process altogether in other areas. If the democratic governments of the region fail to develop effective solutions to these multiple crises, some observers fear a return to authoritarianism or a swing to the political left and away from democracy. The implication for human rights in the region is clear: true egalitarian democracy is a prerequisite for the full protection of human rights.

The nations of Latin America and the Caribbean suffer the highest violent crime rates in the world, and studies show a dramatic increase in the 1990s that continues unabated today. Aggressive and hostile youth gangs are the primary perpetrators of violent crime in the major cities of some countries. The ill-equipped, ill-trained, out-numbered, and poorly paid police and security forces have been unable to control the crime. Judiciaries that suffer from the same ills are similarly unable to investigate crimes and prosecute criminals effectively and efficiently. The problem is only exacerbated by the stench of corruption that is perceived to exist in some of these organizations and institutions. Citizens live in fear; polls show that violent crime ranks as one of the top three concerns across the region. The inability of police and judiciaries to control violent crime by legal means has produced serious setbacks in human rights, as frightened publics call for *mano dura* ("firm hand") policies to restore public security. In the process, overzealous legislation can abridge due process rights of criminal suspects, and aggressive political rhetoric can be interpreted as an invitation to police brutality. A related problem arises when governments order military units to support the embattled police on law enforcement missions. Military forces are not typically trained or equipped for law enforcement duties, nor for control of large crowds and public demonstrations. Governments must urgently invest in adequately manning, equipping, and training—particularly in human rights—security forces in order to avoid widespread human rights violations.

Additionally, numerous terrorist incidents culminating in the unprecedented attacks on the United States on September 11, 2001, have demonstrated that terrorism is one of the most significant threats to the protection of human rights, democracy, and international security in the region.[28] Following the terrorist attacks, governments throughout the region responded with renewed cooperation and solidarity. In June 2002, the General Assembly of the Organization of American States adopted the Inter-American Convention against Terrorism, in which member states reaffirmed the "need to adopt effective steps in the inter-American system to prevent, punish, and eliminate terrorism through the broadest cooperation."

The terrorist threat and the way states respond to it pose unique challenges to the protection of human rights. From a legal perspective, terrorism does not fall neatly into existing categories of human rights or international humanitarian law. Terrorist attacks may take place during times of peace, when all human rights laws are fully applicable. They may occur during times of crisis, when states have the legal right to suspend observance of some rights temporarily to ensure the safety of their citizens. They may even occur in the midst of open conflict, in which case the principles of international humanitarian law would apply. To further complicate matters, states often have difficulty determining the legal status of people accused of perpetrating terrorist acts. Some terrorists may be classified as civilian criminals, and others as lawful combatants entitled to the same protections as any other prisoner of war. Still others may be deemed unlawful combatants and, as such, be legitimately denied many basic legal protections. Until international law evolves to deal more effectively with terrorism of the sort that delivered the blow to the United States in September 2001, such controversy is likely to continue.

While terrorism poses many challenges to respect for human rights, it also showcases military and security forces as the guardians of democratic societies. The U.S.-led war on terrorism demonstrates the need for strong, disciplined, and professional armed forces to protect the democratic institutions that terrorists seek to undermine and destroy. At the same time, military and security forces must always remain aware of the broad range of human rights that may be affected by perfectly legitimate antiterrorist initiatives, among them freedom of assembly and association, freedom of conscience and religion, and property and privacy. Especially in countries where respect for human rights is not firmly entrenched, extra security measures necessary to combat terrorism may also erode confidence in judicial protections and the right to humane treatment during interrogations and confinement. Democracies have a particular interest in honoring their legal obligations under national and international law to respect these rights, all the more so when called upon to deal with a great national or international crisis. For these reasons, Southern Command has adopted its strategy of seeking multifaceted security cooperation activities (exercises, small unit training, academic forums, and visionary initiatives like the Human Rights Initiative) to help mentor military and security forces of the region to attain and maintain good standing in the international community. U.S. Southern Command reaffirms its commitment to ensure its own troops are trained on human rights and to maintain its policy of zero tolerance for human rights violations by U.S. personnel or members of partner nation military forces.

> Democracy is indispensable for the effective exercise of fundamental freedoms and human rights in their universality, indivisibility and interdependence, embodied in the respective constitutions of states and in inter-American and international human rights instruments.
>
> —Inter-American Democratic Charter (2001)

The role of the military in a democratic society is clear: a military exists to ensure the security of the nation while obeying legitimate civilian authority and respecting the rights of citizens and noncitizens. Secondary missions include, among others, contributing to peaceful regional military cooperation and participating in peacekeeping operations around the globe. However, resource constraints drive some governments to assign their military forces nontraditional missions such as disaster relief, environmental protection, riot control, special weapons and tactics operations, and support to traditional law enforcement. Indeed, some of these are even written into national constitutions and law. However, by their very atypical and nontraditional—and thus, not adequately or appropriately trained—nature, these mission areas increase the potential for confusion and mistakes. Strong human rights programs are especially vital when conducting military responses in these types of complex and continuously evolving environments.

The Human Rights Initiative's success can be attributed to the strong desire of regional military forces to move forward in history, establishing better training, inculcating human rights into operational missions, and making a positive contribution to their societies. The abuses of the recent past remain fresh in military and civilian minds. The HRI is an essential tool for achieving the Americas' common vision for a better tomorrow—a tomorrow defined by security, stability, freedom, and prosperity.

U.S. Southern Command is committed to working together with all our neighbors in our shared home who possess these same desires. An important aspect in this process is continuing to support HRI implementation. The command can provide technical support, training, conferences, seminars, and exchanges with human rights organizations, participating national governments, NGOs, and the private sector. In addition, Southern Command is working to strengthen interagency coordination with other U.S. Government agencies and exploring ways to branch out to achieve broader participation from partner nation security forces. To prescribe, adhere to, and enforce when required, laws intended not to restrict human liberty, but rather to enforce human rights, these governments and their agencies will find their strength, their legitimacy, and ultimately their broad-based faith and confidence from the populace in the faithful discharge of these vital yet basic and fundamental duties.

Geography, history, trade, extended families, cultural ties, common threats, and even environmental conditions tie the nations of the hemisphere together and all point to a single, shared destiny. People are central to everything we at U.S. Southern Command do—protecting our nations' citizens is the reason we as military and security forces exist, and ensuring their security in a manner consistent with democracy and respect for human rights is our common mission. As Senator William Fulbright remarked in an address on the Senate floor in 1964, "Foreign policy cannot be based on military posture and diplomatic activities alone in today's world. The shape of the world a generation from now will be influenced far more by how well we communicate the values of our society to others than by our military or diplomatic superiority." Today, we are living in, and are the personal embodiment of, that "generation from now"; as such, we must continue to communicate and uphold the fundamental values of liberty and individual freedom. U.S. Southern Command's intent is to remain at the forefront of human rights training, which will be fully integrated in everything it does. The Human Rights Initiative will be a key component of that training, as it is key to the Partnership for the Americas and essential to fulfilling our common mission.

Notes

[1] Jack Donnelly, *International Human Rights* (Boulder, CO: Westview Press, 1993), 177, n. 1.

[2] Jack Donnelly, *Universal Human Rights in Theory and Practice* (Ithaca, NY: Cornell University Press, 1989), 17.

[3] It has become common to refer to "human rights violations" committed by guerrilla or other irregular forces, such as terrorist organizations. To be precise, when one refers to abuses committed by these groups he or she is referring to violations of international humanitarian law or ordinary crimes. The distinction between ordinary crimes and state human rights violations may be a definitional difference, as the substantive acts may be the same.

[4] The American Convention on Human Rights, also known as the Pact of San José, was adopted by the member nations of the Organization of American States at their meeting on Inter-American Specialized Conference on Human Rights in San José, Costa Rica in 1969. It has since been ratified by

24 of the 35 members, although Canada, the United States, and several Caribbean nations have not ratified it or the two additional protocols.

[5] Donnelly, *International Human Rights,* 6–7.

[6] The Universal Declaration of Human Rights was adopted without dissent but with abstentions by the Soviet bloc, South Africa, and Saudi Arabia. The Soviet Union and its allies abstained because they believed the UDHR placed insufficient emphasis on economic and social rights; South Africa abstained because it objected to the provisions on racial discrimination; and Saudi Arabia abstained because it perceived the references to gender equality to be at odds with Islamic law. Donnelly, *International Human Rights,* 177, n. 2.

[7] The International Covenant on Civil and Political Rights (ICCPR) and the International Covenant on Economic, Social, and Cultural Rights (ICESCR) were originally envisioned as a single document that would codify the rights contained in the Universal Declaration of Human Rights (UDHR). Cold War politics delayed the adoption of the documents for a decade after they were drafted, from 1966 to 1976. The reluctance of the United States to afford the same degree of legal protection to economic and social rights as civil and political rights proved the primary obstacle. In the end, the United States signed but never ratified the ICESCR.

[8] For a norm to become part of customary international law, states must not only uniformly and consistently practice it over a prolonged period of time, but also do so *out of a sense of obligation.* This "sense of obligation" is often expressed by states in their official pronouncements in international forums.

[9] Restatement (Third) of the Foreign Relations Law of the United States (1987) § 702, Customary International Law of Human Rights.

[10] See Makau Mutuna, *Human Rights: A Political and Cultural Critique* (Philadelphia: University of Pennsylvania Press, 2002), 177, n. 30, and Jeffrey F. Addicott and Guy B. Roberts, "Building Democracies with Southern Command's Legal Engagement Strategy," *Parameters* (Spring 2001), at: <http://carlisle-www.army.mil/usawc/Parameters/01spring/addicott.htm>, n. 4.

[11] Most who argue that economic and social human rights should only be viewed as "aspirational" in nature make an exception for the right to private property: an economic right that is so ingrained in the liberal democratic tradition that few separate it from basic civil and political rights. See Donnelly, *International Human Rights,* 28.

[12] The law of armed conflict has both humanitarian and functional purposes. Humanitarian purposes include protecting combatants and civilians from unnecessary suffering, protecting the human rights of people captured by armed belligerents, and facilitating the restoration of peace. Functional purposes include "maintaining the humanity" of those involved in armed conflict, preventing the deterioration of order and discipline within the armed forces, and maintaining the support of the public during a conflict. Jeanne M. Meyer and Brian J. Bill, eds., *Operational Law Handbook* (2002) (Charlottesville, VA: U.S. Army Judge Advocate General's School, 2002), 8.

[13] General Barry R. McCaffrey, transcript of keynote address at the conference entitled "The National Armed Forces as Supporters of Human Rights," U.S. Army School of the Americas, August 10, 1994.

[14] Adapted from McCaffrey.

[15] Professor Michael Reisman, former chairman of the Inter-American Commission on Human Rights, summed up this danger as follows: "I am concerned about [the military] viewing human rights as pragmatic. The moment troops begin to take casualties because they respected human rights, all of this will be down the tube." Quoted in Bruce B. Auster, "Lessons in Killing and Kindness," *U.S. News and World Report* (October 3, 1994), 18.

[16] Richard S. Hillman, John A. Peeler, and Elsa Cardozo Da Silva, eds., *Democracy and Human Rights in Latin America* (Westport, CT: Praeger, 2002), 217.

[17] Senator James William Fulbright, *Address on the Senate Floor,* June 29, 1961.

[18] United States Southern Command, *Policy Memorandum 5–90,* March 19, 1990.

[19] U.S. Southern Command training video, quoted in Washington Office on Latin America (WOLA), *Human Rights Education and Training in U.S. Policy Toward Latin America,* June 15, 1992, 12.

[20] See WOLA, *Human Rights Education and Training in U.S. Policy Toward Latin America,* 12–13.

[21] Jeffrey F. Addicott and Andrew M. Warner, "JAG Corps Poised for New Defense Missions: Human Rights Training in Peru," *Army Lawyer* (February 1993), 80.

[22] McCaffrey interview.

[23] The "Leahy Law" is codified in Public Law 108–447, Section 551 of the Fiscal Year 2005 Foreign Operations Appropriations Bill and Public Law 108–287, Section 8076 of the Fiscal Year 2005 Department of Defense Appropriations Bill.

[24] The six Williamsburg Principles were: "1) Uphold the promise of the Santiago Agreement that the preservation of democracy is the basis for ensuring our mutual security; 2) Acknowledge that military and security forces play a critical role in supporting and defending the legitimate interests of sovereign democratic states; 3) Affirm the commitments of our countries in Miami and Managua that our Armed Forces should be subordinate to democratically controlled authority, act within the bounds of national Constitutions, and respect human rights through training and practice; 4) Increase transparency in defense matters through exchanges of information, through reporting on defense expenditures, and by greater civilian-military dialogue; 5) Set as a goal for our hemisphere the resolution of outstanding disputes by negotiated settlement and widespread adoption of confidence building measures, all of this in a time-frame consistent with the pace of hemispheric economic integration, and to recognize that the development of our economic security profoundly affects our defense security and vice versa; and 6) Promote greater defense cooperation in support of voluntary participation in UN-sanctioned peacekeeping operations, and to cooperate in a supportive role in the fight against narco-terrorism." See "The Defense Ministerial of the Americas" at: <http://www.summit-americas.org/Williamsburg-spanish.htm>.

[25] The Inter-American Institute was founded in 1980 under an agreement between the Inter-American Court of Human Rights and the Republic of Costa Rica, and is based in San José, Costa Rica. The IIHR is an autonomous international academic organization dedicated to the promotion of human rights through education and research.

[26] Final Consensus Document language adopted at Seminar 2002 held in Guatemala City, Guatemala, March 10–16, 2002.

[27] Danika Walters, Foreign Affairs Officer for Colombia, Central America, Mexico, and the Caribbean for the U.S. State Department's Bureau of Democracy, Human Rights, and Labor, telephone interview with author, April 17, 2003.

[28] Inter-American Commission on Human Rights, *Report on Terrorism and Human Rights,* October 22, 2002, at: <http://www.oas.org>.

Chapter 6

Health Engagement and Humanitarianism

Liberty is to the collective body, what health is to every individual body. Without health, no pleasure can be tasted by man; without liberty, no happiness can be enjoyed by society.

—Thomas Jefferson

This unfolding 21st century presents our entire national security structure in general, and U.S. Southern Command in particular, with an unprecedented opportunity to define and shape new means and capabilities that will best achieve U.S. national security objectives in an era of transnational and unconventional threats. We find ourselves at the dawn of new thinking about how we might overcome the inertia and restructure and reposition ourselves—to morph in ways that will improve our own interests as well as those of our partner nations to the south.

To accomplish this, we need a holistic approach to national and regional security—one that encompasses all facets of security, including: personal/physical; economic; political; intellectual; energy; environmental; financial; and health. Broadening the aperture in such a way is necessary to truly understand the different challenges we face and thus the different functions we may perform in confronting them. As such, this requires not only a cultural mind shift among assigned military personnel but also inclusion of new partners. Relationships are important, and such partnerships must be forged by building levels of trust in the ability of all to work together along traditionally unfamiliar, culturally distinct, but strategically important lines outside the Department of Defense.

We need to continue to recognize that the real thrust of 21st-century national security in this region is not vested in war, but in intelligent management of the conditions of peace in a volatile era. While we remain fully ready for combat operations, diplomacy dominates so much of what we do, and development is a mandatory requisite feature of true, long-term stability and prosperity. We need much greater engagement and resultant synchronization with the State Department and USAID throughout the enterprise. This is true in all aspects of security, but increasingly so in the realm of humanitarian assistance and disaster relief (HA/DR) and overall health security. We should undertake no task without first considering the valuable synergy provided when these and other entities work together—throughout the process—as a team.

While expanding our definition and understanding of "security," in addition to seeking greater unity of effort within and among the members of the interagency community, we have also sought to strengthen the bonds of mutual interest and cooperation with our partner nations in the region. Through a long history of training, communication, exercises, and liaison, we have built sturdy relationships that are now ready for expansion into a new realm of partnering arrangements. We have military liaison officers with partner nations now, but we might be even more effective in accomplishing the mission by offering liaison positions for civilian bureaucrats from agencies and cabinet bureaus from all the nations and territories throughout the region. So much of the power of the United States to create successful partnerships in our region is found in the private sector. For example, in May 2007 Microsoft announced a partnership with the Inter-American Development Bank to form a new Latin American Collaborative Research Federation that will create a "virtual research institute." Since then, Microsoft has committed $930,000 to finance the first 3 years of the project, enabling scientists at research institutions throughout Latin America to seek collaborative solutions to socioeconomic problems in areas such as agriculture, education, alternative energy, the environment, and health care.

Health security—the larger term that encompasses the spread of disease, lack of education and awareness of health threats, and equal access to health care, among others—is one key area where we at Southern Command must find ways to work with nongovernmental organizations, private charitable entities, international organizations, and the private sector, striving to become the partner of choice for those who wish to engage and better the region. We should look for ways to integrate this endeavor into key staff nodes. Such partnerships will better nurture common values and emphasize shared interests in expanding economic opportunity, promoting peaceful resolution of conflict, enhancing scientific collaboration, protecting the environment, fighting crime, and combating diseases that respect no border.

Security and stability throughout this region for the foreseeable future will depend upon the creation of a shared and cooperative hemisphere security environment that is inclusive and beneficial to all. We must find ways to focus the collective wisdom of all partners to defeat those groups and forces who want to keep us from reaching our goals. The threats and challenges in our hemisphere are not traditional military ones, and are often interrelated and involve both state and nonstate actors. Thus they require an international partnering and interagency community approach. This vision embodies our belief that our emerging and changing roles and missions require us to enable lasting and inclusive partnerships in order to work collectively to ensure a secure, stable, and ultimately prosperous home in the Americas.

> The health of the people is really the foundation upon which all their happiness and all their powers as a state depend.
>
> —Benjamin Disraeli

Health and Engagement

As previously mentioned, we foresee a regional strategic and operating environment in which the vast scale of challenges that will face the Nation will require the U.S. Government be able to attract people and other nations to support efforts toward shared desired endstates of enhanced cooperative security, sustained stability, and enduring prosperity throughout the Americas. Regional perceptions of the United States will increasingly be critical to our overall effectiveness in these pursuits, and as a result, we will increasingly need substantive, strategic public diplomacy assets with which we can effectively engage the region. In this context, we see a clear opportunity to leverage the Nation's strength in public health to engage the region in a highly positive, concrete, and overt fashion. Health interventions are particularly valuable and visible to the recipients and can have extremely long-term positive effects—especially when delivered in a comprehensive, synchronized, and integrated fashion that ties together the partnership efforts of military and civilian, foreign and domestic, and public and private sectors. Harnessing the capability of multiple disciplines with a shared regional health mission will necessitate greater unity of effort and synergy between U.S. agencies and bodies, rather than perpetuate duplication of efforts. In short, we see much value in empowering a "whole-of-government"—truly, a whole-of-society and ideally a whole-of-many-societies—approach to supporting efforts to increase the level of regional health security through fully recognizing and utilizing shared resources and fostering more effective public health diplomacy.

Global and regional health and its direct impact on national and regional security continue to assume a greater role in our nation's foreign policy agenda, demanding greater insight, knowledge, and a more skilled diplomatic presence in the region. There is an important strategic opportunity for the U.S. Government to better leverage its substantial public health assets found throughout the interagency community to advance humanitarian leadership and protect ourselves and our neighbors from emerging global disease threats and other, broader, and more persistent population-based public health challenges to security. There is a continued need for us to collectively be able to wield this valuable portfolio of health assets in a variety of different circumstances in a more strategic, agile, and facile manner. This will require transcending traditional stovepiped responses to health-related crises and issues, sharpening the ability to identify and respond to key regional health concerns, prioritizing areas for U.S. Government action, and also identifying areas where the United States and its specific agencies will need to perform vital missions in support of another partner, foreign or domestic. Ultimately, our goal is a region whose population is educated in basic sanitation and preventive health strategies; one which has relatively easy access to health professionals; and one whose health professionals have an increased surveillance, predictive ability, and response capacity to confront or even prevent disease outbreaks.

Achieving this endstate first requires a broad, multidimensional definition of public health including, for example, the health-related aspects of agriculture, commerce, the environment, transportation, and the broad population-based benefits that biomedical research yields. Thus, it will require engaging not only agencies such as the Department of Health and Human Services (HHS), the State Department, and the U.S. Agency for International Development (USAID)—which have clear, well-established international health mandates—but also DOD, the Department of Agriculture, the Environmental Protection Agency (EPA), and other Federal Departments and agencies, plus forming and leveraging partnerships with key actors in the private sector and nongovernmental organizations (NGOs) whose programs can have a significant impact on global and regional health. For example, large-scale interagency and public-private sector efforts and ventures are already underway in water and sanitation, malaria, polio, regional disease detection, maternal and child health, refugee and environmental health, and other essential regional health domains.

Once again looking through the lens of U.S. Southern Command, we see we must continue to take a more proactive role in striving to raise the level of health security in the region. In the past, the interests of ensuring national security and the advancement of economic and political objectives consistently have been kept separate and distinct from seeking to achieve humanitarian goals or public health initiatives. Today, because we are more interconnected with our neighbors than at any other time in history, challenges to regional public health represent a growing threat to U.S. health security as well as the long-term stability of weak or developing states. One might even classify "health problems," particularly pandemics, as a growing transnational nonstate actor that has the potential to seriously destabilize Latin America and the Caribbean without a single shot being fired or illicit activity being performed.

For example, according to the 2009 Failed States Index by the Fund for Peace, one indicator of failed states is the progressive deterioration of public services, including health and sanitation.[1] Though not the sole factor contributing to the decline of states, health concerns, if ignored, can become a serious threat on a local, regional, and even global scale. DOD will never be the lead agency in providing health security or increased access to health services—nor should we be. We *do*, however, recognize the growing threats to security posed by endemic health problems. We *do* understand that poor health conditions are a definite factor contributing to rising instability and eventual conflict, and thus we *can* and *must* do all that we can to help create and ensure the conditions of security so that NGOs and other U.S. and foreign agencies can do their jobs in a safe and permissive environment.

Our concepts of "security" and "health" have been viewed as separate focal areas—disconnected, and purposely so. "Security" connotes primarily political, military, and increasingly economic indicators of stability and success, whereas "health" has been relegated to a "merely" humanitarian concern. Health initiatives have focused on improving quality of life in underdeveloped nations, mainly using disease eradication and increased access to health care. Today, though improvement of public health continues to be largely a humanitarian concern, it has also taken on a necessarily more pressing security dimension. An inability to detect and treat an emerging disease, for example, can lead to both a decrease in economic productivity, as well as to an increased probability of exporting this disease and allowing it to transform into a pandemic, particularly in today's increasingly interconnected world.[2] Preventing the spread of infectious disease must be just one of our health priorities as we seek to educate, train, and engage with the military and security forces in the region. Furthermore, although continuing concerns about bioterrorism and pandemic disease tend to dominate discussions of health-related security threats, we also must address the security implications of the state of public health systems in our area of focus.

It may seem at first incongruous for a combatant command, even one which strives to be as interagency-oriented and forward-leaning as U.S. Southern Command, to be engaged in efforts to improve public health. And perhaps it is, particularly if that is how our engagement efforts are expressed or viewed. If, however, we restructure our strategic approach and message to convey that we subscribe to the understanding that "public health" plays a vitally important role in maintaining long-term stability, then we can restate our strategic objectives more along the lines of removing and/or reducing health issues as a potential factor to increased likelihood of conflict. Thus, our continuing commitment to engaging in what some have termed "medical diplomacy" becomes inherently synchronized with our previously stated strategic goals to promote security, enhance stability, and allow for economic prosperity.

And as we continue to emphasize expanding and understanding the definition of security, our roles and missions can and will include a growing list of support functions within the spectrum of public services and institutions. As we have seen, stability, prosperity, and lasting democratic institutions require state security. This, in turn, can be affected and influenced by a wide variety of factors—fed by the two most prevalent and dominant undercurrents and systemic causes of much of the misery and potential insecurity in our region: poverty and socioeconomic inequality. The relatively recent rapid urbanization of Latin America, with its accompanying crowded living conditions, air pollution, and inadequate sanitation, combined with the region's social inequality and poverty, pose increasingly significant health threats. Thus the rate of growth outpaced the ability of society to keep up. These social challenges can also breed discontent as people recognize the tremendous disparity in access to health care and social services to which they should have equal opportunity access.[3]

A recent joint study by the Center for Strategic and International Studies and Massachusetts Institute of Technology showed that poor countries are more than twice as likely as wealthy countries to suffer a political crisis in the next 2 years.[4] This study then correlated infant mortality rates with the degree of poverty in a nation: poor countries exhibited an infant mortality rate in the highest quartile of the global distribution, while wealthy countries possessed the lowest infant mortality rates. Despite few studies existing that directly relate health concerns and violence, reduced productivity stemming from poor health will further increase poverty, which has been linked conclusively to high rates of violent crime. Further, lack of access to health care is often related to high poverty rates, which predict crime.[5] Correspondingly, income inequality is often considered as one of the main factors that increase the prevalence of crime and violence, including gang membership and illicit trafficking.[6]

An Inter-American Development Bank report calculates that violence can cost a staggering amount—up to 6 percent of GDP in some countries—when one accounts for the provision of services for the injured party, the infrastructure to support those services, and the lost productivity.[7] Thus, increasing health security and improving the conditions that would lead to a sustained capability to provide these services for a populace, will have a direct and positive impact on reducing the rates of crime, thereby allowing for increased economic development. Preventing armed conflict is always preferable to fighting one; thus, the more ways we can proactively engage in and support efforts to mitigate the effects of poverty, the farther along we will be on our journey to long-term security and stability in the region.

Southern Command has and must continue to play a vital role as one member of a whole-of-government team carrying out a thoughtfully crafted and integrated health engagement strategy for this region. We must persist in striving to identify optimal ways to address the most pressing health security issues in the region. Our efforts must be handled in a multifaceted manner in order to facilitate a greater sense of "citizen security," which will lead, in turn, to greater national security and enduring stability. Our approach at Southern Command has been to focus on the operational elements of implementation, as well as supporting the development of a holistic strategy that incorporates our interagency, international, and nongovernmental partners. Engagement with the region must continue to occur, and it is imperative for a long-term coherent strategy to be anchored in clearly articulated vital national interests. As with many of the challenges that exist in our region that cannot be restrained by geographic or institutional borders and boundaries, achieving and enhancing health security are greater challenges than any one agency or nation can handle—we need to work in concert with our partner nations, other U.S. Government agencies, and NGOs to be most effective in allocating finite resources toward specific problems.

To this end, our approach at U.S. Southern Command has been to champion and support sustainable development of health resources and care in a context of positive, consistent, and enduring regional engagement. We in DOD possess certain and unique capabilities and the capacity to help partner nations improve their health care capability, especially if we leverage our relationships with NGOs, businesses, and U.S. agencies. Our goal is not to provide health care for the entire region, but rather to build our partners' capability—and then strive to ensure a long-term capacity—for treating their own populations and for responding to health emergencies, both those arising from infectious diseases and those from humanitarian crises.

Our health engagement should be just one component of the overarching integrated strategy for health security and stability as delineated by the State Department and other agencies and organizations. We must refrain from the temptation to "go it alone" or get impatient when the wheels of bureaucracy and diplomacy do not turn as rapidly as we would like. We cannot conduct these health security–related missions and exercises—to include HA/DR and medical and dental readiness training exercises (MEDRETEs and DENTRETEs, respectively)—in an ad hoc or poorly coordinated manner without consideration of other agencies' stability operations. Enhanced and open interagency and partner cooperation is crucial to the success of future security and stability operations.

As previously mentioned, Southern Command's participation in health engagement directly supports our primary focus of achieving and furthering national and regional security objectives. There are also numerous secondary benefits to such engagement—some of which are viewed as equally, if not more, important than health security. First, U.S. military presence that is associated with humanitarian missions, instead of offensive and intrusive military action, will show the United States cares about the region for more than just its own national security—for example, only engaging via counternarcotics or transnational terrorism threats. Such consistent and enduring engagement in the area of health security will show that we also truly care about the long-term security, stability, and ultimately shared prosperity full of hope and equal opportunity for all who call this region home. As shown by DOD's experience in Indonesia after the 2004 tsunami, aid can produce a significant amount of sustained goodwill toward the United States, and particularly toward its military.[8] Putting a face to the U.S. military, especially when the face is that of a doctor performing surgeries, or that of a SeaBees team building a medical center, can only be a force for improving international relations and creating a positive perception of the United States. We should also remember, however, that this strategy is not novel—Cuban doctors have been deploying throughout the region and across the globe for almost 50 years, and have had great success in garnering positive public opinion.[9] We should provide a similar example to be able to display our product in this competitive marketplace of public opinion. We need to do a better job of taking some deserved credit for the countless hours of truly selfless dedication and altruistic pursuits that have an added benefit of helping to reduce security concerns, challenges, and threats to the residents of this hemisphere.

Still another benefit is that continued health care and health security engagements provide outstanding training opportunities for selected U.S. forces and personnel to deploy to a nonhostile area and practice the skills they will need on a battlefield or other high-intensity conflict situation. These skill sets range from logistics planning to construction in remote areas to providing initial medical care that transitions into longer-term sustained health care and rehabilitative efforts. Being able to train and work with the partner nation medical professionals, volunteers, and security personnel on these and other vitally important health-related missions provides a clear benefit to both sides and can be a cornerstone in forging and fostering long-term cooperative arrangements and enduring relationships based on the most human needs. Thus, health engagement in Latin America and the Caribbean provides a moral foundation upon which sovereign nations can build. As they see our lasting commitment to improving the lives of our neighbors and contributing to the betterment of our shared home, perhaps our friends and even competitors will be inspired to contribute in meaningful ways to humanitarian work that enhances regional security and stability, in addition to working to develop and maintain an internal capacity to sustain the skill sets being created through such endeavors.

Southern Command has taken great strides in forming new partnerships with NGOs and we seek to work ever more extensively to maximize the effect of HA/DR missions. NGOs are not necessarily constrained by U.S. Government statutory regulations, and thus their funding usually comes with fewer caveats and restrictions. By cooperating with them, we can learn from them and leverage their expertise and resources to improve our ability to effect improvements in the overall level of health security in an area. Forging trust, cooperation, and teamwork between two nontraditional and perhaps historically noncompatible entities like the military and certain humanitarian-focused NGOs is important as it allows us to present an entirely different image and convey a softer message of engagement instead of presence being construed as occupation or some other imperial pursuit. In return, we are able to offer the NGOs the ability to expand the scope of their endeavors and to conduct health-related missions that would normally be prohibitively expensive or impossible because their desired location for aid or engagement may be a nonpermissive environment because of threats to their personal security. Even by just providing transportation for their personnel and material on a space-available basis, we enable NGOs to devote more of their finite fiscal resources into much-needed supplies and other areas.

Often, opponents of the military's involvement in development operations will argue that aid should only be administered by neutral groups because the military has some Machiavellian intent in conducting any such operation. They claim the military will always be seeking access to a region for its assets or basing rights or "hearts and minds," rather than for purely humanitarian reasons. This is an undeniable secondary benefit of conducting HA/DR and similarly focused missions, but this should not be the primary focus. The intent of providing training, education, and services to populations is not to precipitate a *quid pro quo* situation, but rather to increase health care quality, access, and capacity to facilitate security and stability within our shared home.

Return on Investment

In 2008, a group of experts composed of eight Nobel Prize laureates and renowned academicians met to set cost-effective priorities for increasing global welfare, particularly focusing on developing countries. Their conclusions, titled the Copenhagen Consensus, laid out 30 priorities, of which 12 addressed malnutrition and disease. The solution with the best cost-to-benefit ratio was providing micronutrient supplements for children, with other top solutions including expanded childhood immunization, de-worming and nutrition programs at school, and malaria prevention and treatment.[10] While the panel's findings were not exclusive to Southern Command's region of focus, its recommendations should nonetheless be included in health engagement strategies because: 1) they have been deemed to be highly cost-effective in the prevention of conflict; and 2), the benefits to lives and economic potential far outweigh the required initial investment in care and education.

Further Copenhagen Consensus research assessed that addressing health security issues is not prohibitively expensive; modeling exercises have been done that show that training health care providers on specific protocols for diagnosing and treating common childhood diseases is extremely beneficial when initial quality is low and disease incidence is high—children's lives can be saved for as little as $14 in preventive treatment.[11] Certainly, this is a relatively cost-effective process. Still further, some studies show that 1 extra year of life expectancy gained for a country can produce a per capita GDP increase of 4 percent.[12] This increase can be crucial to economic growth and development, as well as their associated positive effects. As we address health care and its role in health security, we can also look at integrating crime and violence prevention programs into our efforts at improving health education, especially in high-risk zones.

On the other side of the spectrum, other opponents will argue that military resources should not be wasted on missions that fall clearly into the operating lanes of other government agencies. The bottom line is that the military is primarily a war fighting organization; however, if we seek to ensure stability by improving the level of health security of the region, then there should be an undeniable role for the military in humanitarian and other medical and health security–related missions. While relatively expensive compared to other agencies' operating budgets, the missions make up only a small fraction of the total DOD budget. Analysts estimate a recent $20 million humanitarian mission of the USS *Peliteu* to Southeast Asia to be equivalent to just 10 percent of U.S. daily operating costs in Iraq and Afghanistan.[13]

> Not only with the military help that the United States has been offering, but the humanitarian assistance helps to reaffirm the special bond between the American and Colombian people.
>
> —Juan Manuel Santos Calderon
> Minister of Defense, Colombia,
> on board USNS *Comfort*

> This type of diplomacy really touched the heart and soul of the country and the region and is the most effective way to counter the false perception of what Cuban medical teams are doing in the region.
>
> —Elias Antonio Saca Gonzalez
> President of El Salvador,
> on board USNS *Comfort*

We share a vital connection with the wonderful and diverse nations of the Americas. Today, more than ever, common interests interweave the fabric of this beautiful hemisphere. We share common challenges and opportunities; and our futures are inextricably linked. As such, we pursue a host of programs designed to foster security, stability, and goodwill in the region, with the ultimate goal of enabling the spread of true and lasting prosperity to the approximately 460 million people living in this part of the world.

At Southern Command, we are committed to being good partners—and to being the partner of choice throughout the region. Every day, year after year, we dedicate the majority of our resources toward building the security capabilities of our partners, while working to encourage an environment of cooperation among all of the nations in the region. This involves numerous training exercises, educational programs, technology-sharing, intelligence-sharing, security procurement assistance, humanitarian aid, and a myriad of other programs. We endeavor to improve our region's ability to respond to today's and tomorrow's security challenges. Through a steady improvement in security, we can help create the conditions that will enable this region to counter the poverty and inequality that have gripped it for so long.

In terms of military-to-military contact, Latin America and the Caribbean represent many opportunities for U.S. engagement. Of the 31 countries and 10 protectorates in the region, only 2 are land-locked. Maritime engagement has a huge potential for positive effects, especially because the United States has already established a long history of maritime contact and cooperation with most of the region. As a result, we have witnessed numerous positive results from integrating many initiatives originating from nontraditional approaches to the nonconventional challenges we have alluded to thus far. These missions are relatively low visibility, but they can have a huge impact on U.S. military and partner nation military and security force readiness, particularly when they are done in a consistent and enduring manner. Exercises like UNITAS provide excellent forums for military-to-military relationship-building, as well as multilateral HA/DR training, and we have been involved with this wonderful event for 50 years, hosting the 50th Anniversary exercise and celebration in Jacksonville in 2009.

Building confidence, capability, and cooperation among partners is essential to confronting today's security challenges. Our exercise Fuerzas Aliadas (Allied Forces) Panamax has matured over the last 7 years and has become one of our flagship programs. Panamax is a multinational and interagency exercise that focuses on defending the Panama Canal from traditional and nontraditional threats. The exercise began in 2003 as a limited naval exercise with just three participating nations. Due to past successes and efforts to expand partnerships, the exercise has grown to include a roster of more than 20 nations, several U.S. departments and agencies, international organizations, nongovernmental organizations, and multiple military branches of service.

Cosponsored by Panama, Chile, and the United States, this year's exercise formed a truly integrated international force—Multinational Force–South. The force was led by Southern Command's Army component, U.S. Army South, but the maritime components were headed by Admirals from Chile and Brazil. While the exercise scenarios focus on the security of the Panama Canal, this type of integrated multinational training certainly benefits any response to real-world threats in our region—conventional or unconventional. From responses to catastrophic disasters to United Nations–mandated multinational forces, this type of collaborative training has already proven to be indispensable. In addition to the security scenario focused on the Panama Canal, Panamax also included a multinational peace-keeping battalion training event, an interagency Proliferation Security Initiative training event focused on the shipment of weapons of mass destruction, and, what is arguably our most important and farthest reaching mission area, multinational humanitarian training and assistance/disaster-relief training. We integrated the health-security aspects of Panamax to assist the Government of Panama with synchronizing its interagency homeland security exercise, Panamax Alpha, with Panamax and facilitated for the first time the involvement and support of the Defense Threat Reduction Agency, the U.S. Coast Guard, and the Federal Emergency Management Agency.

Joint, international, interagency, and public-private involvement is the essence of Panamax. The collaborative integration of participants and helpful lessons learned this year were exceptional. The increased participation and scope of Panamax over the years underscore the significance the international community places on cooperative efforts and strong partnerships as pillars of worldwide security and stability.

Along these lines, one of our most visible and successful initiatives toward building partner capability and capacity in the health security arena has been Continuing Promise. In 2007, for the first time, we sent a hospital ship—the USNS *Comfort*—with its specifically tailored joint, interagency, international, and private sector crew—on a 4-month tour of Latin America and the Caribbean to bring modern medical care and conduct medical training in 12 countries. It was a tremendous success. Over 385,000 patient treatments were completed, along with 1,170 surgeries, more than 20 community-improvement projects, 17,700 livestock vaccinations, and more than 25,000 dental patients treated. Throughout the deployment, our personnel received vital training, and our message of positive commitment to the region and to its peoples penetrated deep and touched millions. This effort combined multiple military services, multinational integration, and medical professionals from the private sector.

The success of the mission, combined with uniquely integrated medical and construction training for our personnel, spurred the conception of Continuing Promise 2008. Since the Navy only has two dedicated hospital ships, the Navy sourced our request to repeat the *Comfort* mission in 2008 with two large amphibious ships. Building upon the lessons learned from the *Comfort*, we increased mission duration from 4 to 7 months, increased contact time in each port, and integrated more partners for the undertaking.

The two ships carried a mix of military, interagency, multinational, and even nongovernmental medical and health specialists. Along with this diverse medical team, we embarked military engineers, construction experts, Navy and Marine Corps helicopters and crews, and military training experts. This uniquely designed team was tailored to training and humanitarian missions, but had the flexibility to easily transition to disaster-relief efforts should the need arise—which it ultimately did.

One of the ships, the USS *Boxer*, completed the Pacific phase of Continuing Promise with superb results: over 65,000 total patient treatments, including 127 surgeries, 4,000 optometry patients treated, 14,000 dental procedures, medical and military training for thousands of host-nation students, and construction projects at almost a dozen sites. The second ship, the USS *Kearsarge*, completed the Atlantic phase in November, and its joint, international, and nongovernmental medical professionals worked alongside host nation officials to treat more than 145,000 patients in six countries. The crew also dispensed more than 81,000 prescriptions, provided veterinary care to nearly 5,600 animals, and completed various construction and renovation projects in each of the countries visited during the mission.

As an example of the flexibility of this type of venture deployed in our region, after Haiti was struck by successive tropical storms and Hurricane Ike in September, the *Kearsarge* diverted from its planned stop in Colombia to respond to this emergent humanitarian crisis. Supporting relief efforts led by the USAID's Office of Foreign Disaster Assistance, the *Kearsarge* and its crew delivered 3.3 million pounds of food, water, and other relief supplies to Haitian communities devastated by the storms.

In 2009, USNS *Comfort* returned to our waters and again far exceeded everyone's expectations in numbers of patients encountered and treated, numbers of relationships forged, and lasting impact on various host nation populations. With over 100,000 patients seen, 1,600 surgeries performed, 135,000 pharmacies dispensed, 13,000 animals treated, and 37,000 students trained, we were able to engage on a scale previously unimaginable just 4 years ago. But the impact on the host nations was more than just numbers—the *types* of procedures performed and training conducted spoke to the long-term positive effects on society and citizen security as our joint, combined, and integrated crews focused on hysterectomies, thyroids, cataract removals, and education on prevention.

On the engineering side, over 14,000 man-hours were worked by 21 Construction Battalion (SeaBees) personnel as they repaired and improved five hospitals and clinics; provided refurbishments to seven schools; and renovated one baseball field. In addition, in direct support of existing USAID projects, *Comfort* personnel assisted in a laboratory completion in the Dominican Republic and assisted in dock repairs in Panama that buttressed a USAID eco-tourism project. Perhaps even more impressive was the Sea-Bees showcase project at Exporcol School, where they built three classrooms, a kitchen, and a playground from the ground up for the neighborhood of Exporcol in Tumaco, Colombia. The community now has a functioning school which was nonexistent prior to the SeaBees' arrival. As a result, the children of Tumaco will no longer have to attend school in shifts.

From a partnership perspective, during the 2009 deployment, 271 NGO representatives served on board and ashore, 60 partner nation personnel were embarked, and 84 medical essential billets were filled, which increased the overall surgical capacity on board *Comfort* by 30 percent. These invaluable medical professionals volunteered to fill critical roles as medical doctors and nurses, ophthalmologists, veterinarians, dentists, preventive medicine practitioners, plastic surgeons, anesthesiologists, and even a speech therapist. Our engagement and partnering with the private sector also yielded an overwhelming response in the form of donations, as the deployment received over 4 million dollars in contributions, including $1.4 million in high-nutrition meals, medicines and medical supplies, hospital beds and wheelchairs, school supplies, clothing, and first aid kits. Two specific recipients felt the greatest impact as both the Angel Missions and the Children's International Lifeline received more food, medicine, and supplies during *Comfort*'s short visit than either would have received in 3 years of normal operations.

U.S. Navy (Mass Communication Specialist 2ⁿ Class Joshua Karsten)

The USNS *Comfort*—with its specifically tailored joint, international, and private sector crew—sailed on a 4-month tour of Latin America and the Caribbean in 2007, bringing modern medical care and conducting training in 12 countries. U.S. personnel received vital training as well, and their message of positive commitment to the region and its people penetrated deep and touched millions.

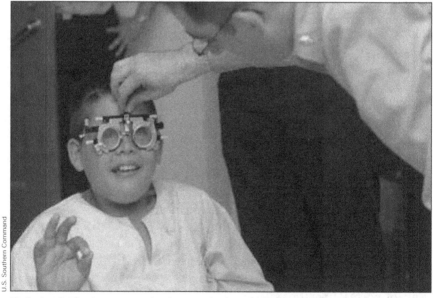

U.S. Southern Command

Medical professionals treat young boy for corrective lenses on board USNS *Comfort* as part of exercise Continuing Promise 2007.

Through postdeployment polling completed by the Center for Naval Analyses, 62 percent of the host nation populations polled reported a significant and positive change in their opinion of the United States, citing the fact that most of the care was focused on previously marginalized neighborhoods and citizens and the personal interaction with and treatment from the medical providers. In addition to creating a lasting impression that the United States cares about the lives of our neighbors and that this type of engagement has continued for 3 consecutive years, other noted impacts of the visits included a demonstration of U.S. goodwill to new governments; a collaborative venue for host nation militaries and their governments; the generation of an interagency planning and execution opportunity for each host nation; and, finally, the definitive change in the attitude of Tumaco residents toward fixing their *own* community. Over the past 3 years, Continuing Promise has been an incredibly successful mission that further advanced our strategic messaging and built confidence, capability, and goodwill in numerous countries in the region serving as a visible and lasting counterweight to anti-U.S. messaging.

More than just a medical mission, these humanitarian service groups (HSGs) have provided dental care to about 50,000 patients, conducted medical training for almost 60,000 host nation students and medical providers, and sponsored over 40 construction and restoration projects at local schools and health care facilities. These visits also extended veterinarian services throughout their journeys, treating and vaccinating thousands of animals, which constitute the livelihood of many families. This shining example of enduring engagement for the greater health security of the region also has become a symbol of goodwill and has brought renewed hope to those who might have given up on a healthy future, as well as to those who might have previously been sympathetic to anti-U.S. rhetoric. Continuing Promise has directly changed the lives of many and indirectly touched the lives of several hundred thousand throughout our shared home.

While our programs and initiatives focus primarily on security—the absolute bedrock upon which the foundation for lasting stability and long-term prosperity is built—increasingly our approach has expanded and is just one effort that supports a broader national approach to true partnering and engagement in the Western Hemisphere. Access to health care is such a critical component of stability and the *Comfort*'s mission is only one of many medical outreach efforts. For example, Southern Command also sponsors MEDRETEs and DENTRETEs, consisting of military medical teams that treat over a quarter of a million patients annually in the region, focusing primarily on needy rural, isolated populations.

These unique training exercises have had tremendous impact inland across the region at over 75 separate locations—changing lives, providing alternative perceptions, and spreading goodwill through quality donated medical assistance. Key to this success is a novel approach to partnering that combines the synergistic efforts of a diverse group of experts from U.S. and international militaries, nongovernmental organizations, and volunteers and donations from the U.S. private sector. This integrated approach highlights the power of creative public-private partnerships to show our true interest in, and eternal commitment to, the people of the Americas. As the new smile upon the visage of every child after facial reconstructive surgery will certainly attest, this is vitally important work and the positive effects can last a lifetime.

Besides medical programs, Southern Command sponsors numerous other humanitarian projects, ranging from planned events such as the construction of wells, community centers, and medical facilities to rapid response missions in the wake of disasters. We also conduct frequent military training exercises with our partners, send thousands of partner military and civilian experts to various leading academic institutions, and provide other critical security assistance to our friends in the region. Throughout the years, Southern Command's Humanitarian Assistance Program has augmented traditional military-to-civilian engagement activities in order to increase our partner nations' ability to respond independently to natural and man-made disasters. Our program helps local populations who could benefit from completed projects such as schools, clinics, community centers, orphanages, emergency operations centers, disaster response warehouses, wells, and potable water systems. In 2008 alone, we completed 49 construction projects and provided critical training programs for first responders, disaster managers, firefighters, and disaster warehouse managers.

A close corollary to the Humanitarian Assistance Program is the New Horizons series of joint and combined humanitarian assistance exercises that U.S. Southern Command conducts with Latin American and Caribbean nations. These exercises provide readiness training for U.S. Engineer, Medical, and Combat Service Support units, but also provide great benefit to the host nation. Each New Horizons exercise lasts several months and usually takes place in remote areas. U.S. Southern Command strives to combine these efforts with those of host nation doctors and civic personnel. In 2007, we conducted these exercises with four nations—Belize, Guatemala, Nicaragua, and Panama. We built on this in both 2008 and 2009, building relationships and capacity in six additional nations.

U.S. Engineer, Medical, and Combat Service Support units participate in New Horizons Guatemala, a joint and combined humanitarian assistance exercise that U.S. Southern Command conducts to strengthen ties with partner nations. These exercises provide readiness training for U.S. units, but are also of great benefit to the host nation. U.S. Southern Command strives to combine these efforts with those of host nation doctors and civic personnel.

Also demonstrating U.S. goodwill, Southern Command directed military forces to provide disaster relief to six of our partner nations in times of dire need. These disaster relief operations, which were integrated with USAID-led efforts and those of the international community, helped alleviate the suffering of many and assisted affected regions in their recovery. Specifically, in one 8-month span in 2008, we provided much needed flood relief to Bolivia in March, quickly provided assistance to Peru following an earthquake in August, and aided Belize after the passage of Hurricane Dean. We were critical first-responders to a Nicaraguan request for relief following Hurricane Felix in September, arranged the procurement of firefighting equipment for Paraguay during a widespread wildfire also in September, and assisted the Dominican Republic after Tropical Storm Noel ravaged the island nation in October.

In almost every case, our Joint Task Force–Bravo (JTF–B), located in Soto Cano, Honduras, was a major contributor to the success of these disaster relief operations. Essentially a small, joint air wing comprised of 18 helicopters, JTF–B is our only permanently deployed contingency force in the region. JTF–B responds to crises as a first-responder and routinely participates in humanitarian assistance, disaster relief, search and rescue, personnel recovery, and noncombatant medical evacuations. JTF–B has a long history of answering the call for assistance and is a tremendously valuable asset to U.S. Southern Command's partnership and goodwill efforts in the region.

In addition to conducting exercises that build understanding and multinational cooperation, U.S. Southern Command conducts a comprehensive Theater Security Cooperation program to develop the capability and capacity of our partners to respond to mutual security threats of many different forms, including those related to health security—either independently or with regional partners. The overarching maritime strategy that encompasses this approach is called Partnership of the Americas (POA), and for 3 straight years, Southern Command has conducted a maritime POA event in our region.

Evolving from the initial 1-month event in 2006, POA 2008 involved a 6-month Navy and Marine Corps mission throughout Latin America and the Caribbean that focused on enhancing relationships with regional partners and improving operational readiness and interoperability. During the most recent deployment, a four-ship multinational task force circumnavigated South America, participated in several multinational exercises sponsored by Southern Command, and conducted theater security cooperation and community relations events on shore. Our POA events serve as visible symbols of U.S. commitment to bilateral and multilateral military cooperation and have evolved into comprehensive engagement missions that maximize exposure to international partners and local communities.

Another multinational exercise—Tradewinds—focuses on transnational threats in the Caribbean Basin. This successful exercise brings together security forces and interagency personnel from 18 nations to practice coordinated first-responder, fire, police, and military responses to security threats. The exercise scenarios emphasize basic security operations, counterdrug activities, and disaster preparedness in a field environment with a focus on regional cooperation.

In addition, we sponsored the pilot deployment of a new U.S. Navy program called Global Fleet Station. This innovative new concept provides a modular platform for sustained engagement tailored to each unique region. This floating theater security cooperation platform hosted more than 5,000 military and civilian personnel and involved a joint, multinational, and interagency approach at each training site. *Swift* has also conducted community relations projects in each port to refurbish local schools and community centers and to deliver tons of donated goodwill materials.

As with *Comfort*, this type of deployment represents the future of engagement—visible, persistent, scalable, and cooperative engagement that trains our personnel and demonstrates the goodwill of the United States while building partner nation security capabilities.

Our region is not all water, however. Thus, to complement our robust maritime programs, we are extremely excited about revamping land engagements with a young program called Beyond the Horizon. This program aims to maximize the impact of our land events by increasing the number of "microburst" engagements—engineer construction, small unit familiarization, subject matter exchanges, medical readiness training exercises—as well as establishing longer-term programs that integrate the efforts of other U.S. Federal agencies, host nations, and the private sector.

We have accomplished much with these exercises, operations, and training opportunities, but there is still much more work that remains. We will look to increase the duration and number of countries visited through Continuing Promise and other similar efforts as part of the Partnership for the Americas, which will build on the successful missions of the *Comfort*, *Kearsarge*, and *Boxer*. These deployments will highlight consistent and enduring engagement with innovative approaches and initiatives that build and leverage strong interagency, multinational, and public-private cooperation. In so doing, we will continue to track along our command heading: understanding the linkages the United States shares with the region; working together with partners to overcome shared challenges; and fulfilling the promise of a secure, cooperating, and prospering hemisphere through innovative and effective strategic initiatives.

> It is a privilege for the second time to be on board this fabulous ship, the *Comfort*—messenger of peace, hope and alleviator of suffering. The ship is an alleviator of suffering and hope for the people, it is a messenger from the United States government for those who suffer from health problems regardless of their ideological or political affiliations but who share the common problem of extreme poverty.
>
> —Jaime Morales
> Vice President, Nicaragua

To continue to be this messenger, we need to communicate effectively that the United States cares about the people of the region—and that we will continue to do our part to help fulfill the promise of the Americas for the duration of the journey. We also need to demonstrate how we are engaged positively on security issues throughout the region. A good portion of our task might simply involve building a wider recognition of all that we currently do in the region—taking some deserved credit if you will—while also developing new ways of connecting with the people of this vibrant and dynamic region. Most importantly, all our endeavors need to harness and emphasize the natural alignments and shared interests between the nations of the Americas. Despite our differences, we continue to grow more economically and culturally interconnected and interdependent and our shared security challenges prove that we are *all*, in fact, on this journey together.

As we look to the future, we see the increasing importance of developing innovative subregional, regional, and hemispheric partnerships to combat transnational security threats. Our current and future security needs require a cooperation that goes beyond mere agreements on the desire to work together. This cooperation needs to be concrete and able to adapt as the willful threat adapts. It needs to combine a multiagency, multinational, and private sector approach to security. But several key prerequisites need to be met before this level of cooperation can take place.

First, we need to earn and maintain trust in order to keep the partners we have and to develop new ones. Our unified approach will require consistent and effective resources, cohesive strategic messaging, and innovative and earnest information-sharing across the board. Second, we need to reexamine the various exercises, programs, and partnerships we sponsor in the region and find innovative ways to make them more inclusive and more effective at communicating our connection to the peoples of the region. Paramount to this effort will be finding the right size and shape of participation with which each nation or agency is comfortable. Participation can range from international peacekeeping operations and humanitarian assistance to large multinational events like the UNITAS and Panamax exercises.

Last, but not least, we need to do a better job of relating and publicizing the efforts of all U.S. agencies and of our own private sector. There is a tremendous amount of good the United States does in the region—from billions of U.S. foreign direct investment, to millions of nongovernmental volunteer hours, to the quarter million medical patients Southern Command treats each year. But often we do not tell our story well, particularly in a way that can help us counter the image that the United States does not pay enough attention to the region. If we employ all of these methods, we will achieve more effective and stronger security partnerships. Coming together and forging lasting cooperative relationships centered on issues of health, humanitarian assistance, and disaster relief offer a framework and opportunity for engagement that exists outside the realm of contentious and highly politicized matters of foreign policy. We need to seize and take advantage of this fact.

U.S. Southern Command hopes to do its part to make these partnerships work. Our evolving engagement strategy commits us to build the security capability of our military counterparts and to expand the capacity for all of us to work together. One way we seek to foster such partnering is an initiative designed to harness the vast potential of public-private sector cooperative ventures in the region. We created a staff structure and engagement plan to tap into these private sector resources and combine their goodwill efforts to our outreach programs. As an example, we use the U.S. Navy's global outreach program, Project Handclasp, to transport materials donated by the U.S. private sector—such as ambulances, school supplies, high-nutrition meals, and children's bicycles—and distribute them as Navy ships pull into ports in our region.

In April of 2009, Project Handclasp, as part of its Million Meals Initiative and Clean Water Initiative, provided the following to hurricane-ravaged Haiti: 1,425,600 high-nutrition meals (which weighed over 217,000 pounds), water filter capability for 350 institutions/homes (each filtration system possesses a 10-year life span), pharmaceuticals valued at over $268,000, medical materials, hygienic supplies, wheelchairs, and stuffed animal toys for children. The expiration dates of pharmaceuticals ranged from more than 1 to more than 3 years from the date of presentation in Haiti.

The high-nutrition meals consisted of fortified soy rice casserole, a product formulated in consultation with Cargill, Pillsbury, General Mills, and Archer Daniels Midland to meet all nutritional requirements for physical health and mental capacity of severely malnourished children, as well as healthy adults. This protein and nutrient-rich formula is a comprehensive and easily digestible product for reversing the starvation process and restoring health and mental alertness. Project Handclasp obtained private sector donations to transport the meals to the ship at no cost. Project Handclasp provided 350 institutions/homes with water for drinking, washing, and bathing for up to 10 years. The filters are portable, easy to use, affordable, and don't need electricity. An analysis of the point-of-use water technologies recognized by the World Health Organization ranked this as the top-rated technology.

Only through building new, capable relationships such as the shining example Project Handclasp embodies—inside and outside government, on both the domestic and international fronts—will we be able to match our strategic outlook to effective unified action, particularly when confronting threats and challenges that do not fall clearly into operating lanes typically reserved for DOD. Only through a robust commitment to partnering will we be able to gain and maintain the critical regional friendships we need for the security of our hemisphere. We truly *are* all in this together—collectively, the nations of the Americas are better poised to meet head-on whatever the future holds in order to bring about a stable, prosperous, and secure future in this special part of the world that we share.

It is difficult to assess precisely the overall impact of training missions with humanitarian benefits of this scale. But based upon the positive local and international press, the number of national leadership visits, and the vast number of people touched by the USNS *Comfort* missions and *Kearsarge* and *Boxer* deployments, we believe they were a significant success. Certainly, there are many lessons learned from these unique and paradigm-shifting deployments to Latin America and the Caribbean—and we will incorporate them into any future deployments—but the integrated and cooperative nature of this mission really serves as a model for the future of engagement and training: *Joint, Combined, Interagency, International, and Public-Private.* We plan to conduct similar missions on a regular basis as part of our continuing fulfillment of our partnership and cooperation with regional neighbors.

With the goal in mind of creating conditions for empowering the population, Southern Command will need to tailor its efforts to include the local health professionals in as many events and projects as possible. Current missions already make efforts to include local health care providers and administrators. Ideally, we envision partner nations' health care professionals deploying on tours similar to Continuing Promise (CP) missions, either in a joint role with the United States, or even perhaps in a self-initiated, sustainable, multinational effort. Before that point, we need to continue building and fostering host nation commitment to the participation in and support of medical missions in the region, both to promote education and to ensure that the mission is seen by inhabitants of the region as a cooperative effort, not an imperial one. Host nation involvement in preparing their populations for U.S.-led missions can make a significant difference in the allocation of services to the right individuals. As seen in CP 2009, if the local ministry of health is engaged and cooperative, the mission's efficacy will be maximized for the local populace.

In addition to recognizing and being pleased with short-term gains and advances in initial health care and security, as well as with local populations' positive perceptions of the United States, we need to always remember to adjust our lens to a longer focal length and ensure we are devoting the proper amount of time, energy, and resources to the enduring strategic objectives. To that end, we can focus more on the education and sanitation components of health care and security. Though the statistics are more quotable when referencing numbers of immunizations given or surgeries performed, many of the Copenhagen Consensus solutions involve longer-term solutions to health security challenges. While the military may not necessarily be able to provide courses of vitamin A supplements (as the Consensus suggests) to every child under the age of five in the Americas—nor should we necessarily attempt to take on such an endeavor unilaterally—our presence in the region *does* give us many opportunities for interaction on a vast array of humanitarian issues.

One novel tactic was implemented during CP 2009 and can be duplicated on a bigger scale. A large fraction of the more than 100,000 patients who came in for a consult were much more interested in receiving a small supply of vitamins and Tylenol for themselves and their children than they were in addressing a serious and/or chronic medical concern. If those people could be identified in the first steps of screening the potential patients, they could be gathered into separate groups for instruction from a corpsman, nurse, or doctor to receive general health education and preventive medicine materials *before* they received their vitamin handout. Considering the mostly generic and nonemergent nature of the patients' complaints, this process could serve to maximize the effective use of our health providers' time and resources while in-country; more importantly, however, it would greatly assist in providing the benefits of long-term health education, basic sanitation principles, and health awareness.

Education can help to create the conditions for empowering local populations to improve their public health milieu. USAID provided $390 million last year to "invest in people and humanitarian assistance," an objective that includes increasing access to health care, basic education, and training. Southern Command should work with agencies like USAID to support their missions; they too have recognized that education and training are central to creating sustainable successes. To further elaborate on this, Ambassador Ivonne A-Baki, the 2007–2009 President of the Andean Parliament, believes that "It is common to view economic development and poverty reduction as two separate issues. Programs and policies for economic development should go hand in hand with programs to reduce poverty. In fact, reducing poverty by investing in education and health care is the best way of achieving economic development."[14]

Another way to assist in the long-term development and sustainment of the level of health care and security is to encourage local buy-in on programs. Continuing commitment to involve local leadership and organizations, especially local doctors, will be essential in promulgating our message and ensuring effective and accurate engagement. Subject Matter Expert Exchange (SMEE) is a program that exists to educate the host nation health care providers by having U.S. military and partner NGOs give instruction on public health, veterinarian services, and advanced lifesaving techniques. SMEE sessions, already implemented on the Continuing Promise missions, offer an opportunity for health engagement missions to continue to yield benefits long after the deployment ends. By doing focused local projects and by training the professional health care providers, we also strive to show to the local populations that they have the ability to take ownership and control over efforts to improve their *own* situation. A series of connected wins in the health care arena, whether they involve vaccinations, new disease control and surveillance methods, or enhancing local treatment capacity, are vital to demonstrating that the United States *does care* about the region in a proactive manner and that we *will continue to care* because we are just one inhabitant of a home we share together.

Finally, as within any home or family, sometimes conflicts can develop between the competing objectives. As alluded to at the beginning of this section, health care and humanitarian missions have traditionally been kept separate and omitted from any discussions involving national security strategy and policy. However, as we continue to have ongoing missions and endeavors like Continuing Promise and others that purposely combine "health" with "security," we are going to increasingly find objectives that seemingly are in direct opposition to each other. Humanitarian assistance and disaster relief (HA/DR) training, improving the health of the population, and public relations are frequently cited as major mission objectives. What matters are the order of importance of these goals and the desired endstate of the region receiving aid. If long-term stability of the region is the ultimate goal, then health awareness, health levels, and health security should be considered the primary focus areas. To that end, medical, dental, and public health professionals should optimize U.S. military medical missions to provide the services that will make the greatest difference for the greatest number of patients and will leave an improved health infrastructure. While there are differences of opinion on how to do this best, the missions must be designed primarily to improve the levels of health education, awareness, access, and overall security—only then can this mission area truly be an enabler toward long-term stability.

HA/DR training goals could complicate and conflict with long-term stability goals, at times. Whereas seeking long-term health stability requires extensive cooperation with the host nation to build capacity, HA/DR training limits operations to addressing only acute threats to health. Since HA/DR is not meant to build health care infrastructure per se, it may actually work against long-term health stability when used in nonemergency situations. It is important that the mission be planned carefully to "first, do no harm" to the existing health security capacity. HA/DR training need not conflict with long-term health security goals, but the offices leading the respective missions should be mindful of the potential for disagreement and working toward cross-purposes. The same can be said over the potential to focus on public relations events to the detriment of increasing patient encounters with those in dire need but perhaps of less "political value." Individual health, including a corresponding access to health care, is a cornerstone of citizen security, and this is and should remain true external to and irrespective of any political system or maneuverings. It is an issue that strikes at the most fundamental of our basic human needs. Thus, it is a perfect mission area to find common ground, come together, and forge lasting relationships toward a regionally shared endstate of security and stability. As Scottish philosopher and author Thomas Carlyle once commented, "Ill-health, of body or of mind, is defeat. Health alone is victory. Let all men, if they can manage it, contrive to be healthy!"

This mission represents not only the cooperation, but the dream, the willingness and the future between these countries that morally share a long history in the future of cooperating and looking for ways to bring people closer and improve the quality of life of the people of the Americas.

—Martín Torrijos
President, Panama

I expect to pass through the world but once. Any good therefore that I can do, or any kindness I can show to any creature, let me do it now. Let me not defer it, for I shall not pass this way again.

—Stephen Grellet (1773–1855)
French-American religious leader

Because of ever-increasing rates of regional and global travel and trade, environmental factors, and growing natural resource constraints, the intensity and regional scope of health challenges will continue to increase in the coming years. Health challenges will also progressively be interwoven with other issues, raising their potential significance for U.S. national security. Finally, we must always remember that for the focused regional public health efforts envisioned in this capability to be successful, they must consistently be planned and undertaken with close consideration of the broader development context of a given host nation or subregion. If this is not synchronized and integrated throughout every level of planning to execution, the tireless efforts amount to little more than episodic events and exercises that have a much shorter shelf-life.

In today's complex global and regional environment, promoting human security, health, and development is the order of the day. Thus, U.S. Southern Command, in coordination with other U.S. Government (USG) agencies, seeks to evaluate its humanitarian assistance and disaster relief programs with the same diligence it gives to military campaigns. We are still in the nascent stages of Continuing Promise and our other health-security and humanitarian missions, but already we can see that improved mechanisms for USG interagency communication and coordination are required. Based upon feedback from each of the deployments and exercises, we learned that operators in the field are starving for information, but there is no consistent place to go to find out who is doing what. For example, teams might show up to build a flood control project in one country, only to find out later that another USG agency has just completed one on the same river, but farther upstream. Equally important is a consensus that monitoring and evaluation need to be implemented for all humanitarian and development assistance programs, using similar terms and techniques across USG agencies, based on international standards and best practices. When we build a clinic, how will we know if it was useful, how the host nation felt about it, or whether it was still functioning a year later?

We need to ensure that each word, thought, and deed is improving the overall well-being of the host nation and is in line with our and the host nation government's overall objectives. As we strive to measure the impact of our health security and humanitarian missions and programs, it makes sense to leverage the lessons learned, best practices, and capabilities in the other agencies. This will undoubtedly enhance efficiency and continuity, and we will be one step closer to a true whole-of-government approach—ultimately, a whole-of-*many*-governments approach—on this important issue. Health engagement is an important strategic opportunity for Southern Command specifically, and for the U.S. Government as a whole. Regional health is a definitive indicator and factor in national and regional security. Being able to mobilize nontraditional, soft power elements and integrate them with more traditional resources and approaches in a strategic manner will be an invaluable asset to better addressing emerging/potential regional and global health threats, while also advancing our public diplomacy as a leader in humanitarian assistance and disaster relief.

Many people argue strongly for making public relations the top priority in our regional engagements, so as to maximize U.S.-oriented goodwill.[15] The difference between aiming toward short-term goodwill or long-term health security may seem to be a false choice to many. "Won't every humanitarian aid mission do both?" is the question frequently posed by those who believe that these missions are a win-win for both the goodwill and the stability goals. A small baggy of vitamins and a 10-day supply of Tylenol certainly curry goodwill, but do they constitute a gain in true health security or any sense of long-term stability? Public relations will be a part of every medical aid mission, but if goodwill supplants long-term security and stability as the ultimate objective, then the focus of the missions will inevitably start to shift from maximizing health gains to maximizing positive media exposure. The result will be seen in everything from the dosage sizes given by the pharmacy to the primacy of distinguished visitor visits over medical operations. During any mission, a vast number of "health encounters" can occur, but the question of efficacy looms large in every physician's mind. Though surgeries, medical consults, and vitamins provide for targeted successes and photo opportunities, they do not constitute enduring, comprehensive solutions to the endemic problems of health care, awareness, and security in many of the countries in this region. This is not an argument against promoting goodwill through medical missions—rather, it is an argument for applying the proper emphasis in the planning phases to ensure the missions are designed to maximize both health gains of the region *and* increased goodwill or perception of the

United States. Since one of the ways we seek shared regional security is through healthy populations, public relations should work with and throughout the core medical operations, not as a separate entity or isolated objective. By law, Title 10 of U.S. Code prohibits the use of military personnel for humanitarian missions that do not directly impact the security of either the United States or the host nation. Good press and positive attitudes about the United States, our intentions, and our commitment to the region will ultimately come as supplementary benefits.

One of the most difficult parts of the entire medical engagement enterprise lies in evaluating the effectiveness of the mission. This can be simple when missions are quantifiable: for example, the doctors on the USNS *Comfort* performed X surgeries or handed out Y pairs of eyeglasses to the local populations. Even days of training can be counted for the Seabees and MEDRETE/DENTRETE teams deployed to the region, or we can count qualifications earned by our personnel. Much more difficult to quantify, however, are the long-term effects of our efforts for the citizens of each nation visited. If our goal is not just regional presence, but rather instilling in the populace and governments that this is part of our constant commitment to enduring engagement, then we must not be dissuaded by a lack of short-term, quantifiable effects or results. Our commitment to a health security mission focused on education and prevention must be composed of a series of engagement events that are focused and synchronized to produce maximum effects. We must remember, however, that the effect may not be immediately visible; nevertheless, it needs to be clearly articulated from the outset and sustained throughout—hence the mandatory coupling of deeds to words in our strategic communication.

Ultimately, the measure of the success of our joint efforts will be the health of the populations in the regions we focus upon, though it will be very difficult to isolate the exact impact of DOD efforts in a sea of competing factors. We could measure changes in the number of doctors per population unit; these currently vary throughout the region from a low of 2.2 doctors per 10,000 people in Guyana, to a high of 38.7 in Uruguay.[16] From a strategic standpoint, success comes in the pragmatic form of incremental gains over time, not dramatic shifts in the efficacy of national health care systems. Evaluation might also be possible through the use of polling in areas where U.S. military personnel have visited, to quantify reactions to our presence and, especially over time, what the impact has been, in terms of both U.S. image and medical care. In fact, polling has been performed after each year's health engagement deployment throughout the region thus far, and we will continue to use this valuable source of feedback.

Though it is far from a comprehensive system of indicators of success, increasing the availability of care in measurable ways can help us assess our long-term positive impact on the region.

Before we can assess effectiveness, or carry out missions designed to achieve long-term national and shared regional strategic objectives, however, we must first *have* that strategy. We need to sit down together, all of us who have a part to play in this vitally important mission area of health security—across the interagency community as well as private sector and NGOs—and create a single, comprehensive, integrated, and synchronized overarching health engagement and health security strategy for the U.S. Government. This strategy would be designed to build both the capability and capacity of our partner's health care systems and accompanying infrastructure to provide lasting health security, as well as articulate and assign supported and supporting roles in executing this strategy. It would also need to clearly identify one single agency to coordinate the humanitarian assistance and disaster relief efforts and resources that come from the dozens of participating agencies and entities.

Until such a lead is designated within the existing framework—or a new office to lead such an effort is created—we at Southern Command must strive to integrate our current range of operations that tend to exist more toward the "hard" end of the smart power spectrum with our partner agencies, organizations, and nations who possess a broader skill set of soft power tools and approaches. We also need to ensure there are integration and synchronization to maximize effects and reduce duplication of efforts. Working with the State Department, we can help to coordinate efforts by USAID, HHS/CDC, NGOs, multinational organizations, and other bodies throughout the region so that we are most effective in delivering aid, providing education, participating in disaster relief, and starting to create a lasting health security capability and self-sustaining capacity. The more coordination that occurs between the participating players, the more likely it is, for example, that a MEDRETE deploys to the region and is timed to complement follow-up visits by AID teams or NGOs—quite a harmonious concert would result when all the instruments are playing off the same sheet of music under one masterful conductor!

The benefits of medical diplomacy are myriad, ranging from the simple fact that medical missions help increase the level of health security and positive U.S. perception, to the complex and interrelated positive effects that better health care, access, and security can have on national health indicators, economic performance, and eventual societal stability. As Southern Command seeks to engage our partners and neighbors in a sustained, positive manner, we need to work with *all* our partners—foreign and domestic, military and civilian, public and private—to synchronize efforts, focusing on efficiency and effectiveness, and on improving partner nation capability and capacity. Humanitarian aid and disaster relief missions also serve a diplomatic mission; administrations that are usually critical of U.S. operations in the region find it difficult to deny the non-threatening and benevolent presence of scores of doctors and literally tons of medical supplies. Health engagement ultimately serves an undeniable security purpose—strengthening local disease surveillance and control systems can help to prevent pandemic disease; encouraging local health education and preventive care can increase the overall level of health and prosperity; and all these provide a cumulative effect to make a country or region less likely to be unstable or to develop into a security risk for any of the inhabitants of our shared home.

We have learned time and again that if we only build the capability of the operational forces—the health care responders and providers—without concurrently building and maturing the corresponding supporting institutional capacity, our partners will never be able to sustain these efforts on their own. As we equip our partner nations physically with supplies, tools, medications, knowledge, and even buildings, we must constantly ask ourselves if the host nations can sustain what we are giving them and what we are teaching them. Is this what *they* need? Does it make sense for the manner of security and the methods *they* use to provide it? Are we really enabling *them* to provide health security for *their own* people?

We must leave the people with an enduring capability and force generation capacity for health security, or they will eventually lose the means to overcome this challenge once we depart. In the end, it is not how well we can achieve health security in the short term (such as the number of vitamin packs, inoculations, and 10-day vitamin packets we provide); rather, it is how well the host nation government and society can provide and maintain health security in the long term—sustained capacity through stability and infrastructure—that will ultimately make the difference. To help accomplish this requires a bit of a paradigm shift on our part, namely, we should not focus as much on generating, giving, or providing a capability *for* them; instead, we should focus on developing *their* ability to generate, employ, and sustain this capacity for themselves. This is the modern day equivalent of the "Give the man a fish and he eats for a day . . . teach the man how to fish and he eats for the rest of his life" parable.

Fred Baker of the American Forces Press Service wrote a wonderful piece on the 2009 *Comfort* deployment in which he describes "teenagers and grandmothers work[ing] side by side with military members from around the world to provide care."[17] This spirit of joint, interagency, international, civilian, and private sector diversity was absolutely critical to the mission, and we at Southern Command firmly believe this symbolizes the way ahead for U.S. efforts in the region.

"My sense is this is the future of operations," said CAPT Tom Negus, the mission commander on board *Comfort*. "If we as a nation are going to hope to have an effect, then we are going to operate in an arena like this, with [nongovernmental organizations] and partner nations . . . all collaborating, all focused on achieving a purpose, having that alignment, that unity of mission."[18]

The United States has established individual relationships with the countries of this region primarily through military-to-military contact. However, during the course of Continuing Promise deployments, we have benefited from working with a mix of agencies and nations—and learning to work through the bureaucracies of each. This unique aspect and resulting relationships will prove valuable in the event the ship is called upon for aid in times of crisis, since "We know firsthand who to call—the people who can make things happen," CAPT Negus said. "That capability makes all of us much more ready in the event of a disaster. But it also fundamentally strengthens the trust between our nations. And the more . . . that we understand each other on so many different levels, then the stronger our ties are with those nations."[19]

And should we get caught up in the typical rush to quantify our results and determine success or failure in terms of sheer countries visited, patients treated, dollars spent, or public relations photos snapped, Baker closes his article with an incredibly poignant image. He uses it to remind us that the *true* impact of the mission cannot effectively be measured in terms of gross numbers, but more so in the individual lives it changes. He writes about the experience of Peggy Goebel, a volunteer nurse working aboard the *Comfort* for her second voyage with Project Hope, one of the first groups to team up with the Navy for these types of missions. I have included the excerpt verbatim below:

> "The difference can't be measured in bottles of Tylenol passed out . . . that's not it," she said. Goebel recalled a teenager she saw in a remote village in Nicaragua. She was 16, poor and hungry. Her baby was swaddled in rags, and at 2 months old,

weighed less than a newborn. The young mother was trying to breastfeed, but hadn't eaten enough to produce milk. The baby was starving, listless and covered in scabies, Goebel said.

A Navy physician at the site took money from his pocket, gave it to an interpreter to buy formula and diapers, and asked the mother to return the next day. When she did, both mother and baby were bathed and clothed. The doctor and Goebel taught her how to mix the formula. They cleaned her only bottle and fed the baby.

More importantly, Goebel made contact with a local Project Hope coordinator, who will follow up with the mother and child to ensure care. The formula the doctor bought was enough to last only a few days, but the follow-up care could mean the difference between life and death for the baby.

"That baby may not have lived a week. That was a life-changing experience," Goebel said. "We can't help them all. We can't do everything. But hopefully, we can plant a seed that we can make a difference."[20]

All of these engagement efforts gain significant power if the United States can achieve broad-spectrum message awareness and reception in the region. As U.S. Southern Command interacts with Latin America and the Caribbean, our message must reflect the promise of sustained commitment and enduring engagement with our neighbors toward shared humanitarian and health security objectives. Because we will continue to operate in a resource-constrained environment for the foreseeable future, effective strategic communication will exponentially increase the value of our engagement endeavors within and throughout the region. Southern Command or DOD will never be the lead agency in U.S. Government humanitarian activities—nor should we. However, we *do* have the potential to do great good as our units deploy throughout the region, and to capitalize on that good to enhance a positive U.S. image within our shared home. Additionally, our international, interagency, and NGO partnerships will give us a better range of possible support activities, and a bigger impact than if we were to attempt to accomplish these missions alone. In short, all of our efforts, combined with the tremendous involvement of other Federal agencies and the huge contribution of the U.S. private sector, show that we are engaging on a large scale with our friends and partners in Latin America and the Caribbean. And it will only get better. As our focus in Southern Command and other Federal agencies shifts from a somewhat unilateral viewpoint to an integrated, multia-gency, public-private cooperative approach, we will better show how the United States has cared, and always will care, about this incredibly worthy region and its diverse and vibrant people.

Notes

[1] The Fund for Peace, "Failed States Index 2009," accessed July 26, 2009, at: <http://www.fund-forpeace.org/web/index.php?option=com_content&task=view&id=99&Itemid=140>.

[2] National Intelligence Council, "Strategic Implications of Global Health," ICA 2008-10D, December 2008, available at: < http://www.dni.gov/nic/PDF_GIF_otherprod/ICA_Global_Health_2008.pdf>.

[3] Laurie A. Garrett, *HIV and National Security: Where Are the Links?* A Council on Foreign Relations Report (New York: Council on Foreign Relations, July 18, 2005), 12.

[4] Jack A. Gladstone and Jay Ulfelder, The Center for Strategic and International Studies and the Massachusetts Institute of Technology, "How to Construct Stable Democracies," *Washington Quarterly* 28, no. 1 (Winter 2004–2005).

[5] Katherine E. Bliss, *Health in Latin America and the Caribbean: Challenges and Opportunities for U.S. Engagement*, A Report of the CSIS Global Health Policy Center (Washington, DC: Center for Strategic and International Studies, April 2009), 10.

[6] Clare Ribando Seelke, *Gangs in Central America*, Congressional Research Service Report for Congress, October 17, 2008, 3.

[7] Mayra Buvinic and Andrew Morrison, "Violence as an Obstacle to Development," Inter-American Development Bank, Sustainable Development Department, Technical Note 4, 2000, page 4. Available at: <http://www.iadb.org/sds/doc/SOCTechnicalNote4E.pdf>..

[8] Tom McCawley, "US Tsunami Aid Still Reaps Goodwill," *Christian Science Monitor*, February 28, 2006, accessed July 4, 2009, at: <http://www.csmonitor.com/2006/0228/p12s01-woap.html>.

[9] Michael Voss, "Cuba Pushes its 'Medical Diplomacy,'" BBC News On-Line, May 20, 2009, accessed July 24, 2009, at: <http://news.bbc.co.uk/2/hi/americas/8059287.stm>.

[10] Copenhagen Consensus Center, "Copenhagen Consensus 2008—Results," 2. Available at: <http://www.cpoenhagenconsensus.com/Home.aspx>.

[11] Philip Musgrove, "Challenges and Solutions in Health in Latin America," Copenhagen Consensus Center and the Inter-American Development Bank, September 12, 2005, 44.

[12] Dean T. Jamison, Prabhat Jha, and David Bloom, "Disease Control Executive Summary," Copenhagen Consensus 2008, 2.

[13] Steven Liewer, "Warship Sets Sail from San Diego on Humanitarian Mission to Asia," *San Diego Union Tribune*, May 24, 2007.

[14] Remarks at "Poverty in Latin America: Challenges, Opportunities and Innovations," hosted by the Millennium Challenge Corporation and Council of the Americas, August 13, 2009.

[15] McCawley.

[16] Pan American Health Organization, "Health Situation in the Americas: Basic Indicators 2008," Washington, DC, 2008. We do not include Cuba because its value, 62.7 doctors per 10,000 people, is artificially inflated by government policy; Cuba exports its doctors for foreign relations objectives.

[17] Fred W. Baker III, American Forces Press Service, "Comfort Care Shapes Lives, Course for International Aid," accessed July 22, 2009, at: <http://www.defenselink.mil/news/newsarticle.aspx?id=55224>.

[18] Ibid.

[19] Ibid.

[20] Ibid.

Chapter 7

Innovation

Together, we need to continue looking ahead to anticipate future challenges and stand ready to face them. Our primary means of engagement is by way of ideas and the flow of information. Therefore, achieving the nation's objectives will rely on innovation.

—Robert M. Gates
Secretary of Defense

The Americas, our shared home, is a strategically vital, culturally rich, and widely diverse and vibrant region of 16 million square miles and 41 nations, territories, and protectorates. To appreciate our linkages, you have only to look at a map. Of course, we benefit from our physical connection by numerous land, sea, and air routes. Our proximity lends itself to a very natural tendency to depend upon each other. But we are also connected by so much more than just physical means—as previously described, we share environmental, cultural, security, and fiscal ties that inextricably link the fates of every nation in our hemisphere. Beyond the physical, economic, and demographic linkages, however—and perhaps most importantly—we generally share the common values of respect for democracy; a belief in the primacy of the rule of law; and conviction in the fundamental principle of inalienable human dignity. By and large, these beliefs underpin the foundations of our governments and remain central to our approach.

Because of these mutual bonds of common beliefs and values, the probability of interstate armed conflict is low. For the foreseeable future, the challenges and security threats we face in this hemisphere fortunately do not include any imminent conventional military threat to the United States, nor do we expect any major military conflict developing between nations in Latin America or the Caribbean. There may be some anxieties between neighbors, but those tensions which arise through the ordinary diplomatic and economic interaction between nations are primarily addressed through nonviolent means. Communication has been a strength in our region, and has proven itself over the last couple years during some of the region's political tensions. This is evidenced by the peaceful mediation and resolution by regional leaders of the crisis between Ecuador and Colombia that occurred in March of 2008. The creation of the new South American Defense Council is yet another indication of the tendency to create forums to encourage dialogue and reduce tension.

Despite this peaceful state of the region from a state-on-state violence perspective, we do face extremely significant challenges that threaten security and stability throughout the hemisphere. The challenges in Latin America and the Caribbean are multiple and complex: among them a broad and growing spectrum of public security threats, the possibility of natural and man-made disasters, and an emerging class of issues such as those relating to the environment. Narcoterrorism, drug trafficking, crime, gangs, and natural disasters pose the principal security challenges within the region. Also, the prospect of transnational Islamic terrorism is of concern and bears due vigilance on our part. One specific area of increasing concern is the nexus of illicit drug trafficking (including routes, profits, and corruptive influence) and terrorism.

Poverty and inequality—particularly when combined with corruption which impedes the rule of law and creates insecurity—are critical issues throughout the hemisphere and leave many searching for the means simply to survive. In many cases, these issues create the conditions from which other challenges arise to threaten democracies throughout Latin America and the Caribbean. Areas with lower levels of economic investment, development, and growth provide a breeding ground for the full range of criminal activities, creating an environment where sanctuaries for terrorist organizations can develop and mature.

The mounting threat from gangs is one such outgrowth of underlying poverty and a lack of opportunity. Gang activity, much like terrorism, transcends borders and affects numerous countries in the region. Gang members are no longer resident solely in Central and South America; they create challenges throughout the Western Hemisphere and number in the hundreds of thousands. Gangs are highly complex organizations imbedded in many types of societies and they use technology in new ways to circumvent lawful authority and travel across national borders with relative impunity.

The global illicit drug trade remains a significant transnational security threat as its power and influence continue to undermine democratic governments, terrorize populations, impede economic development, and hinder regional stability. The profits from this drug trade, principally cocaine, are an enabling catalyst for the full spectrum of threats to our national security, and present formidable challenges to the security and stability of our partners. Drug traffickers are constantly developing new means of preventing interference with their illegal narcotics activities. As we modify our tactics, drug producers and traffickers find innovative methods to develop the drugs and alternate trafficking routes. The drug traffickers of yesterday have become much more lethal today, and this trend is expected to continue. Our success—or failure—in addressing this insidious threat will have a direct and lasting impact on the stability and well-being of both developed and developing countries of the world. Innovative approaches and partnerships are needed to successfully confront this dangerous threat. It will take a coordinated multiagency and multinational strategic approach that brings to bear the strengths and resources of diverse, capable groups to stem the rising tide of the illicit drug trade.

Armed forces are often at the forefront of disaster relief operations and other forms of humanitarian assistance. In many cases, the military is the only resource able to deploy quickly to impacted areas. It can contribute a variety of assets ideally suited for demanding work—transportation, civil engineering, medicine—linked by a highly disciplined and organized command and control system and logistics train. These characteristics highlighted in humanitarian assistance and disaster relief missions are the same attributes that lead governments to task their armed forces with nontraditional missions increasingly distanced from the use or threat of force. Duties in support of public health, critical infrastructure, and the environment are increasingly encountered.

These challenges to collective security, stability, and prosperity have not emerged overnight, nor are they going to go away overnight. The challenges cannot be overcome by any one nation alone; they require transnational solutions. They cannot be overcome by the military alone; they require a truly integrated interagency and even private sector approach. But those challenges that we can link to human endeavors—namely narcotics and human trafficking, international crime, urban gangs, radical movements, and illegally armed groups—are predicated on an environment conducive to their activities. They flourish where governments are either complicit or physically unable to govern effectively. The Americas has a substantial number of these areas—some within the capitals of our partner nations themselves, some on the high seas—but all posing a significant challenge to progress and a promise for security throughout the region.

Specifically for the United States, addressing the challenges posed by gangs, drugs, and terrorist threats requires the application of all instruments of national power. The Nation must also deal with the underlying problems of unemployment, corruption, and a general lack of opportunity. The U.S. Government—particularly the elements of the interagency community—must encourage and assist in building partnerships across the region while working with intergovernmental organizations to ensure success.

Additionally, within this adapting and evolving neighborhood, there exists a "battlefield" of sorts, where traditional state actors, regional power brokers, and even terrorists and criminals share equal footing and are constantly positioning themselves for the ensuing "combat." This struggle takes place in a competitive marketplace of ideas, and as we have seen consistently in the years following the tragic events of 9/11, it is one within which nontraditional actors have become very adept at operating. In this environment, change happens fast. The advantage goes to those who can think, act, and communicate swiftly and in the most effective manner. Leading and synchronizing actions to accomplish any particular mission require thorough knowledge of the current situation as well as a vision for a future environment—one of freedom, security, stability, and ultimately, prosperity.

Taking all this into account, we in the Department of Defense must expand our understanding of conflict beyond lethal means, thereby reevaluating and extending the definition and scope of military operations to include "peacetime" engagement and training activities, as part of a single aggregate strategic skill set. Our self-imposed judicial, political, and moral boundaries that separate combat from criminal activity, domestic from international jurisdiction, and governmental from private interests all provide operational space for innovative and lethal opponents who neither possess nor respect such boundaries.

These are the new fundamental conditions of the 21st-century security environment. This blurring of the lines separating traditional kinetic missions from these nontraditional tasks can be cause for concern, especially with regard to taking on public security responsibilities. National leadership must ensure that roles and responsibilities are clearly defined, and that the forces are adequately trained and equipped.

We cannot expect clear transitions between war and peace—or combat and law enforcement; thus, in certain regions, we need new ideas, approaches, and organizations to manage engagement across the entire spectrum of international relations conditions. Enabling truly joint and interagency and international activities requires additional protocols and authorities to provide effective synchronization of various U.S. Government agency resources, as well as integration among the regional authorities of other governments and nongovernmental actor cells. We need to explore new ways of thinking, communicating, and operating within today's dynamic and challenging international environment.

Countering such threats and reacting to the informational realities require new organizational structures and operational procedures not predicated on traditional notions of war and peace. Our old models and methods provide solutions only when such black and white paradigms are readily distinguishable. Today we operate in shades of gray.

These challenges—transnational and adaptive by nature—must be successfully addressed to provide the security that is an essential precondition to the stability and prosperity we all desire. They require both technological and human innovation to enable cooperative solutions. Furthermore, these solutions will increasingly involve joint, interagency, international, and even private sector approaches that can include nongovernmental organizations, educational institutions, charities, and other stakeholders.

So as we face these challenges at U.S. Southern Command—virtually all require a wide variety of tool sets beyond pure military activity to solve—we are looking for creative solutions to approach partnerships throughout the region. We must innovate in the way we think, organize, plan, and operate; in the way we adapt new technology to ever-changing challenges; and in the way we communicate, including how we describe and frame our challenges both with our partners and with the public in general.

The old adage that "change is a constant" should instead read "change is constantly accelerating." Yet, our core mission has been left unchanged—we remain a military organization conducting military operations and promoting security cooperation in Central America, the Caribbean, and South America in order to achieve U.S. strategic objectives.

We are living in an age of rapid change facilitated by advancing technologies and increasingly networked systems, societies, and economies. In order for security agencies to be successful in this complex environment, those organizations must be flexible, open, and forward-thinking. As globalization deepens and threats emerge and evolve, security organizations will need to continue fostering and building relationships with willing and capable partners to face transnational challenges. The security of the United States and that of our partners depends largely on our capacity to leverage joint, international, interagency, and public-private cooperation—all reinforced by focused messaging and strategic communication.

This unfolding 21st century presents U.S. Southern Command with an opportunity—indeed, an obligation—to define and shape new staff structures and attendant processes that will best achieve U.S. national security objectives in an era of transnational and unconventional threats.

> The achievement of excellence can only occur if the organization promotes a culture of creative dissatisfaction.
>
> Lawrence Miller
> CEO of Forbes

Establishing a "Culture of Innovation"

The aforementioned challenges—transnational and adaptive by nature—must be successfully addressed to provide the security that is an essential precondition to the stability and prosperity we all desire. Meeting them is beyond the capabilities of any one country's military, or for that matter, any one country—they require *both* technological and human innovation to enable cooperative solutions. Furthermore, these solutions will increasingly involve a joint, interagency, and international approach that can include nongovernmental organizations, educational institutions, charities, and other stakeholders. Our hemisphere in particular is one in which we will need to be extremely effective in launching ideas, concepts, and cooperative opportunities for engagement, all of which require innovation.

U.S. Southern Command developed a new strategic plan— "Command Strategy 2018"—based on this very principle. Our commitment to a strategy entirely focused on this integrated approach is manifested in our recent restructuring into a joint and combined interagency security command: an entity casting off large parts of its traditional Prussian-inspired layout reflecting a classic kinetic military, and transforming into a highly adaptable, matrixed organization that brings together armed forces elements and previously labeled "outsiders" under one roof, bonded together by a common cause. It is only through this degree of difficult but necessary revolutionary change that Southern Command can continue to strive to achieve and protect U.S. national security objectives and better strive to become the partner of choice with friends and neighbors in pursuit of a cooperative and shared security, stability, and prosperity.

Innovation is the key to accomplishing and sustaining this change. In a resource-constrained environment, efficiencies can only stretch budgets and labor so far, and the U.S. military, as well as partner nation forces, harvested all the low-hanging fruit long ago. Admiral Sir Jackie Fisher, one of the most innovative minds ever applied to naval operations, remarked early in the 20th century as British budgets were being squeezed, "Now that the money is running out, we must think!"

As previously mentioned, our world is continually shifting and constantly evolving, and this change can be difficult for any large organization to manage. In fact, according to Peter Drucker, "one cannot manage change—one can only be ahead of it."[1] We as a nation must be able to achieve this; further, I believe the United States can and must actively take a role in *leading* this effort. Ideas, both good ones and bad ones, as vetted through a sometimes painful trial-and-error process, led to the cultural and technological innovations that launched this current phenomenon of globalization. It will take more ideas to sustain the engine that drives borderless transactions and interchange, the diffusion of knowledge, and the regional and global redistribution of high-value services that characterize our world today. And it is the successful, pragmatic, and strategically-oriented organization—one that is not adverse to change but, in fact, embraces it—that will promote the generation and exchange of ideas, will foster intellectual rigor, and will create an environment that cultivates passions among and throughout all levels for the scholastic engagement of challenging multiagency and multinational issues. We cannot shy away from these issues; rather, we need to identify them, meet them head on, and be proactive in finding solutions for them *together*.

Change starts with vision, and from that, a strategy to achieve that vision. In 2006, when I took the helm of U.S. Southern Command, one of the first steps I took was to establish my guiding principles for the enterprise—near the top of that list was "Innovate to Improve." Organizational innovation requires both a framework to gather and assess ideas and processes that translate vetted concepts into capabilities. As part of our transformation in this endeavor, we established a Joint Innovation and Experimentation ("Innovation") Directorate. The Innovation Directorate's four divisions—Joint Experimentation, Strategic Assessment, Knowledge Management, and Decision Support—were charged with driving significant performance improvements in how the command trains and fights and how it does business with its diverse stakeholder base. Later, a small Innovation Cell was established within my Commander's Action Group

(CAG) and it was presented with the overarching challenge of creating and maintaining a *culture of innovation* across the entire Southern Command enterprise. My guidance for innovation within the enterprise was then promulgated and followed these four main tenets:

- Innovation would be encouraged and positively recognized at all levels.

- All personnel assigned within the command were requested to dedicate approximately 15 percent of their work schedule to innovative thought (a goal I personally strove in earnest to achieve, as well).

- The Southern Command Innovation Cell would serve as a full-time, dedicated resource to promote innovation within the enterprise and to help foster unity of effort for combatant command (COCOM)–level innovative initiatives.

- Innovative initiatives would be reviewed at the commander level on a monthly basis to provide guidance and top level endorsement where appropriate. Other Southern Command senior leadership would review innovative efforts at least quarterly during every Component Commander's Conference.

To this end, the intent was to use the Innovation Cell as a catalyst, to work at all levels within the enterprise to encourage and promote innovation from all members. To do this, the cell was given three specific innovation-related taskings. First, it was charged with promoting a "culture of innovative thought" throughout the organization and, through this effort, establishing a climate conducive to change. This is a necessary precondition to implementing Strategy 2018. Culture change is undoubtedly difficult to effect and quantify, particularly so in a military organization. Again, however, we must not be satisfied with merely being passively "caught up" in change, but rather striving to lead change. As Drucker points out, "unless it is seen as the task of the organization to *lead* change, the organization—whether business, university, hospital and so on—will not survive. In a period of rapid structural change, the only ones who survive are the *Change Leaders*."[2]

The cell's second main assignment was to take the lead in identifying new and creative ways of meeting the command's missions: in particular, contending with the previously described public security, natural disaster, and emerging nontraditional challenges. This involves exploring new concepts and/or creative use of mature technologies, then rigorously testing possible solutions via simulations and proof-of-concept demonstrations. To accomplish all this requires creating a cadre of individuals (change leaders) who see change not as a threat, but rather an opportunity; who actively search for change, making appropriate decisions on which changes to pursue; and who know how to achieve results that are effective both outside the organization and within it. At the enterprise level, such attributes and actions require the following:

■ Policies to make the present create the future

■ Systematic methods to look for and to anticipate change

■ The right way to introduce change, both within and outside the enterprise

■ Policies to balance change and continuity.[3]

Finally, the directorate was given the primary responsibility for developing validated solutions into an initial operational capability. These can take the form of material, nonmaterial, and combined approaches. I will go into this process more deeply with a couple specific examples, but briefly, in many organizations, innovation tends to follow a "waterfall" or "stage-gate" process whereby solutions development follows a sequential path through a series of discrete phases demarcated by stage reviews. This may work in situations where the environment is relatively stable, incremental progress is the norm, and speed is not essential. Other enterprises, including some military acquisition programs, embrace a "spiral" innovation model that emphasizes fielding a desired operational capability in a series of predefined iterations. While this approach offers significantly more flexibility than the former, it is still inadequate for addressing evolving requirements and incorporating the concerns and contributions of a large number of diverse stakeholders.

With this in mind, Southern Command adopted an "open innovation" model allowing it to integrate internal and external actors throughout its transformation. This collaboration-centric logic ties together the requirements and capabilities of its joint, interagency, and international constituency. Only through such a paradigm can the command harness such a widely diverse group—including military services, intelligence agencies, law enforcement organizations, academic institutions, private enterprises, and nongovernmental organizations—in a manner that is fast, flexible, risk minimizing/mitigating, and cost-efficient.

Introduction to innovation at Southern Command is briefed during every welcome-aboard class at the command to help ensure 100 percent participation in the program. Senior leadership from not only the headquarters, but also the components and joint commands within the enterprise, regularly promote innovation at speaking engagements, publications, and in partner nation relations. We have also seen great benefit from timely, regular, and broadcast recognition being given to those personnel supporting innovation projects.

I am often asked how many people are in the Southern Command innovation program. The answer is, "It depends." It is true that we only have two to three full time members in a dedicated Innovation Cell at the headquarters; however, virtually every subordinate element reporting to Southern Command has formed some type of innovation cell. Recalling my initial request to all personnel to contribute 15 percent of their time to innovative thought, it quickly becomes a fairly large innovation team supporting the desired endstate of promoting, instilling, and maintaining a culture of innovation.

A wonderful example of a widely embraced innovation effort at Southern Command is the relatively recent entry into social networking and social media techniques. This effort strikes directly at the "cultural mindset" target and these pioneering concepts had roots in the Strategic Communications and Public Affairs Departments at the headquarters. Innovative use of social networking has quickly been seized and promoted by virtually every directorate and reporting element within the organization. The initiative has formed its own culture of innovation and, once again, has transitioned to mainstream operations at Southern Command.

Not Just Technology

It is often assumed that all innovation is technology related and therefore occurs primarily at the operational and tactical levels. True, technology has formed a large portion of the Southern Command innovation projects over the last few years, but these have come hand-in-hand with "strategic innovation"—that is, the creative, imaginative, and insightful thinking that targets the organizational, cultural, and paradigmatic levels. Examples of this type of philosophy include initiatives such as process improvements, nontraditional partnering, and business engagement, among others.

As stated earlier, our current strategic environment presents many novel challenges and is dynamic and constantly evolving. Clearly, today's challenges require a broader understanding of all aspects of our national engagement in Latin America, and with this broader view, a better focus on the totality of our efforts in the region. This broader lens includes the enormous contributions of the various members of the interagency community of the U.S. Government. It also encompasses what we think might be the proverbial "submerged portion of the iceberg" when it comes to engaging the region—the vast potential of public-private cooperation. This means we will have to use inventive nontraditional approaches to creating security and stability in this region, largely by working with regional partners abroad and interagency community partners and the private sector at home. One such paradigm shift needs to continue to involve information-sharing and our ongoing transformation from a mindset of "need to know" to "need to share."

Recognizing the interagency character of the task ahead, we have created a new structure in our organization—a robust staff group with direct access to the commander—that is charged specifically with "interagency activity and international partnering." This new division's function is to broaden our awareness of interagency efforts, establish relationships based on trust across the interagency community, integrate other agency experts into the planning process, and ultimately help to achieve a greater synergy of engagement and messaging in the region. This is the first step in our innovative approach.

Meaningful partnerships are based on commitment according to fundamental notions of reciprocity, understanding, and cooperation. The security cooperation partnerships we seek to build and nurture require connectivity, interoperability, and a baseline for communicating mutual understanding. The key is to work toward significantly broader mechanisms of mutual trust with our partner nations. To do so, we need to be able to shed the veil of secrecy, on demand, and to share our technology with partners. Of course, an important caveat to this is the need to retain the ability to restrict access for our own security purposes when for whatever reason those partnerships erode. The time is right to expand our technology base for building partnerships—to build upon a long history of friendship and cooperation—especially in a region in which "combat" is waged and won largely by words and trust, not bullets.

Another example of how we can use innovative approaches is found in the maritime domain, the second-most prevalent and traveled milieu in this hemisphere (behind only cyberspace). As previously described, even with our nation's naval capacity, policing the regional waterways, when combined with our other global commitments, requires more capability than we alone can deliver. Designing a regional network of maritime nations, voluntarily committed to monitoring security and responding to threats of mutual interests, is one of the cornerstones of our Partnership of the Americas.

At Southern Command, years of multilateral fleet and field exercises have provided the basic building blocks for cooperative security in our shared home. For instance, the annual exercise UNITAS first started in 1959 and has been instrumental in establishing working relationships among U.S. and Latin American naval, coast guard, and marine forces. The friendship, professionalism, and understanding encouraged among participants provide fertile ground to promote interoperability, develop a common framework for information exchange, and establish the command and control protocols we will need to achieve what might be called a Regional or even Global Maritime Coalition.

Additionally, Southern Command has served as a test bed for two concepts that are critical enablers for such a coalition concept. We have seen the hospital ship USNS *Comfort* deploy throughout the region twice in the last 3 years, visiting various countries in Central America and the Caribbean, including nations on both sides of the Panama Canal. This tremendous first for our region has provided a highly visible and meaningful symbol of our commitment to the people of this part of the world. We also sent a new type of vessel into the region, a converted car-ferry with enormous cargo space and the ability to reach speeds of 45+ knots, the high-speed vessel HSV *Swift*. This ship carries a wide variety of training teams and gear, repair capability, medical capacity, and exercise coordinators and has paid immediate and large dividends for training, exchanges, building trust, and helping our partner nations enhance their own abilities. These deployments along with others have provided valuable lessons-learned to help the U.S. Navy institutionalize the Global Fleet Station program, which will result in flexible forward presence options to conduct theater security cooperation activities. This kind of "operational innovation" is crucial and we will continue to pursue it.

Southern Command has also pursued innovation in increasing its language capability. We share deep-rooted cultural ties with our neighbors. One only has to look at U.S. demographics to see that over 15 percent of our population traces their heritage to the Hispanic culture, and by 2050, that number is expected to surpass 30 percent. Still, when we conduct military-to-military exercises in the region, we find that success is hampered by language difficulties that diminish real understanding. This is true, of course, throughout all regions of the world.

The difficulty for those who are not multilingual is that trust-building interaction with our partners requires more than mere translation—it requires transfer of ideas that take into account cultural nuances. In other words, it simply is not enough to just see someone else's point of view or perspective; rather, to truly possess their vision, you must be able to see it through *their* eyes. To accomplish this, you must attempt to walk where they walk, eat where they eat, read what they read, and speak how they speak. Only then will you truly be able to think and understand how *they* think.

Across all branches of service and throughout the Department of Defense, language learning is seen as a crucial part of developing cultural understanding. We have a goal at Southern Command for 60 percent of the enterprise staff to gain bilingual proficiency—the DOD average is 10 percent. With the tremendous workload we all face, the objective is nearly impossible to achieve following traditional methods of learning. Obviously, any method used to speed and facilitate language learning can have profound, positive impact on the readiness of our command. A wave of advances in cutting-edge technologies has resulted in an entire range of research disciplines devoted to language learning techniques. Advances like these make it foreseeable that one day we may have something like a "virtual tutor"—a device that provides authentic, real-time interaction and translation, as well as conversational advice and feedback to the learner that encourages self-confidence and independence. As envisioned, such a device would easily rival years of immersion study, which is widely espoused as the best technique available today to achieve language proficiency. This kind of "cultural innovation" is key.

We are also working to amplify the benefits of a number of programs already in place. Besides its many training exercises and security cooperation programs, Southern Command conducts a variety of humanitarian goodwill activities that directly help those in need, while also providing needed training to our team. Each year we construct wells, schools, community centers, and medical clinics in several countries in the region. As an example of our commitment—of our promise to the people of the region—our medical personnel treat about a quarter of a million patients on an annual basis, varying from routine prevention to the most serious emergency cases. We are taking a "blank sheet of paper" approach to finding ways to make these already beneficial programs far more productive and integrated with host nation, interagency, and private activity.

Recently we began another new initiative designed to scratch the tip of the iceberg-like potential of public-private sector cooperative ventures in the region. In a resource-constrained environment, the vast benefits of cooperating with the private sector are obvious. Of course, we need to ensure we create a defensible legal framework upon which we build this cooperation, but through innovative collaboration, we should be able to realize tremendous outreach benefits. An example of just such a venture is the U.S. Navy's global outreach program called Project Handclasp. This unique partnering program takes goodwill materials donated by the U.S. private sector—ambulances, school supplies, high-nutrition meals, etc.—and, at minimal cost to the government, distributes them as Navy ships pull into harbors worldwide on already scheduled port visits. This outreach program is a "people-to-people" endeavor, not "government-to-government"; it connects the people of the United States to the people of the world, and it builds tremendous goodwill toward our service members, since the donations are usually in conjunction with community service volunteer projects like repainting and refurbishing schools, hospitals, clinics, orphanages, and homes for the elderly. In our area of focus, just in 2008 and 2009, Project Handclasp provided almost 30,000 pounds of material for Guatemala valued at $234,000; it provided 225,000 pounds of material for Peru valued at just over $1 million; and in the largest effort to date—the Million Meals Initiative—Project Handclasp provided the following to Haiti: 1,425,000 high-nutrition meals, water filter capability for 350 institutions and homes (each with a 10-year lifespan), pharmaceuticals valued at over $268,000, medical materials, hygienic supplies, wheelchairs, and stuffed toys for children. This tremendously successful program is only a small part of what we can achieve with these types of cooperative ventures. As a nation, we need to tirelessly seek out additional ways to employ innovation and creativity to our national outreach: from ideas like micro-loans, to $100 laptops, to Internet and broadband penetration, to teaching programs, and more.

Another foray into the still nascent arena of public-private and military-civilian cooperation is a ground-breaking effort sponsored by the Southern Command Business Engagement Directorate working with the Business Executives for National Security (BENS). An idea was formed to explore vulnerabilities in the business models used by drug trafficking organizations (DTOs). If we can successfully perform conceptual role-playing as a DTO, we could potentially project how DTOs would act in the next few years and proactively respond to those challenges. Who better to accept this role than a group of highly successful business leaders and professionals? Consequently, the "BENS Cartel" was formed. BENS members worked hand-in-hand with JIATF–S and various partner agencies and departments, including DEA, FBI, and CBP to support this nontraditional initiative. This partnership has the potential to yield positive and rapid return on investment in our ongoing struggle with illegal narcotics producers and traffickers, a major source of death and misery in our shared home.

Additionally, we continue to build on efforts of the past few years in the area of human rights. Several nations in the region are still struggling with the fragile balancing act between peace and justice—focusing on the future and attempting to find reconciliation between former enemies on one side, while being forced to look into the not-so-distant past on the other side to dispense punishment and garner retribution for the abuses committed by uniformed militaries, militias, and guerrilla groups. At Southern Command, we have created a unique and dedicated group of experts working with the nations in the region to improve performance in this vital area. We sponsor a Human Rights Initiative that has created a consensus document on human rights by which the militaries of eight nations and a multinational organization have committed to advance institutional respect for human rights and promote a zero-tolerance environment for violations. We also have proposed legislation to Congress, approved by the Department of Defense and the President, to establish a Center for Excellence in Human Rights. This center will allow us to expand our human rights program and to collaborate with an array of agencies and organizations in public-private partnerships to extend the reach of these critical efforts.

These are just a few ideas about innovation here at Southern Command and in our area of focus: major structural reorganization (with a distinct purpose and desired endstate) to include a Civilian Deputy Commander and an Interagency Partnering Directorate, and *the* gold standard for future joint and combined interagency and international security organizations—JIATF–South; cultural innovation through advanced learning techniques; operational innovation like the Global Fleet Station and exercises like Panamax and Unitas; coalition innovation brought about through sharing information with our reliable partners in the region; technological innovation in terms of precision-guided intelligence; and, even legislative innovation through laws like the recently passed Drug Trafficking Vessel Interdiction Act of 2008, which outlaws unregistered craft plying international waters "with the intent to evade detection." This is truly proactive, aggressive, and game-changing thought and action by our distinguished legislators and teammates in Congress and helps to strengthen the message that we need to develop and instill this culture of innovation across and throughout all levels and instruments of national power.

Spectrum of Innovation

While working toward this overall objective and mindset, a primary goal has been to encourage innovation at multiple levels. Large-scale innovative efforts, such as transforming Southern Command into a Joint Interagency Security Command or deployment of the USNS *Comfort*, have been well recognized and largely embraced. But we also want to encourage creative thinking on projects of smaller magnitude that may not receive nearly as much attention. Project Mirador is one such example.

Mirador was the first deployment of an unmanned surface vehicle used to support real world counterdrug (CD) operations. The demonstration was conducted in less than a month, for less than $250,000, and with the involvement of just two members of the Dominican Republic Navy working with the Naval Undersea Warfare Center (NUWC). It may someday revolutionize how DOD and other applicable agencies conduct littoral water counter–illicit trafficking (CIT) operations, but the project had a very modest start at Southern Command. In contrast, at the other end of the spectrum is our endorsement of long-term projects such as the Integrated Sensor Is Structure (ISIS). ISIS is a very large-scale, multiyear endurance airship program intended to revolutionize intelligence, surveillance, and reconnaissance (ISR) provided to the combatant commands. ISIS is currently sponsored by the Air Force and DARPA. Early expression of Southern Command desires and challenges in this type of large-scale project is equally as important in the spectrum of innovation as the smaller projects.

Further, any worthwhile innovative effort will produce its own set of unique challenges and obstacles that need to be overcome. In most cases, there will be no established procedures or guidelines for integration of a concept that is truly revolutionary. There will be discomfort and a feeling of uneasiness for the prospective innovators, as people leave their established methods and technologies to consider unknown initiatives with no guarantee of success.

Truth be told, we are awash in a sea of this "disruptive technology." Technological innovation is at a fever pitch—in information, in electronics, and most recently in the biological sphere. Each day, it seems, there are dramatic emergent advances trumpeted in various industries: new generation computer chips, smaller communicative and connective devices, genetic enhancements, bioengineering marvels, indestructible polymers and veneers—at times one feels as though tomorrow arrives here newly minted every hour. The hard part is that most, if not all, of these technologies threaten to disrupt existing products and markets, producing turmoil and requiring difficult decisions by managers and planners across a variety of industries—including the military. Yet, they offer ultimately enormous rewards in terms of what they can deliver. It should be remembered that the things we tend to fear most in large, tradition-centric organizations—fluctuations, disturbances, imbalances—are the primary sources of creativity.[4]

How can we leverage the inherent goodness in such disruptive technologies in a way that maximizes benefits and minimizes confusion and failure? This is, of course, hardly a new problem. The emergence of such new technologies—which are potentially threatening to embedded legacy systems and procedural norms—is as old as the notion of business cycles itself. But today, the *pace* of emergence of disruptive technologies threatens to swamp the military's ability to incorporate and use such advancements. We are reasonably capable of inventing and discovering disruptive technology; managing its incorporation, however, is not yet our strong suit and it thus remains a vast and fundamental early 21st-century challenge.

In the simplest sense, disruptive technologies are things that improve on a current product but initially seem too expensive and too limited in capability to make business sense, which leads businesses to "hold on to the old" rather than move to embrace the new technologies. As Roger von Oech urges, "It's easy to come up with new ideas; the hard part is letting go of what worked for you two years ago but will soon be out of date."[5] Understanding what innovation means to an organization and to what degree it is embraced by the leadership defines the innovation process itself. Ensuring success in this process requires that one understands both the political as well as personal innovation philosophies that are inherent within the enterprise. Only then can one start to adequately approach identifying the institutional and cultural challenges, the re-tailoring of methodology, and ultimately the creation of a different environment and landscape. What has worked in the past will need to work better in the future—if it does not or cannot, then it will have to be replaced. This can be painful for those who have grown personally attached and have a personal stake in the existing process, idea, philosophy, or concept. This resistant mindset is what Drucker is referring to when he says the first "change policy" in making any organization receptive to innovation—even organizing it *for* innovation—is to *abandon yesterday*.[6] This policy, which he terms "Organized Abandonment," is centered on "the need to free resources from being committed to maintaining what no longer contributes to performance and no longer produces results."[7] He goes on to add, "In fact, it is not possible to create tomorrow unless one first sloughs off yesterday."[8]

History provides us with many examples, in both the military and civilian worlds, where innovation—both technological as well as cultural—has run smack up against an entrenched industry or mindset that did not welcome its arrival, such as the telephone, the personal computer, ship-to-ship radio communication, the attack aircraft carrier, and cruise missiles and unmanned tactical aviation. How can we in the military best position ourselves to take advantage of disruptive technologies? Essentially, we must establish mechanisms, as business has, to embrace creative disruptive technologies in ways that do not place national security at risk or prematurely discard still vital and useful older systems. One way, recalling Lincoln's quote, is to "think anew." James Bertrand put it slightly differently, though no less poignantly, when he remarked, "Once we rid ourselves of traditional thinking we can get on with creating the future."

Again, at Southern Command, we have found that forming wide-reaching partnerships to help overcome the various forms of resistance to change is one of the critical paths to success for innovation. Partnership compositions may be innovative and diverse themselves, potentially including other COCOMs, members of the interagency community, nongovernmental organizations, academia, corporate America, and various DOD centers of excellence. Our traditional approach of vertically aligned but mutually exclusive cylinders of excellence (stovepipes) prevents us from being able to develop or achieve synergy and leverage each others' excellent ideas and outstanding innovations. Sharing of ideas, planning, execution responsibility, assessment, risk management, and funding resources are just a few of the partnerships benefits.

An ongoing program addressing one of the toughest challenges to counter-narcoterrorism (CNT) operations in our area of focus—denying the use of foliage as a sanctuary to narcoterrorists—is a prime example of the potential payoff of strong innovation partnerships. This program is a combination of the A-160 Hummingbird and the Forester radar. The Hummingbird is a revolutionary project by itself: an unmanned helicopter, able to fly very quietly over the horizon with various sensor packages for almost 20 straight hours. Package the Hummingbird with Forester, a new radar with a demonstrated ability to track dismounts under very dense foliage, and you potentially have a game changer for CNT operations. To accomplish this type of revolution in technology, a formidable set of partnerships has been used. In this case, Southern Command has been extremely fortunate to partner with the Special Operations Command (SOCOM), DARPA, the Army's Research Development and Engineering Command (RDECOM), and numerous other organizations.

Assuming Risk

To truly accomplish revolutionary change through innovation at the enterprise-wide level, there needs to be a willingness to accept a good deal of programmatic, and even *career*, risk. A fair number of proposed innovation projects will not succeed as envisioned and may need to be abandoned. This is perfectly acceptable. We must not allow failures to translate into stifling the new cultural mindset of the organization with a backlash of the old (the "See, I told you so . . . we should have never left the way we *used* to do it"); nor must we allow short-term setbacks to negatively impact the careers of these creative and inventive minds. To thrive in the contemporary security environment, change leaders must adopt an innovative approach—we must aggressively cultivate a professionally safe environment where energetic, pioneering, and inspired individuals can pursue innovation and creativity without fear of failure and its consequences.

Truly, if some level of success is achieved with even one-third (33 percent) of our innovation projects, we should be absolutely satisfied. If every project is successful, then the chances are the innovation program is not pushing the envelope enough in terms of seeking truly revolutionary solutions. As Woody Allen put it succinctly, "If you're not failing every now and then, it's a sign you're not doing anything very innovative." A word of caution and clarity, though: *programmatic risk* should never be confused with operational risk. Each innovation project involving operations undergoes an operational risk assessment to determine likelihood and severity of potential risks for any demonstration. Identified risks are addressed and mitigated or the project is suspended or canceled.

Take, for instance, Project Monitoreo, the first operational deployment of a maritime unmanned aircraft system (UAS) in support of counterdrug operations. Monitoreo deployed to Comalapa, El Salvador, and operated from the international airport alongside commercial aircraft. Careful planning and coordination were conducted to ensure safety at every step before the innovation demonstration was allowed to begin. Host nation review and approval of all procedures were absolute musts. Contingency planning was carefully considered and briefed before each event. Once again, innovation was not easy, and there were several 'bumps in the road' with things not going exactly as hoped or planned. In the end, however, the pioneering effort paid off: Monitoreo successfully demonstrated that a UAS could support regional CIT operations, thereby laying the groundwork for a new generation of aircraft to help support operations.

Second-Order Innovation Effects

Every innovative idea or approach is initially identified to address a specific deficiency or challenge area. However, in the process of demonstrating and transitioning most initiatives, we find second- and third-order benefits beyond the original intent of the innovation. Partner nation capacity- and capability-building during cooperative demonstrations in our area of focus is one of the most valuable second-order effects we have encountered. Ensuring maximum participation and exposure to our partner nation friends during demonstrations by working closely with the Foreign Disclosure Office (FDO) has paid large dividends. Furthermore, innovation projects usually garner a fair amount of media attention and can serve as a means to promote the command's strategic messages. For each innovation project expected to receive media attention, the innovation team works closely with the Public Affairs and Strategic Communication Departments to develop approved sets of project strategic messages to take full advantage of any such opportunities. Finally, innovation projects can serve as a deterrent in mission areas such as CD and CNT. As Southern Command has embraced certain innovation projects, we have seen evidence of both DTOs and narcoterrorists closely monitoring our developments, undoubtedly considering how our new capabilities and concepts could affect their operations. If nothing else, we have momentarily seized the initiative from these groups just by the introduction of creative and potentially game-changing innovation.

Southern Command Innovation Process

The Southern Command Innovation Cell routinely supports a portfolio of around 10 to 15 ongoing initiatives at different stages of maturity. However, there is no intent for the Innovation Cell to be the keeper of all innovative efforts in the enterprise. This is an extremely important point. Each of the directorates, components, joint commands, and military groups within Southern Command is enthusiastically pursuing and developing its own inventive and creative projects across the previously mentioned spectrum of innovation, taking advantage of the autonomy provided by a flatter and more functionally reorganized enterprise. So in essence, there are probably hundreds of these types of projects ongoing within the command and our area of focus at any given time.

Innovation projects, particularly the technological ones, by nature are usually revolutionary and flashy. They capture attention, spur imagination, and inspire people. Projects such as the HSV *Swift*, which has been used by Southern Command to support Southern Partnership Station, fall into that category. There are several other projects mentioned throughout this section, and all serve as examples for lessons learned on how to successfully cultivate and integrate outstanding ideas and personnel to help build into the enterprise what Drucker refers to as a "systematic policy of innovation—that is a policy to create change."[9] The ultimate objective, of course, is to enable the entire organization to *see change as an opportunity*, not as a challenge, threat, or something to be feared.

For any organization, and this is particularly true in our experiences at Southern Command, there is a natural evolutionary progression of improvement over time for virtually any capability or process. In the following diagram, this is represented by the solid line. Some processes improve faster or slower than others, but all share a linear growth pattern. At Southern Command, these capabilities could include humanitarian assistance, disaster relief, counter–illicit trafficking operations, public affairs engagement, strategic communications, or a long list of other areas. The men and women of Southern Command work every day to improve these processes and operations. These "continuous improvements" will inevitably transform the thoughts, activities, and methodologies on the micro level, and the organization as a whole on the macro level. They lead to product innovation, service innovation, new processes, and new second- and third-order follow-on endeavors. Ultimately, as Drucker points out, "continuous improvements lead to fundamental change."[10] One of the intended outcomes of the innovation program, then, is to be a *support organization*, intended to *complement* these established efforts. We break it down into three steps or phases.

Figure 7–1. USSOUTHCOM Innovation Process

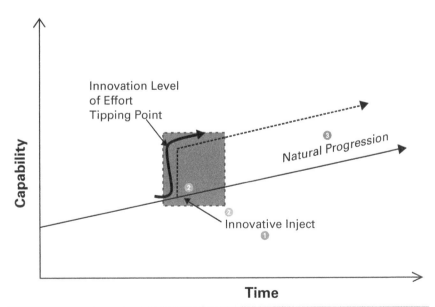

1 - Step one of the process is the *Innovative Inject*. The innovation effort tries to identify new and *revolutionary changes* in the way we currently do business to address the toughest challenges. Proposed innovation injects are solutions that will provide a disruptive change which, if successful, takes us off the *evolutionary* glide path of improvement. Some would call it a step function in capability, or more commonly referred to as a "game changer." There are two keys to success in this phase. First, we adopt the *problem to solution approach*. The key is to prioritize the countless possible challenge areas based on Commander's Guidance and other inputs like component commands, partner nation needs, and lessons learned from ongoing operations and programs. Additional indicators might include regional feedback from the military groups, regular interaction with each of the Service components, and debriefs from DOD and interagency units supporting the command in our area of focus.

Next, it is important to fully understand the nature of a chosen challenge through direct field observation and contact with personnel who know the most about the issues. Second, although perhaps even more important, is identifying a potential revolutionary solution to address the challenge. Once again, creative thought and partnerships are the key—promoting an accepted culture of innovation within the organization allows our personnel to express nontraditional solutions for consideration which might otherwise languish in fear of retribution or failure. It also presents an open door to academia, the private sector, and interagency groups who are eager to find and develop solutions to the truly difficult challenges, in support of regional or national security objectives. These partnerships are absolutely invaluable to the innovation program and need to be constantly nurtured and fortified.

Take, for example, the mission area of counter-narcoterrorism operations. In 2007, one Southern Command Military Group (MILGP) expressed concern that U.S. and partner nation riverine forces were being challenged by lack of intelligence, surveillance, and reconnaissance in the rugged riverine environment. The challenges were researched through the Southern Command service components and by working with our partner nations who held the most experience in riverine operations. Then, working through DARPA, a potential solution was identified. A low-cost, man-portable, maritime-suitable micro UAV weighing approximately 1 pound was proposed to support riverine operators with improved ISR and riverine security during day, night, and adverse weather operations. The project was named "Rio WASP." Working with Peruvian marines and U.S. Navy Special Warfare personnel, the concept was demonstrated and evaluated on the Amazon River and surrounding tributaries. It has since transitioned to real world operations and is a bright spot and success story for the still-nascent innovation program.

2 - Implementation through demonstrations is the heart of the second phase of our innovation recipe. At this point in the diagram, we have injected the innovation in some manner. But our work is decidedly not done—we have to do what Drucker refers to as "organizing the introduction of change . . . that is, to pilot."[11] His thesis is that one cannot market research something that is truly original; neither exhaustive studies nor countless computer simulations can ever be a substitute for the true test of reality. Thus, every new idea, concept for improvement, and groundbreaking invention must first be tested, but done so on a small scale; in other words, it needs to be piloted. The way to do this is to locate somebody within the enterprise or its associates who really wants "the new."[12] As in the example of Rio WASP in Peru, strong regional relations with our partner nations and the largely nonlethal environment in this hemisphere lent itself to an ideal venue for demonstrations.

Additionally, every innovative concept by nature should support ongoing processes or operations, so we need to quickly move from the idea stage to proof of concept. One of the key enablers to successfully accomplishing this is *agility*. In many cases, if we do not quickly take action on new ideas, our adversaries will do so, thus taking the innovative initiative away from us. This is also why the Innovation Cell does not necessarily wait for identified deficiencies to go through the entire vetting process of becoming a stated requirement before attempting to demonstrate potential solutions. Whenever possible, evaluation plans are designed to work hand-in-hand with regional partners and to provide some level of operational benefits, all while safely conducting the tests and evaluations. At the end of each segment, an assessment is conducted to analyze and determine the relative merits of each initiative.

There are two primary challenges to this phase. First, measured expectations are the key to the assessments. Everyone involved needs to understand that revolutionary projects will have hiccups and challenges along the way. Projects should not be abandoned if things do not go smoothly during the demonstration. In the words of Steve Jobs, the founder and CEO of Apple, "Sometimes when you innovate, you make mistakes. It is best to admit them quickly, and then get on with improving your other innovations." Long-term vision and the ultimate *potential value* to the project and also to the enterprise as a whole should be the focus for any innovation project.

Second and more importantly, everyone involved with the demonstration needs to understand that *innovation is not easy.* In *Innovation and Entrepreneurship*, another of his visionary works on this topic, Peter Drucker emphatically states this warning early on: "Innovation is not a 'flash of genius.' It is hard, focused, purposeful work requiring diligence, persistence, and commitment."[13] It takes considerable planning and coordination to introduce any new and revolutionary concept or technology. This is particularly true when organizations are entrenched in a set or current way of doing business and are therefore resistant to change. In the case of Southern Command's innovation program, top-down endorsement of these projects combined with recognition for personnel contributing to this type of work has significantly reduced inertia to innovation projects.

Project *Stiletto*, an afloat research and development platform supporting rapid technology demonstrations, is an excellent example of the value of utilizing a pilot program and maintaining speed, agility, and dedication to a long-term innovative solution. The concept behind *Stiletto* was to determine if a high-speed, low-draft, nontraditional hull form with an "electronic keel" and nontraditional crew could address some of the toughest challenges of maritime CIT operations. Working through OSD's Rapid Reaction Technology Office (RRTO), Army South (ARSOUTH), and JIATF–South, the project quickly went from initial concept to deployment and accomplished a successful real-world CIT interdiction end-game in less than 10 months. Perhaps the most critical key in the entire deployment and demonstration was the partnership enjoyed with the Colombian military. *Stiletto* was based out of Cartagena, always had a Colombian rider aboard, performed cooperative operations with the Colombian Navy, and drew the steady attention of local senior leadership. Recognition was provided at the end of the deployment, as the ship's master was awarded the Army's transportation Warrant Officer of the Year award, in part due to his outstanding involvement with this project. Soon after the initial demonstration of *Stiletto*, the program was transitioned from the innovation cell to the U.S. Fourth Fleet for redeployment.

3 - Thus, transition is the key to the third and final phase of the process. In instances such as Project *Stiletto*, where innovative concepts show promise during the evaluation stage, the challenge is to quickly transition the concept or technology to normal operations. This is the dotted line in the diagram, representing a return to normal operations with an evolutionary improvement pattern restarting after the innovation inject

takes hold. A long-term vision for any innovation project and buy-in from people working within the enterprise are critical in making this a reality. Published demand signals to the service providers by senior leadership have been one tool used to promote promising innovative concepts. Without success in this stage, no long-term benefit will be realized by the innovative program efforts. Dr. Tony Tether, former Director of DARPA, summed up this phase well, stating, "Transitions are a full contact sport."

Another success story can be found in an academia innovation partnership formed with the University of Miami's Center for Southeastern Tropical Advanced Remote Sensing (CSTARS). The concept of using CSTARS was to determine how well access to a constellation of unclassified commercial satellites could support traditional Southern Command missions. Initial demonstrations were conducted with promising results. Subsequent letters of endorsements and demand signals for future use of CSTARS were published and promulgated to various centers of excellence and a funding mechanism was established within Southern Command. Within a year of the initial CSTARS demonstrations, hurricanes ravaged Haiti in 2008 and Southern Command responded with assistance, including an impromptu emergency redeployment of USS *Kearsarge* from its previously scheduled mission. Assessment of inland damage caused by the hurricanes was a critical need to the humanitarian assistance and disaster relief (HA/DR) efforts, and CSTARS provided vital imagery to those operations to quickly determine areas of highest damage and evaluation of inland infrastructure. Unclassified CSTARS imagery and information were then rapidly broadcast and distributed to both DOD and interagency responders via unclassified email. This response was only possible due to the groundwork laid during the initial CSTARS demonstration and a long-term vision for follow-on support made possible by CSTARS to Southern Command.

Both *Stiletto* and CSTARS show the ultimate benefit and return on the investment of persistence and commitment. Belief in your people and their talent, and being able to possess a focal length beyond the tyranny of the present are requisite traits of any change leader. Warren Bennis, an American scholar and pioneer in the field of Leadership Studies, provides this wisdom when he says, "Innovation—any new idea—by definition will not be accepted at first. It takes repeated attempts, endless demonstrations, and monotonous rehearsals before innovation can be accepted and internalized by an organization. This requires courageous patience."[14]

When Alexander the Great visited Diogenes and asked whether he could do anything for the famed teacher, Diogenes replied, "Only stand out of my light." Perhaps some day we shall know how to heighten creativity. Until then, one of the best things we can do for creative men and women is simply to stand out of their light.

—John W. Gardner[15]

The Way Ahead

In a very short time, Southern Command's Innovation Program has delivered tangible results that are already contributing to the organization's mission; furthermore, a constantly growing number of ideas are currently undergoing the transformation from concept to capability. Perhaps more importantly, the program is building the supporting innovation infrastructure—human and technological—to support the command's own transformation. Consistent with the self-stimulating and self-perpetuating nature of innovation, several of the ideas in the innovation pipeline aim to further develop this infrastructure by broadening its reach and accelerating its information flows.

One such initiative aims to create an Innovation Working Group (IWG) concept within the command and our closest partners in the interagency community. The establishment of a single, combined Interagency IWG could streamline the innovation process and serve as an internal clearinghouse, cementing the links between the various networks by institutionalizing their interaction. Relationships founded by individual "Hunter/ Brokers" are linchpins in launching partnerships—the key to growing and sustaining them is to extend the relationship beyond the founding individuals. This is especially true when military organizations are concerned, as it is the norm for their uniformed personnel to rotate frequently.

Another initiative uses technology to help address longstanding workflow management issues within the command. Synchronizing the organization's headquarters, 5 component commands, 6 primary overseas operating locations, 25 offices in a like number of nations, and a multitude of other activities has always been challenging. Several information technology and process control approaches have been implemented with mixed success. A concept under study takes lessons learned from fielding our own internal information management system, as well as ideas underpinning major transaction-based Web sites like eBay to overhaul enterprise-wide task assignment, status tracking, and decision support systems.

On the personal level, a successful change leader should be open to ideas and protective of those who advocate disruptive technologies. We need to work hard to widen the aperture of what is "permitted" in terms of discussion. This applies across the board, from the smallest conferences of mid-grade officers debating programmatic options to the most senior discussions of leadership, to include resources sponsors and requirements assessors on the joint staffs. As part of this spirit of openness, we must encourage the mavericks in practical terms—calling attention on fitness reports and personnel evaluations to innovation, for example. We should pursue with greater vigor programs to send officers into the private sector in lieu of a fellowship or war college—and recognize this in a career perspective as the equivalent of a master's degree.

We need to strengthen our partnerships with the private sector and examine how businesses develop and integrate disruptive technologies over the longer term. We should learn how major businesses are doing this in ways beyond the immediately practical to decide what to invest in for the long term. We also should look for and encourage micro-economic deployment units, fondly known as the "bicycle shops." This is where the mantra of "skip a generation" may actually play out. While the Services do this to some extent with their Tactical Exploitation of National Capabilities (TENCap) programs, clearly this is an area of potential expansion in the context of finding, nurturing, and introducing both innovative solutions and even the innovators themselves.

We should also get strategy and money talking together. This does not happen naturally, as organizations chartered with strategic long-range planning and technological long-range planning are separate entities. Once again, business does this far better than we do, and many corporations are creating specifically chartered "idea factories" to merge strategy and technology at the highest corporate levels. Therefore, perhaps as an adjunct to the innovation cell or part of the IWG, we should create an idea factory on the Service and combatant command staffs. We should consider having this as a direct report at a senior level, populated by a small group of creative and innovative technologists and strategists. Let them identify a series of small, specific disruptive technologies to challenge the orthodoxy. We have thousands of staff officers working on conventional ideas; let's put some resources against the unconventional—our competitors and enemies are doing this daily. These idea factories should be the places where strategy, technology, and money meet; they need access to the full range of current and future plans.

Finally, as we have learned here at Southern Command, there is fertile ground in the area of prototyping and leasing—we should continue exploring and emphasizing this. One key problem with the culture of experimentation is deciding when to buy, and then when to produce en masse. We need an approach that allows cost-effective leasing of commercial possibilities and prototyping of systems we want to try out that are not being produced commercially. Prototyping of weapons systems, platforms, vehicles, devices, etc., allows the possibility that some attempts will fail without doing so on the large scale of full-on procurement. Then, developing and producing the most promising concepts will help to remove hiccups early on, thereby reducing the cycle time from development to transition. It also will promote acceptance of disruptive technologies and ultimately useful systems. We may be able to expand service TENCap and joint advanced concept technology demonstration programs in this regard.

Continuing these gains and achieving success in these and other similar initiatives will require special investment in self-sustaining human innovation. Neither short- nor long-term progress can be sustained without meeting the overarching challenge of developing the right people and skill sets to serve in this environment. We must build a cadre of innovators—people with both pure intellectual firepower and a creative turn of mind who are capable of fusing two disparate disciplines: strategy and technology. Perhaps we should consider building a new curriculum at the Naval Postgraduate School or the Service War Colleges. Furthermore, early 20th-century innovators such as Sims, Moffett, and Mitchell all had career longevity and security—albeit they had enemies and had to fight for position. Again, we must strive to highlight that professionals who display the right attributes to qualify for an "innovation subspecialty" in Navy parlance truly have a career path in this field if they choose it. Each of the Services has created and protected a corps of acquisition experts—AP, or acquisition professional, again in Navy terms—a good step. Now we should consider how to create and protect innovators. Doing so in the military milieu is particularly challenging, as law and custom have long constrained the Armed Forces' ability and agility to change; in fact, the historical and traditional nature of the Armed Forces as an institution creates a self-inflicted resistance to change.

It is the superficial interpretation of this observation that helps give rise to the view that any large, tradition-centric organization is incapable of change, and would therefore never be able to truly embody a culture of innovation. The military in general does a superb job of developing its most cherished resource—its personnel; but without a doubt, we need to do better at promoting the right disciplines and skills among the right people, and putting those individuals in the right place at the right time. In this context, a fortuitous collateral effect of military collaboration with nonmilitary organizations is the cultural cross-pollination—the shared learning—that builds incumbent actors' skills and expedites needed changes in the preparation process. This does not excuse the military from the fundamental responsibility of organizing, training, and equipping their members—rather it reinforces the obligation to adequately prepare their people to work together with the best of partner organizations.

Considering the immense talent, energy, and drive of our human capital, innovation working groups can deliver intellectual economy of force by combining diverse human talents in pursuit of shared problem-solving. These innovation specialists will help facilitate the paradigmatic shifts necessary to transform internal processes and organizational structures into efficient enterprise enablers. They will accomplish this not only by changing the way the enterprise assesses its current programs and performance, but also by maintaining a fresh perspective that sees change as opportunity. This constant striving for continuous improvement, when combined with an understanding and exploitation of innovation, is, therefore, the real benefit and product of a skillfully chosen innovation cell professionally led by visionary change leaders. Ultimately, we as change leaders must always remember, as so eloquently stated by Edwin Land, "The essential part of creativity is not being afraid to fail."[16]

It ought to be remembered that there is nothing more difficult to take in hand, more perilous to conduct, or more uncertain in its success, than to take the lead in the introduction of a new order of things. Because the innovator has for enemies all those who have done well under the old conditions, and lukewarm defenders in those who may do well under the new. This coolness arises partly from fear of the opponents, who have the laws on their side, and partly from the incredulity of men, who do not readily believe in new things until they have had a long experience of them.

—Niccolò Machiavelli

> Every act of creation is first of all an act of destruction.
>
> —Pablo Picasso

Conclusion

One of the challenges to successful innovation or creation is that the outcome is rarely what was envisioned at the start of the process, particularly when external factors are considered. In the hands of a sculptor, for example, "destruction" comes in the form of chipping away from the original form to create beauty. In the hands of a builder or developer, "destruction" comes in the form of leveling any preexisting structure or clearing any field before creating the architect's vision. In both examples, the "destruction" comes from internal application, thus the end result usually remains a constant vision held firmly by the artist himself. However, as seen more often than not in the realm of national security, the act of destruction can also come from external actors, thus forcing us to create and innovate in response.

We need to constantly explore through innovation how to build the new world, making what seems impossible, possible. Many of the creative and innovative examples presented in this chapter were brought about by potentially destructive acts on the part of our competitors. On still others, *we* instituted the "destruction" internally by breaking the mold of preexisting norms and paradigms, as was the case with our enterprise reorganization and transformation. As we concurrently deconstruct and reassemble our role in national security throughout the spectrum of military capability—from nonviolent actions such as military-to-military engagement, security cooperation, and deterrence activities; through crisis response, contingency, and a range of limited operations; up to the highest level of combat intensity in major operations—we increasingly find ourselves redesigning military organizations to meet a "new" reality. These modifications blur the lines between the traditional instruments of national power, as well as the domains within the military instrument.

This blurring of the lines is exacerbated by the fact that the pace of innovation will continue to increase, and eventually biological revolutions will overlay the information and electronic ones we are experiencing today. The relevance of the military as a supporting force and critical enabler in future operations that have not typically fallen into our "bin" will depend on our ability to identify, develop, and implement disruptive technology and other forms of innovative thought. In the end, we will miss many more times than we hit. Rather than the "single great breakthrough," it is far more likely that we will have to manage numerous smaller but still significant changes. Ultimately, the greatest challenge will be letting go of what has so successfully brought us forward to this point. As Admiral Bill Owens has said, "The problem with deep, fast and rampant innovation is not getting people to accept the new, but to surrender the old." Some would say we have difficulty giving up the old because, like a rock climber, we don't have the luxury of letting go with one hand until we have a firm grip with the other: such is the nature in any business with the stakes as high as national security. But there is room for greater innovation and the taking of a few chances in today's world. We should be prepared to sail against the wind.

I have referred to the quality of being "tradition-centric" several times in this chapter. It should not be viewed as necessarily a negative thing. Quite the contrary, there are beneficial aspects of tradition—predictability, standards in the expectations for performance and training, unchanging bedrock and core fundamental values, among others. Peter Drucker explains this concept when he says the traditional institution is designed for continuity—"people need to know where they stand. They need to know the people with whom they work. They need to know what they can expect. They need to know the values and the rules of the organization. They do not function if the environment is not predictable, not understandable, not known."[17] This dependence on continuity also explains why such institutions have an inherent resistance to change to some degree: change for the traditional institution is, so to speak, a contradiction in terms.[18]

Any such institution, then, whether business, university, hospital, or even geographic combatant command, must make special efforts first to be receptive to change and then to be able to imbue all within the organization with the desire to change. And this cannot be done in a vacuum: just as no one agency, military, or even country can face and overcome the transnational and adaptive challenges in our region, so too, no one organization can change rapidly without close and continuous relationships throughout the entire process chain, from innovators to leaders to suppliers and distributors to the end user. Change and continuity are thus poles rather than opposites; that is, the more an institution is organized to be a change leader, the more it will need to establish continuity internally and externally, and the more it will need to balance rapid change and continuity. According to Drucker, "One way is to make partnership in change the basis of continuing relationships."[19]

As stated earlier, there is goodness in tradition and history; there is need for continuity with respect to the fundamentals of the enterprise: its mission, its values, and its definition of performance and results. Precisely because change is a constant in today's environment, any enterprise which attempts to embrace change—and inevitably *lead* change—must have foundations with extra fortification. It is no different at Southern Command—we are still fundamentally a military organization tasked with carrying out missions in support of our national security objectives. That is the "what," and that has never changed, nor has the "why." What *has* changed, however, is the "how" and that is what this chapter has been about: the need to change *how* we think, *how* we perform our missions, and *how* we communicate.

While we must always be prepared to excel in the kinetic domain, we must also accustom ourselves to excellence in areas *outside* the traditional military skill set. Our Armed Forces, particularly in the Americas, find themselves employing nonkinetic tools—instruments of smart power—to achieve their assigned missions. In a theater where we launch ideas, not Tomahawk missiles, the need to "fight to win" may be precluded if we can successfully "compete to *influence*."

Innovation is the key to success in both kinetic and nonkinetic domains. As our Services organize, train, and equip forces, and combatant commanders employ them, senior leaders in each chain must foster a climate of creativity—they must truly become Change Leaders. This requires them to dedicate appropriate resources, build enabling organizations, and implement decision processes using metrics suited for an environment where the desired outcomes are difficult if not impossible to quantify with traditional—typically, attrition-based—metrics. The strategic environment in our hemisphere demands properly timed innovation and a relentless pursuit of emergent opportunities. We must streamline our internal processes, optimizing them for rapid information flows, particularly when it comes to decisions on whether or not to—and then how *much* to, harkening back to the discussion of prototyping and leasing—innovate in response to changes in joint and combined force requirements. We need to sense changes as they occur and react quickly. We must also be able to anticipate these requirements and take a certain number of steps to preempt, perhaps even prevent, these needs.

We must also remain very aware of our competition. *Innovation is a two-way street.* One look at the evolving self-propelled semi-submersible vessels used by narcotics traffickers and it becomes instantly clear that our regional adversaries actively use innovation to support their own agendas. Their innovation groups may not resemble their counterparts in DOD or the members of the interagency community, but make no mistake about their existence or activity levels. In many cases, these groups enjoy the advantage of superior funding, no bureaucratic constraints, and no legal limitations. They are turning inside our circle with incredible ease. They are fast, they are smart, and they are coming at us with ideas. As innovators working at the combatant command level, we must constantly strive to prevail in today's continually shifting and dynamic security environment.

Ultimately, if we are to compete in this marketplace of ideas in our shared home, we need to be relentless in searching for and developing new vehicles and methods of delivery to communicate our strategic message— *we care about you.* Our efforts need a degree of coordination so that in aggregate, they are recognized by the people of the region as the "good" intended and achieved by the United States. Producing this type of understanding will take a broad, coordinated, and continuous strategic communication plan. Leaders at all levels of government—and even outside government—will need to maintain early, persistent, and creative involvement in the communication of our messages. Every innovative thought and deed needs to be packaged with the appropriate message—this will increase the partner nation buy-in that these past examples have highlighted as so vital to development and successful integration.

Finally, we need to leverage the linkages we share with the region to realize the true closeness the nations of the Americas can achieve. Whether it is the mixing and sharing of our cultures, our growing economic interdependence, our shared desires for freedom and prosperity, or our healthy military and security cooperation, we must create an understanding that we are all in this journey together. We need to challenge our staffs, our friends, our shipmates, our allies in this region—the dedicated professionals who work with us every day. Because at the end of the day, we will succeed if we remember that no one of us is as smart as all of us working together. We will prevail if we think about innovation, if we think about how to take the next step, if we recognize that opportunities exist in real time and have a limited shelf-life—we need to be prepared to move quickly in response to emergent opportunities. We've got to out-think our opponents. This is brain-on-brain warfare and that is how we will win in the end—by out-thinking them through innovation. From our broadening viewpoint at U.S. Southern Command, we need to foster innovative approaches that build and strengthen partnerships across the spectrum of options—governmental, international, and private sector—to confront ever-changing and increasingly complex 21st-century security challenges.

Notes

[1] Peter F. Drucker, *Management Challenges for the 21st Century* (New York: HarperCollins, 1999), 74.

[2] Ibid.

[3] Ibid.

[4] Margaret J. Wheatley, writer and management consultant who studies organizational behavior, theories of change, and chaos theory.

[5] Roger von Oech, author, inventor, and creator of Creative Think.

[6] Drucker, 75.

[7] Ibid.

[8] Ibid.

[9] Ibid., 85.

[10] Ibid., 82.

[11] Ibid., 86.

[12] Ibid., 87.

[13] Peter F. Drucker, *Innovation and Entrepreneurship* (New York: HarperCollins, 1985), 15.

[14] Warren Bennis is the Founding Chairman of the Leadership Institute at the University of Southern California and the Chairman of the Board of Directors at the Kennedy School of Government Center for Public Leadership.

[15] John William Gardner served as Secretary of Health, Education, and Welfare under President Lyndon Johnson, and was founder of the White House Fellowship and Common Cause, the first non-profit public interest organization in the United States.

[16] Edwin H. Land, American scientist and inventor, discovered the ability to polarize light; invented in-camera instant photography; and created the retina theory of color vision.

[17] Drucker, *Management Challenges*, 90.

[18] Ibid.

[19] Ibid.

Chapter 8

Youth Matters

Let us remember that our success must be measured by the ability of the people to live their dreams. That is a goal that cannot be encompassed with any one policy or communiqué. It is not a matter of abstractions or ideological debates. It is a question of whether or not we are in a concrete way making the lives of our citizens better. It is reflected in the hopes of our children, in the strength of our democratic institutions, and our faith in the future.

—Barack Obama
President of the United States[1]

Another of the miseries affecting the Latin American and Caribbean region and a close corollary of the spread of illegal drug traffic is the alarming growth of criminal violence. Rising crime is combining with corruption to exacerbate the already deleterious conditions of poverty and inequality, hampering any development efforts and reducing an already stifled economic growth outlook. According to United Nations data, the regional annual homicide rate is one of the highest in the world, with more than 27 homicides per 100,000 people—murder now ranks as one of the five main causes of death in several Central American countries. In comparison, figures for Africa and the United States are 22 deaths and 5.5 deaths per 100,000 people, respectively. The Caribbean registers the highest murder rate of any of the world's subregions, with 30 per 100,000. Recent surveys in Central America now show that two-thirds of the respondents cited crime as the number-one problem facing their countries—six times the number naming poverty.

Contributing to crime rates and severely challenging personal security in many areas is the growing presence and influence of gangs. In Central America, Haiti, Jamaica, and major cities in Brazil, gangs are infecting society's ability to provide basic functions and necessities, and are thus becoming a serious security priority. The overall gang population is estimated to reach into the hundreds of thousands, with the ranks filled primarily by disenfranchised youth. These urban street gangs, colloquially referred to as *maras*, are known for their brutal initiations and extortion of protection money or "War Taxes," as the locals call it. They do not just pose a concern in Latin America—the more sophisticated groups operate regionally with deep reach into the United States, ranging from California to Washington, DC, spreading their tentacles to the very core of suburbia.

The compounded effects of urban violence and transnational gangs are an undeniable threat to our national security and to the larger long-term security and stability of the region. Recognizing this threat, regional cooperation among Central America, Mexico, and the United States is focusing on a new strategy to counter gang-related violence and provide alternatives that encourage young people not to join gangs. The Departments of State, Justice, and Homeland Security and the U.S. Agency for International Development have programs that fit together to augment the efforts of the nations most affected by youth violence. It is important to understand that although the U.S. military is best kept in a supporting role to other lead Federal agencies, U.S. Southern Command still has an important mission in building partner nation capacity. In close coordination with other Federal agencies, we work arm-in-arm with the partner nation military and security forces in the region to build the necessary capabilities to guarantee their own national security and to be able to provide responsible support to civilian authorities when required.

Identifying the Security Challenge

Over the past decade, approximately 1.2 million deaths can be linked to crime in Latin America and the Caribbean. As previously noted, Latin America already has some of the highest per capita homicide rates in the world, with certain regions approaching levels normally reserved for combat zones. Especially troublesome is the killing spree associated with the growth of gang violence and drug-related crime in Mexico, across Central America, portions of the Caribbean, and some areas in Brazil. Violent death rates are higher today in El Salvador, Guatemala, and Honduras than they were during those countries' bloody civil wars. In addition to having a homicide rate that is five times that of the United States and three times that of the world average, a recent study lists Latin America as having the highest homicide rate for people between ages 15 and 24, with a rate 30 times greater than those in Europe.[2] Moreover, every year, approximately one-third of the population falls victim to a criminal act, either directly or indirectly through family members.

In many respects, these security threats are symptoms of the deeper endemic problems of poverty and inequality. According to United Nations statistics, almost 40 percent of the region's inhabitants are living in poverty, defined as an income of less than 2 dollars per day. That is roughly 180 million people—the equivalent of the U.S. population east of the Mississippi—all living on the daily cost of less than a cup of coffee. Moreover, nearly 16 percent are living in extreme poverty—less than 1 dollar per day. Combine these poverty figures with a disproportionate wealth distribution that is second only to sub-Saharan Africa and a high level of corruption, and you have fertile conditions for social and political insecurity. This also becomes a tremendous catalyst for emigration, both legal and illegal, which further reduces a nation's ability to sustain its intellectual, work force, and productivity levels.

Serious violent crime is a growing threat that affects local and regional stability, and is a worsening danger in many countries; the most concentrated gang problem, however, is in Central America and Mexico. The influence of gangs and of youth delinquency in these areas is growing at an alarming rate, with some gang populations reaching over 100,000 in Central America alone. Youth gang membership is also spreading at an increasingly rapid speed—with secondary school enrollment below 50 percent in some areas, a large portion of the youth population is idle and uneducated, making easy targets for gang recruitment. In El Salvador, for example, the youth homicide rate in 2008 was 92 per 100,000 with an average of 10 murders a day. Youth gangs are also on the rise in the Caribbean as children as young as 6 years are participating in gang activity in Jamaica. In recent surveys of the region, delinquency and personal security rank as the top social ill for the majority of countries.[3] This insecurity and its associated costs—not just human costs, but also on the order of $250 billion annually in economic impact—have become a major threat and destabilizing element in many nations in the Western Hemisphere. The level of sophistication and brutality of these gangs is without precedent.

It should be remembered, however, that *maras* are not native to Central America; instead, in the words of General Álvaro Romero, former Honduran Public Security Minister, they are a "phenomenon imported by those who emigrated to another country."[4] General Romero further explains that these gangs were actually born from the mass exodus of Central Americans caused by the political crises and civil wars of the 1970s and 1980s, with most fleeing to the United States. He explains that these children of guerrillas were "raised in a culture of violence and were already predisposed to it. When they arrived in the U.S., they felt isolated. The gang phenomenon grew out of loneliness, being without a family and wanting to find kinship with someone."[5] While these "children of violence" were here in the United States and forming bonds with others who had experienced similar pasts, they learned the "craft" of gangsterism from the more orthodox and organized gangs in places like South Central Los Angeles and similar locations. General Romero sees this as the origin, but then adds, "Their evolution has been constant. Leadership was primarily maintained in the U.S.; they were like Central American subsidiaries of U.S. organizations."[6]

Gangs, despite the fact that they often begin as local delinquent youth organizations, become more organized over time because of this evolution. Some of the more structured gangs function almost like organized crime syndicates, and they routinely cross borders and operate inside the United States. The more efficient groups have emerged as larger criminal enterprises with expanding transnational connections. Dangerous gangs like the Mara Salvatrucha (MS-13), 18th Street Gang (M-18), and the Mexican drug gangs have established criminal networks within Latin America, the United States, and Canada, and are extending their reach globally. Since February 2005, more than 2,000 MS-13 members have been arrested in the United States.

The High Cost of Insecurity

The costs associated with violence in the region are at times difficult to isolate from other ills and assess; however, in 2008, the National Public Security Council of the Salvadoran presidency's office commissioned a comprehensive study compiling the excess direct spending and losses caused by violence in five Central American countries in four areas, namely: increased health care; increased government spending for crime prevention, law enforcement, and justice; spending on private security; and material losses from crime. This landmark analysis found that in 2006, violent crime cost the combined states $6.5 billion—equivalent to 7.7 percent of gross domestic product (GDP).[7] Though all nations suffered significant losses, the total cost of violence varied among countries: $2.9 billion in Guatemala (7.7 percent GDP); $2.01 billion in El Salvador (10.8 percent GDP); $885 million in Honduras (9.6 percent GDP); $790 million in Costa Rica (3.6 percent GDP); and $529 million in Nicaragua (10.0 percent GDP). The GDP losses to crime came at the expense of government investment in social services like spending on development, infrastructure, public safety, and education.[8]

As further evidence of the devastating effect of gangs and crime on the economies in the region, the Inter-American Development Bank (IDB) expanded its scope of survey to include countries from both Central and

South America, and estimated the losses from crime in the region as a whole approached 15 percent of GDP in 2005. The level remained relatively constant through 2008 with the figure being estimated at 14.2 percent GDP. During this same timeframe, the average cost among industrialized nations was only 5 percent GDP. Thus, according to IDB figures, if the nations in Latin America and the Caribbean could lower the losses attributed to crime and violence, it would have a net increase in GDP of approximately 25 percent. This is an economic drain that inhibits efforts to alleviate the underlying conditions of poverty and inequality, but also cuts across productivity and development at all levels of the government and society. In places plagued by gang violence, there is increased level of social disassociation with established support networks. This can spiral into a vicious cycle that if left unchecked, could erode governments into failed states.

Crime also erodes economic growth because foreign investors avoid putting money in places that cannot guarantee the rule of law. According to a 2005 World Bank development report, more than 50 percent of businesses surveyed in the region cited crime as a serious obstacle to conducting business, as compared to only 25 percent of businesses in sub-Saharan Africa and East Asia that cited crime as a major problem. Additionally, tourism is the largest or second largest economic sector and source of income in Central America, and it is becoming particularly vulnerable as vacationers also seek safer regions. Finally, violence dramatically reduces the availability of human capital as skilled workers and managers leave the region because of fear for their personal safety. According to the World Bank, just 11 percent of Central American workers are considered skilled labor and 17 percent of the most qualified emigrate in search of better working conditions. Emigration rates for people with postsecondary education from virtually all Central American countries exceed 10 percent.[9]

Ignoring the problem of gang violence is not an option. Governments, nongovernmental organizations, and communities have been increasing their level of focus and effort on this social ill. In response to tragic crime rates and the globalizing nature of gangs, there have been heightened international attention and renewed desires to help, as well. Unfortunately, there are no simple answers to solve the gang problem—no silver bullet is available to slay transnational criminal networks, nor is there any logical way to declare war on the series of social problems that coalesce to produce youth violence. In fact, given the overwhelming number of variables that criminologists, sociologists, economists, political scientists, and jurists have identified as potential causes, there is probably no single answer to the crisis. More likely, a spectrum of conditions should be present in a society to improve the current situation and prevent future violence. The first step in identifying solutions is to understand the cause of the problem.

Factors Contributing to Gang Violence

Although social scientists have identified many contributing factors associated with the problem of gang violence and despite the fact that much debate still exists about the basic determinants, most scholars agree that income inequality is the strongest predictor of increased violent crime. Areas that have a large percentage of poor people, lack a middle class, and have a small, powerfully wealthy population tend to have high crime rates. It is important to understand that poverty does not cause violence and that poor people are not more prone to violence. However, in cases of extreme poverty and income inequality, some people will turn to armed violence in desperation as an option for advancement. The larger the gap in the standard of living between rich and poor, the worse the crime rate gets. Central American countries, with the notable exception of Costa Rica, have some of the highest income inequality indexes in the world.[10] Although the region of sub-Saharan Africa has the highest disparity, the Western Hemisphere has the highest index of unequal wealth distribution (the United States has the worst income inequality among the highly industrialized nations) and the least progress in reversing that trend. Studies have shown other factors can lead to gang violence in the region, including extreme poverty, high urban population density, lack of legitimate employment, and failure to enforce adherence to the rule of law.

Many NGOs that work closely with at-risk youth focus specifically on extreme poverty, limited access to education, and the lack of productive employment as primary causal factors driving many poor youths to join gangs in growing numbers. In Honduras, for example, 65 percent of the population lives on less than $2 per day and unemployment is over 27 percent. Additionally, very few opportunities are available to the 1.5 million people between the ages of 15 and 24. Compounding these conditions, Honduras has one of the highest murder rates as 53 homicides occur per 100,000 inhabitants, with these murders being attributed largely to juvenile gangs, organized crime, drug trafficking, and social violence. This high homicide rate is coupled with a high rate of physical violence and a growing prevalence of crimes against property.

Another contributing factor associated with greater violence is drugs. It is no coincidence that the worst gang problems in the Americas are found along illicit narcotic-smuggling routes. The Caribbean, Central

America, and Mexico are wedged inextricably between the Andean Ridge, virtually the world's sole producer of cocaine, and the United States, the world's largest cocaine consumer. Nearly 90 percent of the cocaine destined for the United States moves through the Central America–Mexico corridor. Narcotraffickers operating in this transit zone have strong ties to local gangs, as smugglers pay gangs to provide information, protect shipments, and distribute drugs to the local population. Over time, this caustic relationship has opened even more drug markets for traffickers, and generated a larger volume of illegal profits that gangs have been using to buy arms, technology, and recruit new members. The increased illicit capital has also enabled larger gangs to reorganize and expand into more sophisticated criminal ventures like assassination, robbery, kidnapping, and extortion. In the last few decades, drug kingpins have been supplying more and more drugs to traditional "transit countries" where gangs have been pushing the supply through their territory. This illicit business model has developed more powerful gangs, while also generating more extreme violence as well-armed factions compete to control territory and attempt to consolidate illicit distribution networks.

Demographic Trends in Latin America

Countries in the region are experiencing a general demographic transition where the total population growth is slowing and the populace is becoming older. The population change is caused by a decrease in birth rates coupled with an increase in longevity brought about by better access to medical and social care systems. In the middle of the 20th century, Latin America had one of the highest birth rates in the world, but its current levels are below the world average. The dramatically declining birth rates, particularly since the 1970s, have permanently altered the demographic composition of the region's population. Children aged 15 and under comprised 40.2 percent of the population in 1950, and 43.2 percent in 1965. By 1970 a number of factors including increased urbanization, improved access to general health and social services, and subtle changes in sociopolitical attitudes toward families began suppressing birth rates. As the number of people entering the younger demographic sector has decreased, there has been a steadily increasing drop in the size of the under-15 sector: a 3.1 percent decline in the 1970s, a 3.3 percent decline in the 1980s, and a 4.4 percent decline in the 1990s. By 2005, the youngest demographic made up only 29.9 percent of the total population (a 13.3 percent decrease over 40 years), and by 2050 it is predicted to be only 18.1 percent of the total.[11] This decrease in new births has not only reduced the rate of total population growth but has also translated into a generalized aging of the Latin American population.

Combining with the decrease in birth rates is the fact that the population has been living longer. Since 1950, the average lifespan in Latin America and the Caribbean has improved significantly by 21.6 years to 73.4 years for both men and women. The region's longevity rate is only 1.2 years behind Europe's and over 8 years better than the rest of the world's developing countries. Slowly but surely, the population of Latin America is getting older. Although there is still some variation of growth rates between countries, the proportion and absolute number of persons over age 65 has increased and is projected to continue to rise steadily in the coming decades. Between 1950 and 2000, the number of people 65 years old and older jumped from 5.5 million to 28 million; the size of this demographic is projected to reach 108 million by 2050.[12] In fact, the number of persons over age 65 will triple by 2050, when one in every five Latin Americans will be a senior citizen.

These changing demographics present a new set of social and economic challenges for the region. In any society, the population can be divided into those who are working age and those who are too young or too old to work. The working-age population is the one most likely to provide surplus socioeconomic resources through paying more taxes, creating more economic activity, and producing and rearing the next generations. In general, this group pays into the system more than it consumes. In contrast, though still productive, the nonworking population group is far more likely to consume more public resources than it replaces in a given year. This is especially true at the extreme ends of the life span. For instance, a newborn and an extremely elderly person will typically require far more medical and social services than the average middle-aged working adult, yet they are the least able to contribute social services. By combining the old and young into a single group, demographers can analyze relationships between working-age people and the rest of the population, thereby generating a demographic dependency rate.[13] To facilitate comparisons, the demographic dependency rate is always expressed as the ratio of the population younger than 15 and older than 65 to the potentially active population between those ages. A drop in the demographic dependency rate indicates that there is a "demographic bonus" in available resources. This term refers to a situation where the potential burden on the working population is relatively lower than in previous periods.

The declining birth rates in Latin America and the Caribbean have generated a corresponding decline in the demographic dependency rate as fewer young people are competing for social support from the most productive element of society. This presents a short-term boom in available resources—a window of opportunity for countries to be able to invest in their future population by maximizing resources per capita on youth services such as education, pediatric health care, and vocational/technical training. The decreased dependency rate also affords greater opportunities for generating long-term social investments in combating poverty, improving education, and reforming health systems. Unfortunately, the demographic bonus is limited in time because lower fertility rates combined with extended longevity will eventually increase the size of the elderly population. The window of available development resources will continue to close as more and more people join the over-65 group and begin to draw more social service resources.

It is important to clarify that the potential benefit of any demographic bonus is not automatic or even guaranteed. As with any social program, it is totally dependent upon the political-economic realities of each state. There can be no increased development bonus if a country's economy cannot efficiently employ its population. If a government cannot guarantee security, collect taxes fairly, or provide long-term oversight for effective investments in its citizens, this window of opportunity is wasted. In short, the potential benefits of demographics can only be realized by effective, socially responsive governance.

How to Address the Challenge

Population growth, increasing unemployment, poor education, expanding social inequalities, easy access to weapons, overwhelmed law enforcement agencies, and the presence of a large number of persons with military or insurgent training continue to produce increased numbers of militarized criminal groups throughout Latin America and the Caribbean. Since most of our partners in the region exhibit many of these risk factors linked to high violent crime rates, the current problems and related consequences are likely to continue in the near future unless we come together to solve this common and shared threat to our collective security. As criminal drug organizations and gangs expand their power and presence, the spread of violence related to their actions is likely to remain a primary threat to political stability and democracy across the region.

Gangs and youth violence are difficult problems that require integrated and coordinated responses that seamlessly integrate prevention, law enforcement, and development to achieve lasting results, none of which are missions that traditionally fall into the spectrum of military operations. The size and reach of these gangs and criminal elements severely stress regional law enforcement capabilities. In certain instances, governments have called on the military to relieve outgunned and outnumbered police forces. For example, the inability of the police to confront gangs has prompted Guatemala, El Salvador, and Honduras to increase military support to law enforcement and to enact antigang legislation. These militaries then turn to the United States seeking assistance and advice, yet U.S. military forces are legally restricted in their ability to provide such support. For many logical reasons, support for law enforcement functions is provided by the Justice Department, State, or USAID. However, in this region, the Defense Department, through Southern Command, assists our interagency partners to achieve a holistic approach by helping partner militaries develop better capabilities that can support civilian law enforcement and crime prevention programs. We are helping our partner nation militaries and security forces in the Americas with their efforts to instill respect for human rights, develop cooperative planning and information management, and build civil engineering and medical capability and capacity that could be used to support law enforcement. While Southern Command is not the lead agency, its expertise can enhance the coordinated interagency community response.

In addition to regional development and antidrug policies, the U.S. Government has shown commitment to pursuing a broad approach to its foreign antigang policy. The State Department, USAID, and the Departments of Justice and Homeland Security all have programs that address various facets of the problem, namely: diplomacy; coordinating repatriation of criminals deported from the United States; collaborative law enforcement; building partner capability and capacity; and support to prevention and rehabilitation programs.

Additionally, foreign assistance programs need to continue to be designed in conjunction with partner governments to effectively address each nation's individual and unique situation and incorporate the local policing experience of each country's security forces. Furthermore, law enforcement approaches need to be tailored to fit the specific circumstances present in neighborhood crime hotspots. A combination of law enforcement, prevention, rehabilitation initiatives, and alternative development options will prove far more effective than crime prevention or social intervention alone. Support from U.S. Government agencies should help build partner nation capabilities to conduct community policing that effectively integrates prevention, intervention, and law enforcement in ways that are relevant to the specific needs of the community. There must also be an equally dedicated approach that focuses on education stimuli, incentives for remaining in school, youth engagement, and recreation activities. These efforts should be tailored and combined with other programs which provide and develop tools and social skill sets that will be highly valued and sought after for employment in either the public or private sector. We have to provide hope and opportunity as preferred alternatives to joining gangs and the ensuing life of crime and misery. The United States needs to continue to work with our partners in the Americas to identify and improve structural weaknesses in the existing infrastructure across the spectrum from judicial systems and law enforcement to education, youth activities, and development.

Further, because of their transnational nature, criminal gangs and organized crime networks cannot be countered by one nation alone. Instead, the governments and societies in this region need to work together to develop and implement innovative holistic approaches that simultaneously arrest the deteriorating security situation and address the underlying socioeconomic problems that spawn and nurture urban gangs. Thus, they demand cooperative solutions that involve a unified response from the full spectrum of society, including national governments, international institutions, and even the private sector. One such example is a regional organization called the Central American Integration System (SICA), which deals with the economic and social implications of gang-related activity. This organization operates primarily in the diplomatic realm as the under secretaries of defense and security meet regularly to agree on pivotal elements of a coordinated strategy such as information-sharing from databases like Interpol, extradition expediency, communication flow, and regional training centers like the one established in El Salvador.

As shown by the example of SICA, governments throughout the region are working to find the right combination of suppressive and preventive measures to counter the growing threat. Panama, as well as Guatemala, El Salvador, and Honduras have all enacted social programs to counter gang membership. Guatemala and El Salvador have established joint patrols to police gang activity along their borders. Finally, several Central American and Caribbean nations have created a joint database to track gang activity. Thus, there has been successful regional cooperation focused on countering drug-related violence and encouraging young people not to join gangs—this needs to continue and be expanded.

The regional approach to reducing gang violence must be shaped by the larger socioeconomic factors that fuel the problem. The "U.S. Strategy to Combat the Threat of Criminal Gangs from Central America and Mexico"—presented in a special meeting of the Organization of American States (OAS) focusing on gang violence—outlined the following: "Effectively addressing the problem of transnational gangs requires close cooperation, coordination and information-sharing among the countries affected and a comprehensive approach that includes law enforcement, prevention, intervention, rehabilitation and reintegration."[14] Thus, success in this arena requires a balanced approach that combines existing law enforcement and crime prevention efforts with positive socioeconomic options for troubled communities. These efforts must also be integrated regionally to support broad transnational development that prevents criminal networks from simply transferring their corrosive presence to neighboring countries. U.S. Southern Command, in partnering with interagency teammates and the militaries and security forces in the region, continues to support increased hemispheric solutions by actively engaging with national governments, the OAS, and the Central America Integration System.

Improving Public Security

To ensure social integrity, several nations in the region have committed military forces to help counter threats that normally would be the responsibility of the police. Although this is clearly not a preferred solution—particularly because it could complicate the protection of human rights—the growing trend is born out of the necessity to counter increasingly powerful and socially destructive gangs, drug cartels, and criminal organizations. In most cases, the military has been deployed as reinforcement for overwhelmed law enforcement units. Although the military should expect to support civilian authorities in times of national crisis, this should not naturally extend to militarizing domestic law enforcement roles.

It is thus increasingly important to work across the interagency community and partner with regional governments to develop modern law enforcement capabilities and strengthen judicial systems. In coordination with the State Department, several other U.S. agencies have been supporting their international counterparts' efforts to face the challenges of gangs in the Americas. The FBI is working with Mexican and Central American authorities to improve regional information-sharing and increase training for investigators and law enforcement officers. Enhanced cross-border cooperation has helped Federal agencies like Alcohol, Tobacco, and Firearms (ATF),

Immigrations and Customs Enforcement (ICE), and the Secret Service combat growing international criminal networks. These sustained efforts weaken the grip of terror that gangs maintain on communities by denying them access to criminal profits and weapons. Preventing crime and enforcing the rule of law is a critical component to combating gang violence, but being "tough on crime" is not enough. Regional efforts also need to focus on targeting the root causes of poverty that provide fertile grounds for criminal organizations to thrive and flourish.

> I ask myself: who is our enemy? Our enemy . . . is the lack of education; it is illiteracy; it's that we don't spend on the health of our people; that we don't create the necessary infrastructure, the roads, the highways, the ports, the airports; it's that we are not dedicating the necessary resources to stop the deterioration of the environment; it's the lack of equality which we have, which really makes us ashamed; it is a product, among many things, of course, of the fact that we are not educating our sons and our daughters.
>
> —Oscar Arias
> President of Costa Rica[15]

Targeting the Cause, Not Just the Symptom

The primary cause and origin of most gang activity can be traced to a perceived lack of positive economic outlook in the community, which in turn stems from observed chronic problems like poor education, structural unemployment, and limited access to social services. Many young people join gangs as a survival mechanism because they lack other viable opportunities. The best way to help troubled youths is to first create a safe and secure environment where the rule of law and educational and other social services can be offered. This is where the majority of our efforts in DOD can continue to be focused—working with our partner nation militaries and security forces to build their capacity to provide and ensure the conditions of security. Once these requisite parameters have been established or restored, then the other elements of national power can begin their work toward stability and development. USAID, for example, is coordinating a number of initiatives focused on improving access to social services and sustainable economic development

SOUTHCOM All-Star players pose with a group of Panamanian little leaguers during a baseball clinic in Curundú. More than 500 local kids took part in the clinic. The SOUTHCOM team, comprised of top military baseball talent, went on a goodwill tour to the Dominican Republic, Panama, and Nicaragua.

that empower communities to offer positive alternatives to a life of crime. The collaborative efforts in Guatemala and El Salvador are two cases in point that illustrate the integrated approach that is common in the region.

In Guatemala, USAID is partnering with the national government, local NGOs, and the private sector on a program that focuses on deterring youth from joining gangs and helping rehabilitate former gang members. USAID's cross-cutting youth activities are designed to address the needs of adolescents and young adults between 10 and 25 years of age living in rural areas, marginal urban areas, and indigenous pockets.[16] The USAID contributions are augmented by support from the private sector to provide academic scholarships, leadership training, and funding programs to teach English and entrepreneurial skills. In his speech in Cairo in June 2009, President Obama addressed this issue when he said, "no development strategy can be based solely upon what comes out of the ground, nor can it be sustained while young people are out of work. . . . All of us must recognize that education and innovation will be the currency of the 21st Century." William Fulbright took this notion still further when he remarked, "We must try to expand the boundaries of human wisdom, empathy and perception, and there is no way of doing that except through education."[17]

Hand-in-hand with, and complementary to, education programs, Guatemala is also a test bed for a project that tries to emphasize the idea of rehabilitation as an alternative to mere repression or law enforcement. Currently, gang doctrine stipulates that religion and death are the only accepted methods to leave the *maras*; furthermore, as discussed previously, the lack of opportunities for education, employment, and other development is usually the primary motivator for young people to join gangs in the first place. Attempting to confront all these elements of the larger gang challenge is a project USAID funds through the Global Development Alliance. The effort focuses on youth at risk and has two primary objectives, namely: 1) deterring these youth from becoming involved in gangs; and 2) rehabilitating and providing developmental programs and opportunities for former gang members. The project runs several youth houses where former *mara* members receive counseling and basic education, as well as several crime prevention councils that organize curricula with schools and get youths involved in sports.

In El Salvador, USAID is working with local agencies to restore the rule of law and citizen confidence in the justice system and state institutions. The main thrust of this effort is to support criminal justice system reforms that stimulate more effective community partnerships with business and governments to prevent crime and offer alternatives to gang membership. The program strives to improve government ethics and anti-corruption efforts that promote greater transparency, accountability, and more responsive governance within the country. The multifaceted approach also includes providing support to government programs designed to increase private and public investments in health and education. This effort also provides a huge cost-savings benefit, as, according to a recent Human Development Index for El Salvador, it costs the state $1,200 a year to keep someone in prison, while spending on education and secondary school ranges between $200 and $250 a year per child.[18]

These are just two examples—there are a number of similar development efforts throughout the region. In each case, U.S. programs in development, crime prevention, and partner-nation capacity-building are closely linked to national and regional antigang efforts. Education is a key focus as it provides the path and the tools to enable a successful journey toward hope and opportunity, and away from the misery, violence, and death of gang life. In the words of President Barack Obama during the opening ceremony at the Summit of the Americas in April 2009, "unless we provide opportunity for an education and for jobs and a career for the young people in the region, then too many will end up being attracted to the gangs and to the drug trade. And so we cannot separate out dealing with the . . . law enforcement side from the need for critical development in our communities."[19]

Building Partner Nation Capacity and Capability

It bears restating that this challenge area is not one that falls within the spectrum of operations typically assigned to the military; rather, this skill set resides with our extremely capable partners at the Departments of Justice, Homeland Security, State, and USAID. That means we in the military need to do all we can to assist agencies and organizations that are better suited and properly trained in such mission areas. Further, the complexity of the challenge facing the U.S. interagency community and partner nations only reinforces the need for coordinated interagency and international solutions. Thus, our role at U.S. Southern Command is to support and help where appropriate and needed—we are committed to pursuing multinational, multiagency, and public-private partnerships that can better confront the challenge of gangs and embrace the opportunities of the Americas. Southern Command spends a great deal of resources building the security capabilities of partner nation militaries to meet 21st-century challenges. This includes helping to build professional security forces that respect human rights and are fully capable of functioning throughout the spectrum of operations—particularly in the more nontraditional roles from peacekeeping and disaster response to supporting civilian law enforcement and emergency relief.

To this end, Southern Command conducts a wide range of bilateral and multinational exercises, as well as numerous international exchanges, to strengthen regional partnerships and collective capabilities that are integral to U.S. national security and that of the region as a whole. There are no major exercises focused specifically on training to provide military support to civil authority efforts to counter crime, but many of the military skills that are best suited to provide this support are honed in existing exercises. There are also many military capabilities that can augment civilian efforts in crisis situations. By training these core military competencies—including civil engineering, medical management, maritime interdiction, logistics support, campaign planning, and information management—not only are we strengthening the region's capability to effectively operate together in times of conflict, but we are also generating a positive capability that could provide support to civilian authorities in the future.

Using an integrated international, interagency, and public-private approach that listens to and engages with our partner nation militaries and security forces, we are able to more accurately identify needed equipment and training exercises to build military capabilities that reinforce law enforcement and prevention programs. For example, Southern Command works closely with partners to ensure that militaries and security forces in Central America and the Caribbean are capable of controlling national borders and littoral areas, providing support to civil authorities in times of crisis—particularly civil engineering, logistics, transportation, and maritime and aerial patrol platforms.

Beyond the Horizon is one such example, and the newest evolution of Southern Command's tradition of humanitarian assistance exercise programs. To support Beyond the Horizon, U.S. military engineers and medical professionals deploy to Latin American and Caribbean nations in order to conduct advanced training on the best ways to provide military support to humanitarian assistance. Part of the exercise involves military staffs carefully planning and conducting logistical operations to support large deployments of personnel and materiel to remote regions to provide medical and engineering services alongside partner nation military and security force units. Medical teams deliver a full range of medical, surgical, dental, pharmacy, and veterinary services, as well as training of host-nation medical professionals. Engineering troops build schools, clinics, community centers, water wells, and other quality of life enhancement facilities. In any given year, about 400 U.S. Service members participate in Beyond the Horizon training with their counterparts in nine countries.

In past decades, these types of exercises were only coordinated between military forces, with little consideration of how they fit into larger development plans. This oversight limited the long-term sustainability of our humanitarian assistance. Quite honestly, the lack of broader coordination with civilian agencies ignored an opportunity to make lasting social impacts in the Americas—the focus was simply to provide units world-class training. It was wonderful that citizens in need received medical care, and gained some useful infrastructure in the process, but there was little thought given to long-term effects; thus, return visits and progress reports were nonexistent. Although units received great training, when the event was over, there was no follow-up. Over the years, the U.S. military has treated thousands of patients and built scores of buildings in the region; unfortunately, however, most of these great works were completed without integrating these efforts into existing sustainable programs. The social impact dissipated drastically once the military left. In some cases, the bridges, schools, and clinics built were never fully used because the bridges may not have been on a proper farm-to-market route; or there were no books or teachers available to take advantage of the new schoolhouse; or no doctors or nurses or supporting infrastructure were available to sustain the clinics.

By coordinating our program closely with partners, we can identify better ways to cooperate to ensure that we are mutually supporting efforts. The whole-of-government approach to planning and executing Beyond the Horizon can achieve more realistic training and provide greater opportunities for sustainable results with the same investment. In actuality, what we are talking about is closer to "whole-of-society" planning and integration that includes not just the U.S. interagency, but also NGOs and other cooperating organizations. The military can still gain great engineering training, but by building a youth center, school, or clinic in the right spot where it supports a USAID community-based prevention program, the project takes on an additional long-term benefit. If the military is going to build a bridge, it is logical to coordinate activities to ensure they fit into the nation's development plan, and do not duplicate efforts already funded by other agencies or efforts in the private sector. The intent is not to become a contractor for development agencies, but rather to maximize collaborative opportunities. Every dollar DOD or any other agency places on the ground frees up limited resources from other agencies to focus elsewhere, all still confronting the same shared challenges. Similar return on investment from more effective and efficient use of resources occurs when nations coordinate, deconflict, and synchronize efforts to better take advantage of finite resources and capabilities.

Beyond the Horizon missions are designed to foster goodwill and improve relations between the United States and the governments of the region. The program builds upon those previous efforts, adding a series of engagement events for U.S. troops to exchange knowledge with host-nation officials that generate better government-to-government and people-to-people relations. Another feature is a 3-year phased support strategy in each nation that will result in better humanitarian support, stronger local relationships, and more persistent community involvement. The more we work together, the better we can focus our effects and respond to rapidly and constantly changing environments.

New Opportunity to Share Lessons in Support of the Rule of Law

An emerging opportunity for collaboration being explored between USAID and the Defense Department is through the National Guard Bureau State Partnership Program (SPP). The SPP links U.S. states with partner countries to support common security cooperation objectives. The program's strength is the unique civil-military nature of the National Guard, which facilitates interaction with both civilian and military forces of foreign countries. While most of the military is not geared to directly support the rule of law, each of our states' Guard forces explicitly provides this very service when directed by their Governor. Collectively the National Guard has hundreds of years of experience providing critical functional support to law enforcement during emergency situations. Through the National Guard's State Partnership Program, these lessons can be shared with partner nations. By coordinating through the U.S. Ambassadors' country teams, and other agencies as appropriate, the National Guard can provide support tailored to meet the objectives of both the United States and its partner nations.

Recently, USAID has been working with the National Guard in the eastern Caribbean to strengthen local programs targeting youth violence. The goal is to go beyond National Guard training for military units and share ideas on effective youth programs. In cooperation with the Florida National Guard and U.S. Southern Command, USAID held a Youth Service and Crime Prevention Workshop in Saint Lucia and Antigua and Barbuda. The events linked a broad spectrum of experts from local organizations focusing on youth violence with professionals from Florida who oversee similar programs. Specialists representing the State Prosecutor, the Police Athletic League, several sheriffs' offices, and the National Guard's Youth Challenge Program shared their lessons learned from years of working with at-risk youths in rural and urban counties. This initiative highlights not just the vibrant partnership between the United States and these Caribbean island nations, but also the seamless linkages that exist between the civilian and military, Federal, and state governments and private and public sectors of our own society. This type of multifaceted cooperation is essential to tackle the complex causes of youth gang violence. Wherever possible, we at U.S. Southern Command will continue to seek to work with our military and civilian partners to develop international, interagency, and public-private action to achieve such synergistic results.

The preservation of our free society in the years and decades to come will depend ultimately on whether we succeed or fail in directing the enormous power of human knowledge to the enrichment of our own lives and the shaping of a rational and civilized world order. . . . It is the task of education, more than any other instrument of foreign policy to help close the dangerous gap between the economic and technological interdependence of the people of the world and their psychological, political and spiritual alienation.

—William J. Fulbright[20]

Gangs are a phenomenon of imitation, an imitation of young people. . . . What sustains a gang? They must have human resources. It is necessary to prevent young people from joining them. You must have a policy of security that monopolizes the minds of young people so they are not attracted to gangs and so there are other options for them.

—General Álvaro Romero

The Way Ahead

We at Southern Command are focused on current threats and challenges that most certainly fall within the spectrum of military operations. But we cannot avoid or ignore warning signals and trends that may fall outside those operating lanes but still have definite impact on, and implications for, our national security. Drugs, violent youth gangs, and poverty are placing future generations at risk of growing instability and a lack of security. Our commitment and promise to the next generation are that they will have a future—one of hope and opportunity. But in order to do so, we must ensure they have the requisite capability and capacity to nurture their own potential.

As we have seen, the best strategy in this pursuit is a phased approach that has three main pillars: the appropriate and timely use of force (providing and ensuring security), balanced development (setting the conditions for stability), and education (creating the tools to build a lasting prosperity). In simpler terms, "Our tools to knock down this wall of insecurity should be the control of territory and the fortification of moral values."[21] The use of force, either by military units or by security teams, is where we at Southern Command can play a large role in helping our partner nation military and security forces to train and build such a capacity that has at its core a fundamental respect for human rights and the rule of law. In this regard, we are wise to take lessons from past conflicts—military troops are not the proper implement when confronting problems of a political or social nature. True, in some cases, to eradicate a problem, it might be necessary to start at the base and to do so with force; however, there must be consistency, we need to remember deterrence cannot be achieved by law enforcement alone, and we also need to remember that the stick works most effectively when paired with the carrot.

To that end, we must coordinate our activities with other agencies and other governments to ensure that development efforts are evenly distributed and avoid duplicating or exacerbating the preexisting inequality of income and standard of living. This infrastructure- and stability-building phase would then segue directly into the final phase referred to as the "propagation of ideas." Culture and education must be promoted because today's world is competitive and technological; however, many countries in the region are still primarily rural and education does not yet reach everybody, as evidenced by the nearly 30 percent illiteracy rate with a functional literacy rate approaching 50 percent. According to General Romero, "the movement of ideas is fundamental," and this movement is impossible with such a dearth of education and literacy.[22]

Finally, as with every strategy, there needs to be a single, common message that interweaves every action and gets communicated firmly and widely. We need to broadcast our message that we, collectively, will not tolerate the existence of violence in our neighborhoods and the stealing of our youth. We are not without compassion, but we are firm in our resolve. We will be at the same time no greater friend, and no worse enemy: friend to any who want to leave the world of misery, poison, and violence behind and rejoin a peaceful, secure, and prosperous society; and enemy to all who disregard the rule of law, attempt to corrupt the next generation, and make the remainder of us live in fear. Focusing on the importance of leveraging the media in this strategic communication, Romero points out, "The heroes of the young people are themselves young, able to easily promote themselves within the media. They are not the Nobel Prize winners for peace or for medicine. The media, in general, is promoting that young people, delinquents and those who exhibit aggressive behaviors are the heroes of our time. They should not be permitted to promote themselves with such ease."[23]

The promise of the future lies in our youth; and that promise begins with education and continues through solid institutions of democracy, the respect for human rights, adherence to the rule of law, and the infrastructure that supports development. How can one run a developing country and enter a globalized economy, however, if—as one country's President in our region asked me—as many as 90 percent of your high school graduates leave the country? A nation needs the imagination and energy of its youth, or it is doomed to stagnation and failure. A nation needs to provide hope and opportunity that show a path away from drugs and gangs, or it is destined to wallow in the misery of violence, lawlessness, and crime. A nation needs to educate its youth, or it will be banished to a future forever trapped outside a globalized, industrious, and advancing economy, marketplace, and society.

Every neighbor in our shared home needs to spend more time thinking about the youth. Neither Southern Command specifically, nor the Defense Department as a whole, is or should be the lead in such pursuits. We can, however, be helpful in connecting with youth—through sports and military engagement programs like our traveling Southern Command baseball and soccer teams, and through what we might term junior ROTC programs throughout the region. We must continue to provide support to augment the valuable and extensive efforts by USAID, State, Homeland Security, and other agencies who are actively engaged in the region in various programs and efforts, all designed to restore security, to begin to provide stability, and to work with our partner nations to lay the foundations for hope, opportunity, and prosperity for the next generation. We must continue to strive to be the partner of choice in seeking to fulfill the Promise of the Americas.

Notes

[1] President Barack Obama, "Opening Ceremony Remarks," Summit of the Americas, Hyatt Regency, Port of Spain, Trinidad and Tobago, April 17, 2009.

[2] Latin American Technological Information Network, *Map of Violence: The Young People of Latin America*, November 2008.

[3] Latinobarómetro. Available at: <http://www.latinobarometro.org/>.

[4] Interview with retired General Álvaro Antonio Romero Salgado, extracts of which were published in "Gangs," *Dialogo* 19, no. 1. General Romero is professor of politics at the School of National Defense of Honduras and was Minister of Defense (1990–1991). He served as Honduran Ambassador to Nicaragua (1992–1993), Presidential Chief of Staff (1994–1998), and Minister of Public Security (2006–2007).

[5] Ibid.

[6] Ibid.

[7] *Los Costos Económicos de la Violencia en Centroamérica* [the economic cost of violence in Central America], El Salvador, 2008, 13–14.

[8] Ibid., 14.

[9] W. Carrington and E. Detragiache, "How Extensive Is the Brain Drain?" *Finance and Development: A Quarterly Magazine of the IMF* 36, no. 2 (2007), 19.

[10] World Bank, *World Development Indicators 2008*. Available at: <http://go.worldbank.org/XUR6QHSYJ0>.

[11] United Nations Economic Council on Latin America and the Caribbean, *Demographic Observatory: Population Projection*, April 2007, Table 9, Latin American population under 15 years of age by country, 43.

[12] Ibid., 22.

[13] United Nations Economic Council on Latin America and the Caribbean, 21–22 and 188.

[14] Permanent Council of the Organization of American States, Committee on Hemispheric Security, *U.S. Strategy to Combat the Threat of Criminal Gangs from Central America and Mexico*. Presented at the Special Meeting on the Phenomenon of Criminal Gangs, January 17, 2008, 1.

[15] Oscar Arias, President of Costa Rica, Speech at the Summit of the Americas, Trinidad and Tobago, April 18, 2009.

[16] Indigenous is self-identified as pertaining to one of Guatemala's 24 indigenous ethno-linguistic groups.

[17] William J. Fulbright, remarks on the occasion of the thirtieth anniversary of the Fulbright Program, 1976.

[18] *Los Costos Económicos de la Violencia en Centroamérica* , 17.

[19] Obama, "Opening Ceremony Remarks."

[20] William J. Fulbright, *Prospects for the West* (Cambridge: Harvard University Press, 1963), 43.

[21] Interview with General Romero, 12.

[22] Ibid.

[23] Ibid.

Chapter 9

Looking to the Future

If we choose to be bound by the past, we will never move forward. And I want to particularly say this to the young people of every faith, in every country: you, more than anyone, have the ability to remake this world.

All of us share this world for but a brief moment in time. The question is whether we spend that time focused on what pushes us apart, or whether we commit ourselves to an effort—a sustained effort—to find common ground, to focus on the future we seek for our children, and to respect the dignity of all human beings.

—Barack Obama
President of the United States[1]

The nations of the Americas have never been as important to each other as they are today. With exponential advances in technology and strong natural connections, our societies are bound together more closely across the entire spectrum of human contact than they have been at any other time in history. From migration and demographic changes, to a record level of commercial interaction and interdependence, to shared transnational security challenges, our countries' futures are wedded together.

During my 3 years at U.S. Southern Command, we tried to focus on the strengths of this hemisphere—the enormous diversity, beauty, and potential—while also seeking effective and cooperative solutions to the complex security challenges that traverse borders throughout the Americas, most notably crime, gangs, and drugs. At the same time, we understood that the realization of our hemisphere's long-term security, stability, and prosperity will only come through addressing the underlying conditions of poverty, inequality, and corruption that affect vast portions of the region today.

The Americas is our home—our *shared* home. There are many inhabitants sharing this residence; in fact, about 500 million people, one-half of the hemisphere's population, live in the 41 nations, territories, and protectorates of Central and South America and the Caribbean. By the year 2050, the actual population in real numbers may grow to 768 million, approximately 10 percent of the world's population.[2] While each of us celebrates our uniqueness and diversity across the hemisphere, we also share tremendous linkages and natural alignments that bring us closer together with each year that passes. Simply looking at a map underscores the obvious physical connection between our nations. However, we are tied together in ways far beyond physical and sociological proximity—the accident of geography; our hemisphere is linked demographically, economically, socially, politically, culturally, linguistically, and militarily. These shared qualities and beliefs connect us and provide the basis for addressing the common challenges that affect the security and stability of all nations in the region today. These common traits also enable strong partnerships as we look to the promise of tomorrow, and serve as the foundation for the enduring relationship we will need as we face the challenges of the future together.

U.S. Southern Command is responsible for conducting military operations and promoting security cooperation in Central America, the Caribbean, and South America in order to achieve U.S. strategic objectives. Successfully accomplishing this mission enhances the security and stability in the Western Hemisphere and ensures the forward defense of the United States. Our motto is simple: *Partnership for the Americas*. These four words capture our vision and overarching strategy, objectives, and themes. This vision defines where the organization must go if we are to achieve our goals in the future. As we look forward, Southern Command seeks to continue evolving into an interagency-oriented organization striving to support security and stability in the Americas. This vision embodies our belief that the challenges we face require us to enable lasting and inclusive partnerships in order to work collectively to ensure security and enhance stability in the Americas. Our efforts are significantly influenced by our understanding of the complexities of the hemisphere and our ability to foster cooperation, with and among, willing and capable partners. As globalization trends continue, we are certain that our security will involve deeper cooperation with multinational, multiagency, and public-private partners. As our hemisphere "virtually" shrinks, each of our nations—working together—becomes more important in facing the challenges posed by this new century.

Our mission is derived from national guidance; our strategic vision and approach rely on interaction and exchange with interagency community partners and, increasingly, on those partners in the international community and private sector. We use this input from all these stakeholders to ensure partnership, cooperation, and synergy are inherent in everything we do. Our living and evolving strategy was crafted to respond to the ever-constant mandate to meet joint military requirements while also recognizing the growing need to integrate all instruments of national capability and capacity to meet the challenges of the future throughout the hemisphere. As we move into the future, we are committed to helping build a focused, collaborative approach that will enable all of us to work together to fulfill the promise of the Americas.

The word *promise* has two different, but equally important, meanings. The first meaning is a mutual agreement between parties—an unbreakable bond. The second meaning is the potential expressed in the intent to accomplish a mission or to do something vital and important. Southern Command has been and will continue to be fully committed to meet both definitions: we *promise* to be a reliable partner throughout the hemisphere as we face tough challenges together; and we will also work with our partners to help unlock the *promise* of the future.

Partnering—military and civilian, public and private, foreign and domestic—is an essential component of the Southern Command mission. It enables all of us in the enterprise to fulfill our full range of missions while effectively supporting our friends and teammates in their own endeavors. These partnerships have been based on shared understandings and common interests and we will endeavor to build and further develop them. We must also remember, however, that while we do not—and will not—agree on every issue or every problem, we *will* work together in cooperative and supporting efforts to resolve shared problems to all our betterment. These agreements, understandings, and bonds will yield valuable insights, will enable us to prioritize and synchronize our efforts in a resource-constrained environment, and will contribute to the development of a comprehensive and synergistic strategic approach that is holistic and integrated in a cooperative manner with our partners. And throughout, to facilitate and perpetuate this environment of collaboration and teamwork, we need to better communicate not only what we are doing, but also *why* we are doing it, to audiences both internal and external. Every thought, word, and deed needs to be synchronized to convey the same message—we are all in this together, we share the same fate, and we will work together to achieve shared security and stability.

In the preceding chapters, I have described the intricacies and the dynamism of the diverse region in which we live and operate. I have highlighted the tremendous linkages that we share with Latin America and the Caribbean—important geographic, cultural, economic, and geopolitical linkages. I have outlined some difficult underlying conditions faced by the region, led by poverty and unequal wealth distribution, and how they contribute to specific challenges such as crime, violence, and illicit trafficking of drugs, people, and weapons. In the remainder of this final chapter, I would like to share my personal opinions on where I see the future taking us—a forecast of sorts for our region: I will highlight the trends I believe our strongest linkages will take, address the main challenges we still face, and talk about actions we can take—leveraging the potential of some of Southern Command's key initiatives already underway, and further developing and maturing them—to help us and our partners meet current and future security demands.

This is the right time for all of us, inside and outside the U.S. Government, to work together on the challenges facing this hemisphere. By doing so, we can realize the true promise of the Americas. It all begins with building and communicating real understanding, leading to a real and vibrant Partnership for the Americas.

> Our governments know that the truly great challenges of our day can best be met by marshalling our complementary strengths and abilities in the service of our shared goals. Our hemisphere's potential is enormous and our success is linked intimately to the success of our neighbors.
>
> —Condoleezza Rice
> Former U.S. Secretary of State[3]

The countries of the Americas are, and will increasingly be, important to daily life in the United States. Shared connections and opportunities for working even more closely include economic growth, jobs, equity, energy, citizen security, migration, democratic governance, and the rule of law. We also need to recognize and understand, however, that some of the most important issues in relations with Latin America are in many ways domestic issues for the United States, namely, immigration, drugs, energy, and trade. A steady drumbeat throughout these chapters has been the importance of maintaining a strong U.S. commitment to strengthening democratic governance, the rule of law, and respect for human dignity— and doing so through patient, nuanced, cooperative, and primarily multilateral processes and instruments.

We need to continue examining these unfamiliar—particularly for the military and security forces—processes and sharpen our focus and strategic approach by investing time and resources into strengthening and, where necessary, creating new multilateral tools to support the establishment of security, democracy, and liberty in the region. But this is going to require a significant shift in thinking *away from* traditional bilateral channels of diplomatic pressure and assistance, and *toward* multilateral cooperation with likeminded partners. One of the ways to find cooperation and partners is to focus on the number of strong linkages which already exist and provide ample opportunity for collaboration, interaction, and exchange as we confront shared challenges.

Linkages *and* Challenges

The majority of the countries in the Western Hemisphere are at a crossroads, having fluctuated over the past decades between authoritarian and democratic governments. The combination of endemic poverty, gangs, corruption, illicit trafficking, transnational crime, and other illegal activities has stressed the ability of several of the democratic governments of the region to fully exercise their sovereignty. In order for these countries to thrive and provide for their people, they must enjoy a stable and secure environment.

As we have discussed, there is a considerable range of important issues, all of which need to be coordinated through multiple levels in more than one agency and in more than one nation. This is a prerequisite for any project or any overarching approach to the region: each issue needs to be assessed as part of an interconnected and unified strategy. For example, the illicit narcotics issue cannot be adequately addressed in isolation from issues of migration, arms trafficking, money-laundering, and radical ideological terrorists. Our strategy has become an overarching framework based on the affirmation of common values through institutional cooperation within the hemisphere: democracy, liberty, and human rights; additionally, our strategy includes learning lessons from the past while looking to the future—perhaps even anticipating problems before they erupt with overwhelming urgency.

Economics

International commerce and trade between the United States and Latin American and Caribbean countries are strong, and experts expect this growth to continue. The total of all merchandise imported from Latin American and Caribbean countries to the United States increased 24.3 percent from 2004 to 2005, and exports from the United States to the region increased 17.6 percent during this same period.[4] Total mercantile trade between the United States and Latin America was $409 billion in 2004, up from $301 billion in 1999, and accounting for approximately 17 percent of total U.S. world trade.[5] Economic partnerships are strong today and experts expect U.S. trade with Latin America to exceed trade with Europe and Japan by 2011.

The economies in Latin America and the Caribbean are increasingly tied with the global economy, with particularly close linkages to the United States. Now, Latin American economies are beginning to feel the negative impact of the current economic downturn in the United States and Europe. Although the duration and impact of these economic problems are difficult to predict, any global or regional slowdown or reduction in demand and prices for commodities will naturally have an adverse effect on this region. Economic data from late 2008 showed that commodity prices that had risen until mid-July 2008, had recently fallen. Wheat and corn futures were down 70 percent, oil prices dropped 55 percent, and several metals were down 50 percent.[6]

The fall in commodity prices will ease some inflationary pressures, but combined with other economic factors, it will negatively impact the region's growth and cause near-and long-term challenges for the region's leaders. Near term, they will have to cope with the economic slowdown and its inherent challenges: reduced exports, tighter access to financing, stock market devaluation, less foreign direct investment, and reduced migrant remittances. Long term, if these economies continue to falter, they will have to deal with the electorate's disappointment, and in some cases reduced overall security and stability. They will also face a challenge in fully implementing positive economic reforms that many of the region's governments have attempted to implement over the last two decades.

Although 2009 and the next few years are forecast to be more difficult economically in our region, 2010 shows promise for recovery and growth. Each country will vary in performance depending on its own situation, policies, and political leadership. Many of the larger countries in our region are well-prepared to weather this adverse economic situation due to recent economic reforms and an increased integration with the global economy, particularly the U.S. economy. Our interdependence with the region should, over time, dampen individual economic shocks, and foster sustained economic growth.

On a broader scale, globalization can be seen as "plate tectonics"—a force that *can* be interrupted, but not stopped by anything less than a true world catastrophe. Left to its own, globalization will increase due to the sheer weight of market forces. Then there is the notion that as the global economy grows and expands, the beneficiaries will be greater in number. History, however, paints a different picture. Although poverty rates have been modestly reduced over the last 15 years—from 48 percent living in poverty in 1990 to an estimated 35 percent in 2007—with increases in population over the years, the absolute numbers of people living in poverty (living on less than 2 U.S. dollars a day) have risen slightly overall in the region. The number of people living in indigence—or extreme poverty (living on less than 1 U.S. dollar a day)—has also climbed, affecting an estimated 12.7 percent of the population.[7]

Combined with this poverty is a disproportionate wealth distribution that is second only to sub-Saharan Africa. The richest 20 percent of the Latin American population earns 57 percent of the region's income, earning 20 times that of the poorest 20 percent. By comparison, the richest 20 percent in high-income regions of the world earns only 7.7 times that of the poorest group.[8] This inequality gap negates any positive impact of growth on poverty reduction. The cumulative effect of poverty and income inequality in Latin America and the Caribbean serves as a catalyst for insecurity and instability. Although these figures vary from country to country in the aggregate, poverty and inequality make whole regional populations vulnerable to the influence of illicit activity—such as drugs, crime, gangs, and illegal immigration. Additionally, there are extra-hemispheric factors that affect the region as well. For example, many nations buy Latin American raw material and agricultural goods and then transport them outside the hemisphere for their own use. These short-term gains fail to create the jobs needed for sustained growth and do not offer any incentive for reinvestment in Latin America and the Caribbean.

Thus, in some ways, globalization will continue to be a divisive factor if it perpetuates disparities—the gap in the global standard of living between the "haves" and the "have nots." This could lead to a backlash against the "haves," potentially creating more anti-U.S. sentiment and anti-Westernism. As the security-related problems of globalization become more important and more prevalent, our ability to influence the global rule sets and to help contribute to the global security agenda will become attenuated. We as the different members representing the larger U.S. Government need to work with our partners to devise new, mutually beneficent, multilateral pacts on labor regulations, environmental rules, and other agreements that are important for commerce, trade, defense, and the like. We have a window of opportunity to work with our neighbors to make globalization secure.

The hemisphere shares other economic linkages in addition to trade relationships. For example, Latin America and the Caribbean are the largest sources of legal and illegal immigrants into the United States, and these immigrants often send remittances back to their countries of origin. Inter-American Development Bank studies estimate $45 billion in remittances flowed from the United States to Latin America in 2006. This is another sign of economic interdependency throughout the hemisphere.[9]

Technology provides both an economic and social linkage. The Internet enables a connectivity that did not exist 20 years ago, and the hemisphere has embraced this new opportunity. From 2000 to 2007, growth of Internet use in Central America was 623.9 percent; South American growth was 326.7 percent; Caribbean growth was 704.4 percent; and North American growth was 114.7 percent. Additionally, English and Spanish rank as the first and fourth top Internet languages in the world, respectively.[10] Rapid communication exchanges and the growing use of the Internet are clearly contributing to increased interactions and constitute a strong linkage. However, technology can be a double-edged sword, as a growing technology gap will undoubtedly widen the poverty gap; thus, as we make advances, we need to ensure we share and exchange those advances to the betterment of our entire neighborhood.

Energy is another factor involved in the strengthening economic linkages within the hemisphere. According to the Department of Energy, three of the top four foreign energy suppliers to the United States are located within the Western Hemisphere—Canada, Mexico, and Venezuela. Further, as reported by the Coalition for Affordable and Reliable Energy, the United States will need 31 percent more petroleum and 62 percent more natural gas in the next two decades.[11] As the United States continues to require more petroleum and gas, Latin America will become a global energy leader with its large oil reserves and oil and gas production and supplies.

Prosperity requires basic resources. We currently are well positioned, but resources tend to be scarcest where they are free. It will be critical for the region and the world to properly price resources that once were (are) free, seek alternate energy sources, recycle, and use other methods. We are not in a "finite supply" situation mindset, yet; rather, we are in a "reuse and recycle" system, but there will still be a constant scramble for resources, which could contribute to a keen competition for energy, water, and land. In extreme cases, this could lead to an eventual conflict over them. The cost of oil and consumption trends are two macro forces that are already raising this region to new prominence levels, as indicated by the presence of China buying up as much of the available resources as possible. New economic interests are based on energy supplies and access to other resources. As we continue to curb our own dependency on the rest of the world for such commodities, we need to remember that some key resources come from our region and conflicts will arise to ensure foreign access to them.

Social and Political

In addition to demographic and economic ties with Latin America and the Caribbean, we share social and political views rooted in a common commitment to democracy, freedom, justice, and respect for human dignity, human rights, and human values. The foundation for enabling these fundamental tenets rests upon a representative form of government. The citizens of this hemisphere believe the best form of government is a democracy that truly represents the population and is more than just action at the ballot box. The first article of the Inter-American Democratic Charter clearly articulates this belief: "The people of the Americas have the right to democracy, and their governments have an obligation to promote and defend it. Democracy is essential for the social, political, and economic development of the peoples of the Americas."[12]

Corruption, however, is a huge impediment to improved governance by obstructing adherence to the rule of law and creating insecurity, thus negating the gains of even the strongest economic ties. Various studies point out that reducing corruption could save some nations in the region billions of dollars annually. Trust in politicians and political parties is particularly low throughout the region and this distrust shows no signs of relenting. This stimulates discontent and disenchantment with the system, which can lead to confusion and rejection of "democracy." To prevent backsliding toward authoritarian rule, democracy assistance needs to translate into real tangible improvements in the judicial systems, accountability of public institutions and leaders, and greater transparency and improvement in public services. One method to accomplish this is to leverage the positive perception of other international actors— the United Nations, the Organization of American States, and the European Union. Strong governmental institutions organized around transparent policies and processes, legitimate justice systems, and ethical leaders in all elements of the government are the components necessary to defeat corruption. The people in this region want this transparency and legitimacy—it is just up to the leaders in positions of power to make this occur. For our part, we need to listen, engage, and function as equal partners in joining hands with our neighbors. In some cases, we may need to surrender short-term benefits for long-term gains.

Today, democracy is practiced in varying degrees in almost every country in the hemisphere. We are fortunate to be united by democratic principles, the inspiration of liberty, and the people's desire to have human rights respected by their governments. Of course, there are differences in form and style among our governments, and the democratic scorecard may differ greatly from nation to nation. While our hemisphere contains many representative governments, there are some relatively significant differences in what we each think of as democracy—elections alone do not guarantee democratic rule. However, compared to three decades ago when the form of government in the majority of the countries was not democratic, the region's similarities outweigh the differences. Nations across the region agree that in true democracies, free governments should be accountable to their people and govern effectively. We need to continue to build on and develop these similar beliefs, using them as cornerstones as we craft new institutions dedicated to the rule of law, freedom, and opportunity. Governmental institutions that eliminate corruption and protect the civil rights and freedoms of those they govern are more likely to enable future security and stability.

Culture and Language

In this hemisphere, we are fortunate to share similar main languages and interwoven cultural linkages. Although there are many different dialects, this area uses four primary languages: English, Spanish, Portuguese, and French. While the United States is thought of as primarily an English-speaking nation, it now has the largest number of Spanish-speaking citizens in the world after Mexico. The United States and the rest of the region have significant cultural ties today and these will grow even stronger in the decades ahead, as evidenced by the previously cited United Nations report that predicts people of Hispanic heritage will comprise approximately 30 percent of the total U.S. population by 2050.

Because of the physical and the sociological proximity of the many nations of the Americas, reinforced by the growing influence of a range of Hispanic and Caribbean diaspora populations within the United States itself, we can draw on the immense and diverse sources of goodwill and shared aspirations that potentially link the many nations across the hemisphere. We are very much moving toward becoming a bicultural and bilingual nation, which will only strengthen the bonds we already share in this neighborhood.

However, we still need a greater emphasis on public diplomacy—using those shared languages to ensure our words reach the desired audience and convey the right messages. This may take a long time to have an effect, but it can start with extending the level of culture-to-culture diplomacy, including educational exchanges and interaction between leading people in academia. In the words of Senator William Fulbright, "The essence of intercultural education is the acquisition of empathy—the ability to see the world as others see it, and to allow for the possibility that others may see something we have failed to see, or may see it more accurately."[13] Fulbright goes on to explain that the purpose of the exchange program is to "erode the culturally rooted mistrust that sets nations against one another" because educational exchange can turn nations into people, contributing as no other form of communication can to the "humanizing of international relations."[14]

> Over the long term, the United States cannot capture or kill its way to victory. Where possible, what the military calls kinetic operations should be subordinate to measures aimed at promoting better governance, economic programs that spur development, and efforts to address the grievances among the discontented, from whom the terrorists recruit.
>
> —Robert M. Gates
> Secretary of Defense

Military

As a traditional military jurisdiction, USSOUTHCOM's area of responsibility is notable by its current and foreseeable lack of conventional military threats; but the region's persistent conditions of poverty, inequality, and corruption provide fertile soil in which international criminals and terrorists can recruit and flourish. Throughout this area of focus, security threats take forms that we more readily associate with crime than war. In the region's growing gang activity, we see criminals and the disenfranchised band together in innovative ways that threaten U.S. national security. In the very capable hands of resourceful, well-trained criminals and extremists, activities such as kidnapping, counterfeiting, human trafficking, and drug trafficking concoct a dangerous blend that leave human tragedy in their wake. The growing threat from gangs is an outgrowth of underlying poverty and a lack of opportunity, and until these fundamental causes are addressed, the symptoms will continue to increase in severity. Gang activity, much like terrorism, transcends borders and affects numerous countries in the region.

Drug trafficking will also remain a hemisphere challenge. While we have made great progress in the fight against drugs, we have not yet eliminated the threat. The illicit drug industry alone accounts for nearly 20,000 deaths in the United States each year. The demand for drugs in the United States remains strong and creates incentives for illegal activities. The Andean Ridge remains far and away the leading supplier of the world's cocaine and a provider of heroin consumed in the United States. Drug traffickers are constantly developing new means of preventing interference with their illegal narcotics activities. As we modify our tactics, drug producers and traffickers find innovative methods to develop the drugs and alternative trafficking routes. The drug traffickers of yesterday have become much more lethal today, and this trend is expected to continue.

Areas with lower levels of economic investment, development, and growth provide a breeding ground for terrorism and the full range of criminal activities. Poverty, inequality, and corruption create an environment where sanctuaries for terrorist organizations can grow. Narcoterrorists like the FARC in Colombia and Sendero Luminoso in Peru are one form of active terrorism and derive their funding and power from the sale of illicit drugs. These organizations and a number of extremely violent gangs have driven up the rates of homicide and kidnappings throughout the region and do not operate within traditional nation-state boundaries—they live among and terrorize the populace, and take advantage of ungoverned and undergoverned spaces without any regard or respect for national sovereignties.

Additionally, jihadist radical groups are present in a number of these areas within the hemisphere—many in urban areas. These terrorist operations are supporting Islamic radical groups worldwide, and there is potential for terrorists to use permissive environments within the Western Hemisphere as launching points for devastating attacks. Groups in these areas raise money by both legal (religious donations, donations from local Arab businesses) and illegal means (extortion, insurance fraud, drug trafficking, weapons sales, document sales, commercial piracy) to support terrorists worldwide.

In addition to the growing impact of crime, gangs, drugs, and terrorism, environmental disasters such as hurricanes, earthquakes, volcanoes, floods, tsunamis, and drought also loom as an ever-present danger. In Latin America, because of rapid population growth, the size of the populace in cities has increased significantly since the 1980s, escalating demand for water, land, and energy. Fast-growing settlements outpace the societies' ability to provide the basic infrastructure to maintain adequate quality of life and health conditions that are essential to human development. People in urban centers consistently endure dangerously high levels of air pollution, severe water contamination, and catastrophic mudslides resulting from rapid deforestation on the periphery.

None of these challenges falls into mission areas traditionally associated with the military; but addressing them effectively in a 21st-century way requires the application of all instruments of national power. Therefore, we have to be innovative in our approach to best leverage the inherent knowledge and capabilities present within our partner agencies. Furthermore, when you analyze the challenges we face together in the region, you quickly realize that not even one *nation*, big or small, can successfully overcome them. Illegal drug trafficking, criminal activity, gangs, human smuggling, terrorist financing and recruitment, natural disasters—none of these stops at a nation's border. These challenges require cooperative solutions and partnerships. Our unified and cooperative team must also deal with the underlying problems of unemployment, corruption, and a general lack of opportunity.

Thankfully, there is a long tradition of security cooperation, combined with very little state-on-state military conflict, in our shared home. The healthy military and security force relations throughout most of the region provide an outstanding vehicle for cooperation in diverse missions, such as peacekeeping, counternarcotics, disaster response, and humanitarian operations. As I have attempted to show through the preceding chapters, we at Southern Command have found that, hands down, the most effective and durable responses to nearly all of these challenges and threats we face in this region can best be achieved through reinforcing the capacity for our partner nations to govern justly, create and sustain lasting economic and social infrastructures, and sow the seeds for an enduring sense of hope and prosperity.

The key to the future of this great region is *understanding*—understanding each other, understanding shared challenges, and understanding the promise of security cooperation for our shared future. At Southern Command, we study the numerous and compelling linkages to the people and societies in the Americas and communicate their importance as we strive to build and strengthen relationships in the region through effective strategic communication and interagency partnering. Everything we do at Southern Command must encourage and assist in building partnerships across the region, while working with intergovernmental and public-private organizations to ensure success.

Southern Command is committed to being a good partner in a military-to-military sense. Every day, year after year, we dedicate the majority of our resources toward building the security capabilities of partners, while working to encourage an environment of cooperation among all of the nations in the region. We conduct frequent and wide-ranging multinational exercises and international exchanges with our partners, send thousands of partner military and civilian experts to various leading academic institutions, and provide other critical security assistance to our friends in the region. All of these are done as part of strengthening regional partnerships and collective capabilities we believe are integral to U.S. national security and stability of the Western Hemisphere. These exercises focus on confronting regional threats such as maritime insecurity, terrorism, illegal migration, and illicit trafficking. At the same time, they are increasing partner nation ability to support peacekeeping, disaster relief, and humanitarian assistance.

Panamax, for example, is the world's largest multinational training exercise. More than 20 nations focus on improving the hemisphere's ability to provide air, sea, and land forces to assist the government of Panama in its excellent work of securing the Panama Canal. Another large-scale exercise we support is UNITAS, which trains participating forces to ensure maximum interoperability in future coalition operations. The 2009 iteration involved 7,000 international sailors and mariners and included Canada and Germany; it marked the 50th Anniversary, making it the longest running multinational maritime training exercise in the world.

In addition to our robust maritime programs, we are extremely excited about revamping our land engagements with a young program called "Beyond the Horizon." This program aims to maximize the impact of our land events by increasing the number of "microburst" engagements—engineer construction, small unit familiarization, subject matter exchanges, medical readiness training exercises—as well as establishing longer-term programs that integrate the efforts of other U.S. Federal agencies, host nations, and the private sector.

We will look to increase the duration and number of countries visited through Continuing Promise and other similar efforts as part of the Partnership of the Americas, which will build on the successful missions of the ships *Comfort*, *Kearsarge*, and *Boxer*. These deployments will highlight persistent engagement with innovative interagency, multinational, and public-private cooperation.

We will continue our Regional Airspace Integration (RASI) initiative with a focus on improving Central American capability to detect and monitor aircraft in the predominantly unmonitored airspace. This endeavor involves integrating the civil, military, and security air domain in the region, modernizing air traffic management, and building a multinational common operating picture through a regional surveillance center and new surveillance radars. A complementary program to RASI is the Regional Aircraft Modernization Program (RAMP), which conducts surveys to identify gaps in the aviation capability of our partners to respond to transnational threats. Ultimately, RAMP aims to promote regional air sovereignty through increased cooperation, interoperability, and modernization of regional air security assets, with cooperating nations better prepared to perform humanitarian and air sovereignty missions.

Again, our role in the military is to work with partner nation military and security forces to ensure the requisite conditions of security are in place so stability can start to take root. We endeavor to improve the region's ability to respond to today's and tomorrow's security challenges. Perhaps the most dramatic example of building partner capacity is Colombia's mounting success against illegal armed groups. Southern Command has provided training and logistical and technical support to increase the capability of Colombia's forces, enabling a string of victories over the narcoterrorist groups. For the first time in decades, the Colombian government is providing services in all of its municipalities, and the Colombian people have a renewed confidence in their future. As Colombia "wins its peace," the entire region benefits because the narcoterrorists lose capacity to grow and transport drugs.

With each new success and triumph, momentum is built. Through a steady improvement in security, we can help create the conditions that will enable this region to counter the poverty and inequality that has gripped it for so long. The foundations for this can then perhaps be exported to other parts of the globe where similar conditions and challenges exist—for example, can overcoming the tendencies toward state failure in Haiti provide lessons learned and the promise that the situation will not worsen in Afghanistan, Somalia, and other places? If we can demonstrate a credible and effective rule of law and whole-of-society response to armed insurrection and the drug trade that fuels it in Colombia, what prospects for a similar success might there be for containing the heroin traffic and lawlessness of Central Asia?

While our programs and initiatives focus primarily on security, increasingly our approach has broadened to support stability and development efforts as part of a larger national path to true partnering and engagement in the Western Hemisphere. We pursue a host of programs in support of other lead agencies and government entities to include numerous training exercises, educational programs, technology-sharing, intelligence-sharing, security procurement assistance, humanitarian aid, and a myriad of others. In addition, Southern Command conducts a variety of humanitarian goodwill activities that directly help those in need while providing needed training to our team. As an example of our commitment to the people of the region, our medical personnel treated almost 700,000 patients in the past 3 years, varying from routine prevention to the most serious emergency cases. A key aspect of the mission is the partnership of military personnel with other government agencies and nongovernmental organizations. Furthermore, we sponsor numerous other humanitarian projects, ranging from planned events such as the construction and/or refurbishment of wells, schools, community centers, and medical facilities to rapid response missions in the wake of disasters.

All of these efforts contribute to showing goodwill, to building relationships, and perhaps most importantly, to building understanding. Underlying these endeavors and fundamental to their success is a novel approach to partnering that combines the synergistic efforts of a diverse group of experts from U.S. and international militaries, nongovernmental organizations, and volunteers and donations from the U.S. private sector. Such diversity of humanitarian expertise enhances mission effectiveness. It also lays the foundation for relationships that could pay dividends in the event that the United States responds to a potential humanitarian crisis in the region. Finally, this integrated approach highlights the power of creative public-private partnerships to show our true interest in and deep caring for the people of the Americas.

Building our partners' military and security force capabilities, as well as their capacity to sustain and develop these capabilities on their own, is our primary purpose as we focus on security cooperation. We need to continue the great efforts described in the preceding pages, but we also need to ensure we are doing more than just creating activity and establishing presence. There is a high level of determination and professional camaraderie and a growing sense of teamwork among the military and security forces in this region. I have personally borne witness to the building regional consensus that recognizes threats like illicit trafficking, terrorism, and organized crime are not just one nation's problems, nor are they isolated to one particular facet of a larger issue. For example, there are not just "source nation" issues and "transit nation" issues in the flow of illicit narcotics—rather, they are all subsets of larger, overarching transnational and region-wide issues. Therefore, neither one government entity within a single nation, nor any one solitary nation by itself, is the proper solution. We cannot use just military capabilities and authorities to effectively address these threats; nor can they be addressed exclusively through law enforcement or other government agencies individually.

These dangerous threats and challenges look to exploit natural, political, and institutional seams of authority, operation, and capability throughout all levels of government. Thus, countering these types of obstacles to security, stability, and prosperity in the Americas requires strong and enduring partnerships across the whole of government, and across the whole of many governments, working together in cooperation and synergy. To accomplish this, we will need to expand our thinking and our interagency and international cooperation. Our challenge, therefore, is *intellectual* as well as *institutional,* and I truly feel we can learn a great deal from the professional military and security forces in this region.

Our collective success in this pursuit will not be measured merely by the number of countries who participate, or the number of ships, aircraft, and people who show up for the exercise; that is a good start but, going forward, success will be determined by a measurable increase in the level of performance and capability of each unit or country from year to year, exercise to exercise, conference to conference. Thus, the purpose is to truly generate and build the requisite capabilities to provide security for each partner's populace, and then to develop the capacity so that this will be self-sustaining and advanced within each partner nation as we face the growing number of shared transnational challenges to the security of the Americas.

> Many people have assumed that because the House of Representatives the Senate and the President have declared for collective security, the job is done. But the establishing of order and the making of peace does not consist merely of a solemn declaration of a well-drafted constitution.
>
> The making of peace is a continuing process that must go on from day to day, from year to year, so long as our civilization shall last. Our participation in this process is not just the signing of a charter with a big red seal. It is a daily task, a positive participation in all the details and decisions which together constitute a living and growing policy.
>
> —J. William Fulbright
> Senate Address, March 28, 1945

Looking Ahead

The dawn of the 21st century presents the U.S. Southern Command with an unprecedented opportunity to define and shape new means and capabilities that will achieve U.S. national security objectives in an age of adaptive, nontraditional, and transnational threats, challenges, and opportunities. As the smallest, most nimble geographic combatant command, charged with responsibility for an area characterized by unconventional military missions, USSOUTHCOM *today* is well equipped to develop a new, interagency model for addressing and confronting these challenges. Having developed a culture of bold and continuous innovation, USSOUTHCOM *tomorrow* will lead U.S. defense and security transformation by setting standards for effective joint, interagency, and multinational partnering solutions.

We live in a dangerous age. Driven by unprecedented technological advancement, globalization will continue to simultaneously disenfranchise and empower radical actors who will attempt to coerce representative governments through criminal and terrorist tactics. Defeating crime, gangs, illicit narcotics, and terrorism is a significant challenge for the United States because established national security tools—centered on military-backed diplomacy—are largely ineffective against this asymmetric threat. Preventing crime, defeating terrorists, and eradicating the sources from which new generations of threats sprout requires a multifaceted approach that reduces existing resources and capabilities while simultaneously improving the underlying conditions of poverty, inequality, corruption, and ignorance that otherwise create and breed future criminals, gangsters, traffickers, and terrorists. Currently, no single arm of the U.S. Government has the ability or authority to coordinate the multiple entities required to execute an effective international campaign. Local, state, and Federal security officials struggle to envision new roles and responsibilities for organizations designed to address the challenges of a different era.

We must never allow the appearance of a somewhat peaceful regional environment to fool us—threats and challenges to our national security as well as to the region as a whole do exist, lurking in our blind spots. This is not the future of "conflict" as the U.S. military has historically envisioned it, or for which we find ourselves adequately organized, trained, or equipped. At times, we find ourselves without adequate legal concepts or authorities, sufficient funding mechanisms, or mission statements. At others, we find ourselves performing missions clearly outside the skill sets to which we traditionally train, but which strategic and operational situations dictate as necessary. As those chartered to employ lethal force in defense of the Nation, we in the DOD must accept "conflict" and all the nuanced challenges to security as it exists today and redefine ourselves for the challenges at hand even though they may not match our self-conceptions as warriors.

As we chart our way into the next decade of this century, we will hold steady to our course of persistent engagement, partnership-building, enabling understanding, and positive strategic messaging—all propelled by our interagency-support approach. I believe our efforts are making a difference in the hemisphere and for the security of the United States. I truly feel that our superb Soldiers, Sailors, Airmen, Marines, and Coast-guardsmen—Active, Reserve, and Guard—as well as our talented civilians are daily living up to the trust the American people have placed in them. They are all volunteers to serve their country, and I am honored and blessed to serve with them every day. Our people are our greatest strength, and I thank them and their families for their tireless efforts and selfless service to this Nation.

From everything that has gone before, we have the basis for imagining how the future might look for global security. The combatant commands we have today appropriately seek to maintain a vital regional perspective on security issues. However, enabling truly joint and interagency activities in the future will require additional modalities and authorities to provide effective synchronization across the spectrum of U.S. Government agencies' resources. We need vastly better integration across the entire government of the United States, and we need better coalition integration.

Imagine all the actors who wield the instruments of national power—what many call "the interagency"—clumped together in the form of a huge, amorphous iceberg. Science tells us that a typical iceberg has only 1/8 of its actual size showing above water. In Latin America, the military is that tip of the iceberg. The vast majority of the "force" that will be brought to bear in this pursuit is comprised of doctors, lawyers, businessmen, financiers, construction workers, and educators—not soldiers or policemen. To further progress, we need to institute a new process and paradigm that will bring all instruments of national power to bear in meeting current and future regional challenges. This unfolding 21st century presents our entire national security structure in general, and U.S. Southern Command in particular, with an unprecedented opportunity to define and shape new means and capabilities that will best achieve U.S. national security objectives in an era of transnational and unconventional threats. We find ourselves at the dawn of new thinking about how we might overcome the inertia and restructure ourselves—to morph in ways that will serve our own interests as well as those of our partner nations to the south.

For our part, as included in this continued evolution, we "test drove" a new model. Southern Command was perfectly suited as a test case: we could easily transition over a relatively short period to a more integrated posture that expanded our strong interagency perspective and capacity. To accomplish this, we needed an operating picture with persistent, accurate visibility of all U.S. Government and nongovernment activities ongoing throughout our region. Broadening the aperture in such a way required not only a cultural mind shift among assigned military personnel, but also inclusion of new partners. Relationships are important, and such partnerships must be forged by building levels of trust in the ability of all to work together along traditionally unfamiliar, culturally distinct, but strategically important lines outside the Department of Defense.

Specifically, here is what we initially envisioned and continue to foresee for Southern Command and any other like-minded, interagency-oriented security organization.

Interagency Cooperation

We envisioned a true interagency team, with senior representatives from each key agency and cabinet actually holding command positions throughout the organization. Instead of historic J-coded directorates suited solely for military operations, we have organized directorates reflecting the kinds of missions we want to undertake in the 21st century, namely, *Partnering*, *Stability*, and *Security and Intelligence*. More will follow as our priorities and skill sets adapt and transform.

The Three Pillars of Democracy—Diplomacy, Development, and Defense

We need to continue to recognize that the real thrust of 21st-century national security in this region is not vested in war, but in intelligent management of the conditions of peace in a volatile era. While remaining fully ready for combat operations, diplomacy dominates so much of what we do, and development is a mandatory requisite feature of true, long-term stability and prosperity. We need much greater engagement with the State Department and USAID throughout the enterprise. We should undertake no task without first considering the valuable synergy generated when these and other entities work together—throughout the process—as a team. The importance of this notion has been exemplified by establishing a 3-star equivalent, post-Ambassador Deputy to the command, and having another post-Ambassador as the commander's primary economic advisor.

Public-Private Linkages

Much of the power of the United States to create successful partnerships in our region is found in the private sector. For example, Microsoft creates tremendous, positive impact in the region. Nearly 850,000 people work in Microsoft-related jobs—roughly half of the information technology market in Latin America and the Caribbean. Between 2003 and 2007, Microsoft awarded over $27 million in grants and software to help more than 30 million people in 19 countries in our region. Moreover, in May 2007 Microsoft announced a partnership with Inter-American Development Bank to form a new Latin American Collaborative Research Federation that will create a "virtual research institute." Since then, Microsoft has committed $930,000 to finance the first 3 years of the project, enabling scientists at research institutions throughout Latin America to seek collaborative solutions to socioeconomic problems in areas such as agriculture, education, health care, alternative energy, and the environment. Innovative ideas like this come from industry all the time. At Southern Command, we must find ways to work with nongovernmental organizations, private charitable entities, international organizations, and the private sector—to become *the* partner of choice for those who wish to benefit in the region. We should look for ways to integrate this endeavor into key staff nodes.

High-Speed Staff Process

Using new methods of connection and a flattened organization that links the staff to move at mandatory speed in the era of the 24-hour news cycle has also been a prerequisite for success. Stovepiped, hierarchic, redundant, and serial processes that characterized the organization in the past have begun to make way for collaborative, integrated, matrixed, and parallel decisionmaking in our new structure. Key enterprise-wide functions (e.g., planning, resources, and assessment) have been led by functional directorates responsible to prevent gaps and seams while ensuring unity of effort toward the overall strategic objective. Eliminating duplicative and excessive multilevel reviews has started making the whole enterprise more lean, more flexible, and more adaptive to the changing environment. A matrixed process has shown it can lend itself to a healthy competition of ideas on major issues among directorates; at the same time, a vigorous dedication to teaming along the way has helped to prevent such "creative friction" from bogging down decisionmaking. The whole organization is striving to be mission-focused, informed and guided throughout by strategic communication, as well as integrated by function. As we continue to learn and improve, this new way of doing business will more fully incorporate the political, military, economic, humanitarian, ecological, and diplomatic dimensions of regional operations into a single, coherent strategy.

Strategic Communication Focus

Strategic communication is the ultimate team sport—it must be done as part of a joint, interagency, and commercial system. It does no good whatsoever to have a perfect strategic communication plan that is ultimately contradicted by other U.S. Government agencies, as is often the case, unfortunately. Each plan must be vetted properly and become a combined effort. It should take into account what private industry is doing in a given country or region so that inherent contradictions between public and private institutions do not undermine the entire effort. It must be crafted in a sensible, collaborative, collegial way and done in an appropriate voice.

We must instill communication assessment and processes into our culture, developing programs, plans, policy, information, and themes to support the U.S. Government's overall strategic objectives. To this end, Southern Command has worked tirelessly to integrate communications efforts horizontally across the enterprise to link information and communication issues with broader policies, plans, and actions. We need to continue to emphasize that this type of assessment and strategic thinking needs to be considered at the front end of planning, not conducted as an afterthought. We need to continue to focus on synchronizing words and actions, ensuring deed mirrors thought, and doing so across and among all elements of national power. The way we tell our story needs to be viewed as a vital extension of national policy. The narrative matters deeply.

Additionally, at least for strategic communication that goes beyond the shores of the United States (a safe assumption for virtually everything we do in this arena), the international community must be considered and often consulted. In other words, the impact on individual countries and international organizations should be considered, and—if possible—they should be part of the plan. In particular, international organizations have resources that can be used in execution and even in planning. Similarly, little success can be achieved in a foreign land without the cooperation of the host nation and regional organizations. Often, they can contribute to strategic messaging and should be consulted for their expertise and their understanding. While there will undoubtedly be exceptions to this approach, such consultations and cooperation can frequently pay enormous dividends.

Ultimately, we in the business of national security must work together to arrive at a shared understanding of what constitutes strategic communication in an international context. This is an effort that must involve practitioners at the Department of Defense, Department of State, and indeed at all Cabinet organizations and national agencies engaged in international strategic communication on behalf of the United States. It is also an effort that can be informed by those in private industry who work in this milieu.

Sustained Engagement

As discussed throughout this piece, the capability to forge willing and capable partnerships throughout the region and to create a sense of goodwill toward the United States is essential to achieving the mission. In order to do this, we need sustained engagement. We plan to conduct deployments similar to the USNS *Comfort*, USS *Kearsarge* and *Boxer,* and HSV *Swift* on a regular basis. We need military and civilian, public and private exercises and initiatives throughout the region, with more microbursts of assistance, as well as long-term initiatives integrated across the Federal Government. In short, we need coordinated, whole-of-government, persistent, and continual efforts that meld with the efforts of the international community and the private sector.

In order to strengthen and/or gain partners, first we need to earn and maintain their trust. This will require a unified approach with consistent, effective, and flexible engagement. It will require innovative and earnest information-sharing across the board. It will require innovative ways to make our various exercises, programs, and partnerships more inclusive and more effective in reinforcing our connection to the peoples of the region. Finally, it must be more than just episodic visits stemming from political or public relations goals—it will require a simple and clear long-term commitment of time, resources, and presence that is designed to generate a lasting connection and develop a true capability and capacity for security cooperation within each of our partners.

As our partners build capability and capacity, we need to assist them in being able to deny transnational threats from using their sovereign territory. We need to help them be able to "see" these threats, whether on land, in the air, on the sea, or in cyberspace. This involves the appropriate awareness systems—coastal radars and air surveillance radars, for example—as well as physical assets such as patrol boats and aircraft with crew trained and proficient to operate and maintain them. It will also require the ability to share information with the United States and with adjacent neighbors in order to build a common operating picture in a regional sense.

We also need these partners to be able to help conduct peacekeeping operations. Already, we see many nations in the region contributing to international peacekeeping in places such as Haiti. By developing a regional capability, we will reduce the demand for U.S. forces to perform peacekeeping missions, while also increasing the legitimacy of peacekeeping forces by diversifying international representation.

Combined/International Contacts

While planning and transforming our new organization, we have sought to strengthen the bonds of mutual interest and cooperation with our partner nations in the region. Through a long history of training, communication, exercises, and liaison, we have built sturdy relationships that are now ready for expansion into a new realm of partnering arrangements. We have military liaison officers with partner nations now, but we might be even more effective in accomplishing our mission by offering liaison positions for civilian bureaucrats and diplomats from agencies and cabinet bureaus from all the nations and territories throughout the region. Such partnerships will better nurture common values and emphasize shared interests in expanding economic opportunity, promoting peaceful resolution of conflict, enhancing scientific collaboration, fighting diseases and crime that respect no border, and protecting the environment.

Besides the ability to fuse information and efforts across the command, we also need to create an environment where the various U.S. Government agency representatives are willing and authorized to integrate into our efforts. We need to create a whole-of-government program where integrated planning and career exchanges are the norm. It should be a positive career step for someone from the military to fill an exchange in one of the other Federal agencies, and the converse should be equally true. By working together and building a regional focus point for policy implementation, we should be able to reduce redundancy, gain resource efficiencies, and ultimately better ensure our security and that of our partners.

Continued globalization and the diffusion of high technology have made it certain that the United States cannot ensure its forward defense by itself. Working alone, we cannot stop drug traffickers from penetrating our borders; nor can we locate and neutralize terrorist threats abroad without capable partners willing to cooperate with us. Sustained engagement will go a long way toward building willingness, but we also need to identify capability shortfalls with these partners and flexibly expend resources to build overall regional security capability and capacity. Just as important, we need to be able to rapidly address capability shortfalls with key partners to meet emerging transnational threats.

> It is as much by the force of ideas as the force of arms that we will secure our future. And the principal idea is this—that people of different faiths, cultures and creeds can live together peacefully.
>
> —Tony Blair
> Former UK Prime Minister
>
> Barricades of ideas are worth more than barricades of stones. There is no prow that can cut through a cloudbank of ideas. A powerful idea, waved before the world at the proper time, can stop a squadron of iron-clad ships, like the mystical flag of the Last Judgment.
>
> —José Martí[15]

Seizing the Moment and Gaining Consensus

In short, all of our efforts, combined with the tremendous involvement of other Federal agencies and the huge contribution of the U.S. private sector, all show that we are engaging a great deal and on many levels with our friends and partners in Latin America and the Caribbean—and it will only get better. As our focus in Southern Command and other Federal agencies shifts from a somewhat unilateral viewpoint to an integrated, multiagency, public-private cooperative approach, we will better show how the United States has cared, and always will care, about this incredibly worthy region and its diverse and vibrant people. But we cannot rest on the laurels of our valiant efforts this far—there will always be a need for new programs, new ideas, and new understanding. Right now is the perfect time for all of us, inside and outside of the U.S. Government, to collaborate on the challenges and opportunities we face together in the Americas.

Meeting today's and tomorrow's challenges required organizational change for Southern Command—and that change is continual. Further, this change needs to be much more than mere cosmetic surgery: it needs to be real change that matches the unique threats and opportunities of the 21st century. We recently completed the first real phase in transforming the entire command into a leading interagency security organization, with interagency, multinational, and private sector partnering as core organizing concepts. Given the worrisome security trends in this hemisphere, the transformation of Southern Command into a more capable and comprehensive security organization has been a critical step in a needed transformation of the greater U.S. security apparatus.

We have implemented this model at Southern Command within a rather short span of time, drawing upon immense cooperation from other agencies, Congress, and senior leadership within our Department. Doing so has become a useful experiment in creating new organizations to meet 21st-century security challenges. Perhaps over time, the model will form the basis for change at other national security organizations, much like U.S. Africa Command. Clearly, we should at least consider rethinking the fundamental structure and approach of joint, combined, interagency, and even international security organizations, ensure we integrate and coordinate with commercial and nongovernmental entities, and then seek to leverage lessons learned for the future. We are moving in this direction now, but much remains to be done.

Only through building new, capable relationships inside and outside government, on both the domestic and international fronts, will we be able to match our strategic outlook to effective unified action. Only through a robust commitment to partnering will we be able to gain and maintain the critical regional friendships we need for the security of our hemisphere. Through this partnering, continued dialogue, and sustained and persistent engagement and exchange, we ultimately will develop the ability to understand the region, know what transpires, and know how to act or interact with our partners. Modern information systems, extensive language capability, and cultural training and study are the tools necessary for this command to achieve this understanding.

The importance of Latin America and the Caribbean to the United States cannot be overstated. It merits frequent high-level visits to see firsthand the tremendous linkages and challenges we share and to demonstrate U.S. interest and commitment to our partners in Latin America and the Caribbean. We can assist in this endeavor through raising awareness of the strategic importance of this region with Members of Congress, key interagency community decision- and policymakers, and the United States public in order to garner the support needed to achieve strategic objectives and convey the proper messages. We truly *are* all in this together—collectively, the nations of the Americas are better poised to meet head-on whatever the future holds in order to bring about a stable, prosperous, and secure future in this special part of the world that we share.

> Power derives from strength and will. Strength comes from the transformation of resources into capabilities. Will infuses objectives with resolve. Strategy marshals capabilities and brings them to bear with precision. Statecraft seeks through strategy to magnify the mass, relevance, impact and irresistibility of power. . . . The practitioners of these arts are the paladins of statecraft.
>
> —Chas W. Freeman[16]

Final Thoughts

The transnational nature of threats and opportunities will continue to draw the nations of our hemisphere together. In the process of striving to forge ever stronger bonds through security cooperation and stability-building endeavors, other areas like diplomacy, commerce, development, and communication will undoubtedly benefit as well. Commerce, commodities, information, and ideas now travel across borders on air, maritime, space, and cyberspace highways, bringing unprecedented benefits to previously isolated individuals and communities. This same connectivity that brings and promises progress, however, also enables threats in multiple nefarious forms to move, hide, adapt, and sustain themselves with greater ease than ever before.

We are engaged in a set of ideological conflicts—and we are not good at these. They do not play to our traditional strengths or exist in our "sweet spot" or "wheelhouse" of skill sets. To prevail against these conflicts and overcome these challenges, we have got to get better at partnering, supporting, communicating, listening, and helping, when asked—there will be no greater friend. However, we are first and foremost a combatant command and we still maintain our traditional military core competencies. When our enduring vital national interests are threatened, we need to make very clear to all who wish to do us harm, that there can be no greater enemy.

The coming decade will see fundamental changes in how we base and employ forces—both traditional military forces as well as the increasingly joint and combined military/civilian teams; it will also require new methods for how we weave the thread of military power alongside the diplomatic, informational, and economic threads to form a more complete fabric of interaction with our partner nations in Latin America and the Caribbean. Southern Command is optimally positioned, structured, and manned to be at the forefront of these changes, synchronizing our actions, programs, and messages with the other agencies of the U.S. Government, as well as with those of the other inhabitants of our shared home. We will continue to ensure the forward defense of the United States, establish regional partnerships, and help enhance regional hemispheric security and stability so that the United States and partner nations may extend the benefits of secure democracies and economic prosperity to all the citizens of the Americas.

During my 3 years at the helm of U.S. Southern Command, I have been extremely fortunate to work closely with and learn from civilian government and military leaders, as well as with our partners to the south to improve the security and stability of the Americas. Together we have sought multinational, "whole-of-government" and in some cases "whole-of-society" approaches to create a secure and stable environment that set the conditions for long-term prosperity for the Americas.

This region continues to play a critical role in the continued security and prosperity of the United States. Despite some challenges, I believe that through the sharing of ideas, economic interdependence, cultural understanding, and harnessing innovation and our existing strong ties and bonds of friendship to build an integrated approach to partnering, U.S. Southern Command will continue to be a welcomed military partner of choice in this hemisphere—we will certainly work hard to help make this vision a reality. There are many opportunities to improve hemispheric security cooperation ahead and we are committed to pursuing multinational, multiagency, and public-private partnerships to confront the challenges and embrace the opportunities of the Americas. We dedicate the majority of our resources to building the security capabilities of our partners while encouraging an environment of cooperation among the nations in the region. The mutual benefits of these partnering efforts are profound.

Southern Command will continue to improve on its model of interagency, international, and public-private support, facilitated by the forthcoming completion of the command's new state-of-the-art headquarters building. The new facility will enable still deeper partnerships

Rear Admiral Joseph D. Kernan (center) salutes Admiral Stavridis during the Fourth Fleet reestablishment ceremony held at Naval Station Mayport on July 12, 2008. Rear Admiral James W. Stevenson, Jr., relinquished command.

with academic, business, and civil-society leaders as we seek innovative and proactive solutions to the complex challenges we face in the Americas. I'm proud of what we've done, our valiant efforts thus far—but much more work remains.

Thanks to the support of Congress, joint service teammates, interagency community partners, international friends, and allies and our growing relationship with the private sector and NGOs, the future appears promising for Southern Command and the pursuit of our mission in the region. We will continue to conduct numerous multinational exercises, exchanges, and humanitarian events. We will eagerly build on lessons learned from previous years and will be relentless in further integrating joint, multinational, interagency, and public-private efforts into as many of our actions as possible. We will continue to track along our command heading: understanding the linkages the United States shares with the region; working together with partners to overcome shared challenges; and fulfilling the promise of a secure, cooperating, and prospering hemisphere through innovative and effective strategic initiatives.

As I conclude my watch and my time with you in these pages, I would like to leave you with some personal reflections. First, what I will remember:

- Seeing the look on the faces of Marc Gonsalves, Keith Stansell, and Tom Howes as they came off the aircraft into freedom, after 5–1/2 years in captivity at the hands of narcoterrorist FARC thugs.

- Visiting an eye clinic in Panama supported by one of Southern Command's health engagement outreach activities, and watching a 5-year-old boy put on his first pair of glasses, and finally being able to see and saying to his mother, "Mami, veo el mundo"—Mom, I see the world.

- Watching our partners take down a semi-submersible submarine, part of stopping 700-plus tons of cocaine from coming into the USA.

- Seeing a two-star Admiral, Joe Kernan, the first commander of the U.S. Fourth Fleet, carrying bags of rice ashore in Port au Prince from USS *Kearsarge* after hurricanes ripped through Haiti in the summer of 2008.

- Walking through the ruins of Machu Picchu and thinking about all the history and culture of this region, and the importance of the indigenous societies.

- Eating *feijoada* in Rio with my Brazilian friends like Admiral Moura Neto.

- Riding to a seafood restaurant in Cartagena with General Padilla and Admiral Barrera, talking with them about how to help our Colombian friends.

- Working with the Coast Guard—Thad Allen and Dave Kunkle and Rob Parker—learning what interagency cooperation is really all about.

- Briefing Secretary Gates on our plan to reorganize the command on an interagency path and winning his approval.

- Watching the new headquarters rise up in the field across from our current location.

- Pinning a third star on Glenn Spears as a Deputy and welcoming Ambassador Paul Trivelli as our first civilian Deputy.

- Smoking cigars with Dominicans and discussing the finer points of Dominican, Honduran, and Nicaraguan cigars.

- Learning Spanish and Portuguese, and reading for the first time Gabriel García Márquez in his native tongue.

- Watching the helicopters of Joint Task Force Bravo bringing victims of landslides out of danger.

- Sitting in Secretary Gates's office as he told me my next assignment and realizing suddenly that all of this would come to an end for me—the sadness of that coupled with the excitement of a new challenge.

Now, what I have learned:

- That in this part of the world, true and lasting security is so seldom delivered by the barrel of a gun.

- That here, thankfully, we are not launching Tomahawk missiles, we are launching ideas.

- That everything we do must be international, interagency, and public-private. All must be undergirded by strategic communications.

- That, above all, we must innovate.

- That our opponents are smart. They innovate. They wake up each morning seeking to come up with a new idea. We need to match that.

- That 21th-century security is brain-on-brain warfare. We cannot spend our way to success—we must outthink our opponents.

- That we must move faster, always faster—the only thing we cannot accelerate is the speed of trust.

- That, as with any relationship, trust must be built over time—one step, one exchange, one exercise at a time.

It is this trust, I firmly believe, along with transparency, friendship, and perpetual cooperation that will, in due course, deliver on the promise of the security, stability, and ultimately, prosperity we all desire. So we must take great care in building it up and do what must be done to avoid tearing it down.

Only history will judge whether or not our deeds and actions, as well as our partnerships, will bear good fruit in this region. Our approach at U.S. Southern Command has been simple: international, interagency, public-private. This approach has been woven together throughout by strategic communication. It is my humble opinion that only through a sustained and dedicated commitment to this course of action can we truly chart a path that delivers us to our ultimate destination: the realization of the promise of the Partnership of and for the Americas.

Finally, I would like to close with a word about the superb U.S. Soldiers, Sailors, Airmen, Marines, Coastguardsmen—Active, Reserve, and Guard— and civilians who serve in the region. They are volunteers and patriots, and I am proud and lucky to serve with them every day. Our greatest strength is our people, and I ask that we always remember their own and their families' sacrifices in service of our great nation.

> For all those brave men and women struggling for a better life, there is—and must be—no stronger ally or advocate than the United States of America. Let us never forget that our nation remains a beacon of light for those in dark places. And that our responsibilities to the world—to freedom, to liberty, to the oppressed everywhere—are not a burden on the people or the soul of this nation. They are, rather, a blessing.
>
> —Robert M. Gates
> Secretary of Defense

Notes

[1] Barack Obama, "A New Beginning," Remarks at Cairo University, Cairo, Egypt, June 4, 2009. Available at: <http://www.whitehouse.gov/the_press_office/Remarks-by-the-President-at-Cairo-University-6-04-09/>.

[2] *World Population* in 2030 (United Nations Department of Economic and Social Affairs/Population Division, 2005), 33.

[3] Condoleezza Rice, "Remarks at Pathways to Prosperity Plenary Session," Panama City, Panama, December 10, 2008.

[4] Trade Stats Express—National Trade Data, Office of Trade and Industry Information, Manufacturing and Services, International Trade Administration, U.S. Department of Commerce, 2005, December 18, 2006, available at: <http://tse.export.gov/NTDCChartDisplay.aspx?UniqueURL=h1fog2 55vklrl55zk5jlhqf-2006-12-18-16-29-57>.

[5] Stephen Johnson, *The Heritage Foundation, Candidates Briefing Book Issues 2006, Latin America*, December 8, 2006. Available at: <http://www.heritage.org/Research/features/issues/issuearea/LatinAmerica.cfm>.

[6] Ibid.

[7] Economic Commission for Latin America and the Caribbean, "Social Panorama of Latin America 2007." Available at: <http://www.eclac.cl/publicationes/default.asp?idioma=IN>.

[8] The World Bank, 2008 *World Development Indicators*, April 2008.

[9] Inter-American Development Bank, Press Release, Migrant Remittances, October 18, 2006, December 7, 2006. Available at: <http://www.iadb.org/NEWS/articledetail.cfm?Language=En2&artTyp e+PR&artid=3348>.

[10] Internet World States, "Usage and Population Statistics," September 18, 2006. Available at: <http://www.internetworldstats.com/stats.htm>.

[11] Coalition for Affordable and Reliable Energy, "Energy—The Lifeblood of America's Economy," December 10, 2006. Available at: <http://www.careenergy.com/energy-facts-statistics.asp>.

[12] Organization of American States, "Inter-American Democratic Charter," September 11, 2001, at: <http://www.oas.org/OASpage/eng/Documents/Democratic_Charter.htm>.

[13] J. William Fulbright, *The Price of Empire* (New York: Pantheon Press, 1989), 47.

[14] Ibid., 53.

[15] José Martí, Cuban author and leader of the Cuban independence movement. This was from '*Nuestra América*' (Our America), in *La Revista Illustrada de Neuva York*, first published on January 1, 1891.

[16] Chas W. Freeman, Jr., *Arts of Power: Statecraft and Diplomacy* (Washington, DC: U.S. Institute of Peace Press, 2007), 3.

About the Author

Admiral James G. Stavridis, USN, assumed duties as Commander of the United States European Command and as the Supreme Allied Commander, Europe in 2009. From 2006 to 2009, he commanded U.S. Southern Command in Miami, focused on Latin America and the Caribbean.

ADM Stavridis is a 1976 distinguished graduate of the U.S. Naval Academy and a native of South Florida. A Surface Warfare Officer, he commanded the Destroyer USS *Barry* (DDG 52) from 1993 to 1995, completing UN/NATO deployments to Haiti and Bosnia, and a combat cruise to the Arabian Gulf. *Barry* won the Battenberg Cup as the top ship in the Atlantic Fleet under his command. In 1998, ADM Stavridis commanded Destroyer Squadron 21 and deployed to the Arabian Gulf, winning the Navy League's John Paul Jones Award for Inspirational Leadership. From 2002 to 2004, he commanded Enterprise Carrier Strike Group, conducting combat operations in the Arabian Gulf in support of both Operation *Iraqi Freedom* and Operation *Enduring Freedom*. Ashore, he has served as a strategic and long range planner on the staffs of the Chief of Naval Operations and the Chairman of the Joint Chiefs of Staff. He has also served as the Executive Assistant to the Secretary of the Navy and the Senior Military Assistant to the Secretary of Defense.

ADM Stavridis earned a PhD and MALD in International Relations from The Fletcher School of Law and Diplomacy at Tufts University, where he won the Gullion Prize as outstanding student. He is also a distinguished graduate of both the National and Naval War Colleges. He holds various decorations and awards, including two awards of the Defense Distinguished Service Medal, the Defense Superior Service Medal, and five awards of the Legion of Merit. He is author or coauthor of numerous articles and several books on naval ship handling and leadership, including *Command at Sea* and *Destroyer Captain*.